D. Padgett
3/1/02

Anna Deavere Smith

TALK TO ME

Anna Deavere Smith is an actor, a teacher, a playwright, and the creator of an acclaimed series of one-woman plays based on her interviews with diverse voices from communities in crisis. She is the founder and director of The Institute on the Arts and Civic Dialogue at Harvard University, and is the Ann O'Day Maples Professor of the Arts at Stanford University. Her works include *Twilight: Los Angeles, 1992*; *Fires in the Mirror*; and *House Arrest*, and she has written for *Newsweek* and *The New Yorker*, among other publications. She lives in San Francisco.

also by Anna Deavere Smith

Twilight: Los Angeles, 1992
Fires in the Mirror

TALK TO ME

TALK TO ME

Travels in Media and Politics

Anna Deavere Smith

ANCHOR BOOKS
A Division of Random House, Inc.
New York

FIRST ANCHOR BOOKS EDITION, OCTOBER 2001

Copyright © 2000 by Anna Deavere Smith

All rights reserved under International and Pan-American
Copyright Conventions. Published in the United States by
Anchor Books, a division of Random House, Inc., New York,
and simultaneously in Canada by Random House of Canada
Limited, Toronto. Originally published in hardcover in the
United States by Random House, Inc., New York, in 2000.

Anchor Books and colophon are registered trademarks of
Random House, Inc.

The Library of Congress has cataloged the
Random House edition as follows:
Smith, Anna Deavere.
Talk to me: listening between the lines / Anna Deavere Smith.
p. cm.
ISBN 0-375-50150-9 (acid-free paper)
1. United States—Politics and government—1993– 2. Political
culture—United States. 3. Political culture—Washington (D.C.)
4. National characteristics, American. 5. Presidents—United
States. 6. Press and politics—United States. 7. Politicians—
United States—Interviews. 8. Interviews—United States.
I. Title.
E885.S63 2000
306.2'0973'09049—dc21   00-055306

Anchor ISBN: 0-385-72174-9

Book design by Barbara M. Bachman

www.anchorbooks.com

Printed in the United States of America
10 9 8 7 6 5 4 3 2 1

THIS BOOK IS DEDICATED TO MY MOTHER, ANNA Y. SMITH,

A TEACHER IN THE BALTIMORE PUBLIC SCHOOLS, WHO WAS ALSO AMONG

THE FIRST PEOPLE TO TALK TO ME.

ACKNOWLEDGMENTS

To my hosts in Washington, the Honorable Amory Houghton and Priscilla Dewey Houghton, for welcoming me into their home and for giving me a base from which to work. For their spirit, humor, friendship, and generosity.

My editor, Ann Godoff, for introducing me to another kind of writing, another way of looking at character, another way of creating voice, another way of inhabiting words and talk.

My agent, Gloria Loomis, for being there, always, with her particular, unique combination of savvy and grace.

Kate Niedzwiecki, for her constancy and her editorial assistance.

Sarah D'Imperio, Ann's assistant.

Jessye Norman, for conversations that influenced the formation of some of the ideas in this book. For her performances, which have taught me many lessons about the relationship of a single voice to an audience. For her passionate interest in this country. For how she speaks to us, all over the world, in our souls, through songs—songs in different languages, songs from all over the world—songs written now, songs written in the past. Some of those songs come from the United States: spirituals about hope in the presence of suffering and unfairness, and then patriotic songs about glory and promise. Songs that she sings and has sung in the acoustic perfection of concert halls, in churches, in opera houses, in schools, against the granite background of monuments, in the huge coldness of convention halls. Songs that manage to bind us, even through our differences. For the magic of her communication to our hearts, beyond words, beyond cultures, across boundaries.

The presidents who were willing to meet with me, and their staffs who made it possible: President Jimmy Carter, President George Bush, President Bill Clinton.

Stephen Rivers, for his diligence in helping me move around the beltway world. Peter Osnos, for early conversations about this book, and his encouragement. Diana Walker, for her humor, inspiration, and generosity, and for her perceptive, sometimes theatrical, photographs of presidents since Carter. Catharine Stimpson, for her common sense. Stephen Hess, at the Brookings Institute, for being the first to translate Washington for me. Riley Temple, for giving me confidence from time to time, right on time.

With gratitude to, and in memory of, Maynard Parker, former editor of *Newsweek,* and Charles Lyons, former chair, Department of Drama, Stanford University.

Alison Bernstein, Andrea Taylor, Christine Vincent, Barron Tenny, and all of the people at the Ford Foundation, for conversations and experiments about how to enliven democracy and the ways in which we talk to one another across the lines of power, race, class, and difference; in institutions, cities, and countries; and between individuals.

Suzanne Sato, a patron saint and wise woman, for helping so many of us take risks—intellectually and artistically—in our disciplines, forms, and communities. For being forward-looking.

The Rockefeller Foundation, Bellagio Study and Conference Center on Lake Como, Bellagio, Italy. Special thanks to Gianna Celli and Susan Garfield for my residency there.

Adria Popkin, for her clerical assistance on the first draft of this book.

David Chalian, Stacey Shorter, Roberta Goodman, Kimber Riddle, Diana Alvarez, Sandra Smith, Jane Kennedy, Irene Mecchi, and Shana Waterman, for their intelligence, friendship, and support.

The artists, core audience, and staff of the Institute on the Arts and Civic Dialogue, who have been experimenting for three summers with the art of conversation in public.

Colleagues and deans at Stanford University, for being flexible and making it possible for me to take the time needed to research, prepare for, and follow the '96 campaign.

The students in my Arts and Civic Dialogue class, Fall 1999, for their energy, inventiveness, openness, appetite for civic responsibility, and, most of all, idealism.

Stephen Richard, Kitty Eisele, Nora Connell, Marcos Najera, Lynette Turner, Matthew Francis, Andrew Goodman, Cori Nelson, Stacey Schwandt, and Eryn Rosenthal, for the research and creativity needed to develop an understanding of the presidency and the press in history and now. For all the logistics and long hours provided to move me through the presidential campaign trail in '96, and to the South, where churches had burned that summer.

This book was inspired, in part, by a project I developed called the "Press and Presidency Project." One of its dimensions was as a project for the theater. It was originally commissioned by the Arena Stage Theater: Doug Wager, artistic director; Stephen Richard, managing director. It was subsequently produced at the Arena Stage Theater, the Mark Taper Forum, and the New York Shakespeare Festival. Its development was also supported by the Intimann Theater and the Goodman Theater. Many thanks to all of the theaters, artistic directors, managing directors, boards of directors, the "Friends of the Press and Presidency Project," and the actors, designers, dramaturgs, historians, stage managers, production assistants, staff, and audiences that dedicated their time, commitment, and talent to giving that project a life—financially, logistically, intellectually, and artistically. Its life in the theater (a play called *House Arrest*) provided the opportunity to represent ideas in the form of character, spoken words, and metaphor in front of live audiences. It also provided the opportunity to talk to actors and other theater artists about language and character in new and different ways. Finally, it provided the opportunity to talk to audiences after shows and to invite them to talk to me, and to one another.

Stanley and Betty Sheinbaum.

Stephen and Daryl Roth.

Gordon Davidson.

Cinder Stanton, Monticello.

The White House.

The Maryland Correctional Institute for Women.

Maggie Williams, Judy Woodruff and Al Hunt, Mike McCurry, Sheila Tate, Jody Powell, Peter Mirijanian, John Sullivan, Susan Mercandetti, Tina Brown, Rhonda Sherman, Wendy Smith, Robert Kaiser, Ben Bradlee and Sally Quinn, and Don Graham.

To all of the people who invited me to their homes, their favorite restaurants, their parties, their offices, and their prison visiting rooms in and around Washington. For your fellowship and your generosity in opening doors that otherwise would have been impossible to open.

I interviewed more than four hundred people in the course of working on this project. To all of the people who provided interviews—most of which do not appear in this book—those hours of interviews, your words, are the heart of the project and the foundation for my work in general. Thank you for talking to me.

CONTENTS

Prologue: Wild Waves and Bonfires   3

Washington, D.C.   13

Culture Shock   22

A Trochee in the Second Beat   35

The Three Questions   46

Talking to Jesus   60

Segregation   67

Garrison Junior High School, Baltimore, Maryland, 1961   80

The East Coast Corridor   88

Theater and Politics   95

Orientation: Dinners and Lunches   108

A Briefing   116

Locked Up   120

The Power of Muteness   125

Grandpop's Nigger   131

Slaves on P Street   141

Creating Fictions   145

Metaphor's Funeral   158

Policing   164

Swinging   179

Theater History   211

Performing for the President   218

Culture Wars and Domestic Beatings   231

"That's Not My Job"   239

Talking to the President   241

The Death Drive: It's the Mad Hatter's Tea Party and
    Tom DeLay Is Pouring   252

Everybody's Talking   270

A Medley   273

Epilogue: Playing Clinton   293

TALK TO ME

WILD WAVES AND BONFIRES

1971
BALTIMORE, MARYLAND
A HOWARD JOHNSON'S PARKING LOT NEAR I-95

PACKED AN OVERNIGHT BAG AND COUNTED OUT EIGHTY DOLLARS, all the money I had in the world. My mother drove me to a Howard John-son's near I-95. A car pulled up with four friends, each of whom had come from a different point north of Maryland. At age twenty-one I left my family, my hometown, and, with my four friends, took off for California. We wanted to see America and to make sense, each in our own way, of what to do with all the breakage and promise that had been released through the antiwar movement, the assassinations of Martin Luther King and Bobby Kennedy, the beginning of the environmental movement, and the bra-burning, brief as it was, of the women's movement. And there was the masculine glamour and fashion of the black liberation movement. Years later I would talk to some of those Black Panthers. One of them mused openly, "I think we got caught up in the theater of it. We began to believe we were in a movie." One of the Chicago Eight would similarly say, "It was theater, until the cops showed us the difference between reality and theater, and hauled some of us off to jail."

Was it theater or not? I took off to see for myself. Quite apart from the theater, the sexiness of the antiestablishment voice was another promise, a serious promise that was eking out from under all the chants, all the music, all the pageantry. What was promised, after all was said and done, was a larger idea of "we the people." What was promised was that more voices would matter, that the patrician white male would not be the only one to hold the chair. This promise was made by none other than ourselves, so if we were to ever be disillusioned again, we would have to be the cause of that disillusionment.

My mother tells me she sat in the car and cried for a long time after I left. Her life's work had been to educate me, my four siblings, and hundreds of others who had passed through her classrooms all over Baltimore. Her goal had been to position us firmly in the black middle class.

Her trajectory was one that had been formed in the depression—a colored girl growing up poor in a family of eight in a tough, segregated Baltimore. My father, more fortunate, had been the son of a businessman who had an eighth-grade education and had started a business with a pushcart. His shop had eventually held its own on Pennsylvania Avenue, the street for black businesses during the day and good jazz at night. My grandfather had managed to send all six of his kids to college. My mother and her siblings, too, all went to college.

I suspect that some of those kids my mother taught in the Baltimore public schools, she only wanted to keep out of trouble, heartbreak, and illiteracy. (She never believed there was such a thing as a nonreader.) As for me, she had spent many nights helping me read and write, and I could tell she had faith in me. But life is more than reading, writing, and putting the correct answer on a test. Especially when the tests and the books themselves become suspect, as they did in Wagnerian proportions round about 1968.

It was a rocky road, and I, as the first child, was to make the first solid step. It wasn't to be the step my mother expected. My college education answered few questions. It created many. I came out of college with debts, and, rather than a five-year plan, or even a foothold in the next generation of black success, I had about fifty years' worth of questions about the world I came from and the world I live in. I am still in the process of answering those questions.

WHAT I REMEMBER MOST ABOUT AMERICA ON THAT TRIP WAS THE gorgeous tapestry of autumn in the West Virginia hills, the hamburgers in Texas, and the poverty in Oklahoma, which was beyond anything I could have imagined. We landed finally on Coronado, an island off San Diego, and stayed in the home of a friend whose husband was in the

Navy and out on duty somewhere dangerously close to Vietnam. The place was in stark contrast to what I thought California would offer. Everyone seemed to ride bikes, play tennis, and have blond hair. It was as if nothing of the sixties push to color American culture had happened there. We did boring "survival" jobs during the day and watched the sunset over the Pacific every night, until each one of us figured out, singly, which route we should take next.

One by one we left one another. It was sad. As each person parted, I knew that I may have been watching a series of dreams deferred. I had watched my friends speak their dreams each night. They started out with bluster, and, as the days rolled on, rather than constructing the dreams into plans and realities, they began to leave their sentences unfinished, taking drags on a cigarette where words used to follow, sipping water or wine where a fist used to be pounded, or sighing where a guffaw used to come. The conversation was melting.

One night, in a van that we had driven to a beach in Baja California, just south of the Mexican border, I could feel the palpable pull of the known. It weighed on all my friends. I could feel the weight of it in my own heart. It was an ache. It was time, for them, one by one, to get back to the boyfriend, father, or mother who had caused them to have questions in the first place. They would return with the questions unanswered. This was very different from my project, which was to take, at its word, and with both eyes open, and at the same time one eye piercing suspiciously, the movement's promise to give more voice to more people. I left the van and sat on the beach, with its wild waves and bonfires. The roar of each was wilder than anything I had experienced on the East Coast. I began to fear that my own dreams would meet the air undone. I decided not to speak them to my friends, although that had been the purpose of my trip. The trip with eighty dollars and an overnight bag had been meant to speak my dreams out loud until I had a plan. But dreams don't have to be spoken, they only have to be seen.

Soon after we got back to Coronado, I said good-bye, and went north.

1973

GEARY STREET

SAN FRANCISCO, CALIFORNIA

I arrived, in June 1973, at a five-story building that sat above several store-fronts on Geary Street in downtown San Francisco. Among the store-fronts were a glitzy deli with mounds of chopped liver in the window, called David's Delicatessen, an art gallery, a soup place called Salma-gundi's, and a bar just to the right of that called The Curtain Call. I couldn't afford to buy anything in any of those places. Even for a cup of coffee or an apple, I had to go up the block, where it was fifteen cents cheaper. There were two theaters across the street. One was the theater operated by my school, the American Conservatory Theatre. The other brought the big road shows from New York. Our theater did all the "au-thentic" stuff, the "real" theater, with "real" acting, "real" intellect, "real" art, and it evoked and used "real" feelings. The other stuff was thought to be mere "spectacle."

You could hear the cable cars and the brassy whistle of the hotel doorman across the street, sharply signaling for cabs as the guests stood waiting in their polished shoes, manicured nails, and perfectly clipped hair. We were a motley bunch, to say the least, in the midst of that down-town finery. But we were just blocks from the Tenderloin, with its myriad tragic stories—drug addicts, prostitutes, pimps, the downs of the down-and-outers—on every corner. Not so destroyed as they would be in the eighties, with the invasion of crack cocaine, but nonetheless in a vari-ety of states of despair, loss beyond repair, and physical and psychological danger. There was the dramatic reminder of hope in the form of the glo-rious choir that belted out from the Glide Memorial Church. Glide wel-comed the richest and the poorest, the luckiest and the most challenged. Some of us went there on Sundays to get a burst of inspiration and to hear good speaking—who knew, you might find Maya Angelou in the pulpit. We could also hear great singing.

SUMMER 1996
THE CAMPAIGN TRAIL

Twenty-three years later I would travel back to San Francisco on a press swing with President Clinton, and I would leave the trip as Clinton went in to visit the Glide church. America seems to me to be addicted to hope. Presidents from time to time visit places like Glide, where hope lives and where someone seems to be tending to those who missed out on the American dream. I wonder how often they visit the places where there is no hope, no hope whatsoever. Has a president in office ever gone without a chaperone to press the hand of a person in profound need?

And then I think about those who have "everything." What are they yearning for, another dollar, a sunnier day? happier progeny? Are they still in the hopeful state, or are they prisoners of their ambition? Is ambition, drive, the same as hope? Does hope exist only for those who are "lost," "lost causes"? Those who have hope are perhaps the motor, the air, the breeze under the soul of the nation.

1973
BEETHOVEN'S NINTH
SAN FRANCISCO

In that summer of '73, we carried sweaters on our piles of scripts and dance clothes because the breeze from the bay was very cold at night, almost like in winter. We had so much to talk about, so many people to talk to—the shoe shine man across the street with the incomprehensible European accent (last time I walked by, in early 2000, he was still there), Tennessee Williams, who was visiting (I actually saw him for real in the elevator), or perhaps one of those people sitting on a corner in the Tenderloin. In this pre-AIDS-consciousness time, it was romantic in all ways, physically, spiritually, intellectually, aesthetically. The twenty-four-hour murmur of electricity under the ground of the cable car was the perfect metaphor. And the foghorns spoke to the darker, lonelier side that could visit you too.

We were 210 students, all there to study identity, change identities, to learn to "be." There are a variety of ways to describe what acting is. "Being," "Seeming," "Becoming," "Lying," "Truth Telling," "Magic," "Transforming." We were new. Some among us had known the building for an hour longer than the others of us. No one ever arrives at the same time as everybody else. We were going to learn how to talk to each other onstage, and through all of this how to take our own special message to the *world*.

On one of the first days I was coming into the building, a tall, thin, aristocratic-looking white woman who appeared to be about my age, and whom we ultimately referred to as the Katharine Hepburn among us, came breathlessly down a narrow hallway, saying to me (whom she had never seen except in that one instant), "Do you know where I can get a drink of water?"

She said this as if she had known me all my life, as if I were a sister, a brother, a friend. She may even have grabbed my hand. I wasn't put off by the fact that she was a stranger. Her presence in that question made me feel in an instant as if I had known her all my life. Having grown up in segregation, I found it odd that a white person would approach me without her own barriers up, and without the expectation that I would have barriers. I was so stunned by her presence that I didn't speak. Besides, I didn't know where to get a drink of water. Just as rapidly and as urgently, she vanished down the hallway and out into the street. I thought that perhaps this was what acting was. Because, as real as it was, realer than real, it also seemed like a moment out of a scene from Chekhov's *Uncle Vanya*, or as if one of Tchaikovsky's symphonies had burst into speech. *Urgency* is the word. And it's one of the top ten in the vocabulary of acting.

Acting is the furthest thing from lying that I have encountered. It is the furthest thing from make-believe. It is the furthest thing from pretending. It is the most unfake thing there is. Acting is a search for the authentic. It is a search for the authentic by using the fictional as a frame, a house in which the authentic can live. For a moment. Because, yes indeed, real life inhibits the authentic.

I knew intuitively that this was metaphorically what it was all about. Later I would learn fancy words for it. I would learn, in all the reading I did about acting, what Joseph Chaikin, a great director, had to say—that presence is the gift of the actor. Presence is a "kind of deep libidinal surrender which the performer reserves for his anonymous audience."

Presence is that quality that makes you feel as though you're standing right next to the actor, no matter where you're sitting in the theater. It's the feeling you have that the performer is right in front of you, speaking to you and only you. It's that wonderful moment when Jessye Norman sings in a quiet, so quiet you can hear a pin drop concert hall to an audience that is attentive like no other. It's a moment when she seems to be singing as she's never sung, and the audience seem to be listening as they've never listened. It's the moment when it's clear that everyone is there for the same reason. It's not that frenzied desire for the diva, but a sudden calm that hits the hall, like it did in one performance I saw in Paris, where they love her so much they named an orchid after her. These moments have a kind of authenticity, because they reach the heart. They speak to us. They speak to us not because they are natural in the sense of normal. They speak to us because they are real in their effort to be together with a very large *you*, the *you* being all men and women.

Politicians have tried to borrow those skills, and they have misused them and ended up speaking to very few.

That genuine moment, that "real" connection, is no small thing. It is not something that happens every day. Is it rare because it calls for a special talent? Is it a moment that can happen only when we don't know each other, when we have so much to learn about each other that we hang on every breath together? It is hard to find those moments in our culture because we think we know so much about each other. Perhaps it is a moment that is dependent not only on the performer or the leader, but on the audience as well. Does this era of focus groups and polls, this desire to get at and quantify the mysteriousness of that "deep libidinal surrender," make it nearly impossible to find those moments of true engagement? Does the overdetermined nature of our time, and the inherent desire to control the public, to control their thoughts, particularly how they work those thoughts into actions that are favorable to the marketplace, create an atmosphere where only the predictable can occur? Those moments of deep libidinal surrender are in fact all about that which is not predictable. And there *is* no anonymous audience. At least that's what the pollsters would like, what commerce would like. They would like to make the anonymous audience *fully* identifiable. With no anonymous audience, there can be no deep libidinal surrender.

Politicians have tried to get the benefit of lessons that performers have learned, presumably because they would like to create the feeling with their audiences that great actors and singers create. They would like to make us feel as though they are speaking to us and only us. But they fail at it. I was surprised to learn that one of Clinton's coaches in 1996 was a graduate of the Yale School of Drama. I wonder if the audience also has that libidinal surrender that they reserve for that one special performance that they so long to adore, to be with, to be enchanted with. If the possibility for surrender is deep, and libidinal, and therefore natural, why is it so hard to find in political life these days? Is it all used up for movie stars? Or money? Or is it simply profoundly in reserve? We're having a hard time connecting in public.

I never knew a group of people like the people I met in the summer of 1973—those 210 actors and all of our trainers. One night I went to hear Beethoven's Ninth performed. I had never heard it live. It was in Grace Cathedral, which sits like a great princess atop Nob Hill in San Francisco. It was so exciting. At one point, as you know, that single human voice comes out after all that music. A tenor exclaims, from the orchestral beauty that has preceded, *"Freunnnnnnden!"* Which means "friends." And then the choral part of the symphony begins—after his call.

When I went to yoga class the next day, I complained of a hot feeling on my forehead. I hadn't been able to sleep. I thought I was feverish and was getting the flu. My yoga teacher listened attentively, looked me square in the eye, and calmly said, "It sounds to me like one of your chakras is opening."

Who ever heard of a piece of music making you feverish? I liked her explanation. Not that I had ever had a chakra open. Many fevers and chakras later, I know, whether it was a fever or my chakras, Beethoven caused it, and that's thrilling. Not only is communication possible across cultures, it is possible across centuries. No great desire to communicate ever dies.

Perhaps it was the sound of the tenor singing *"Freunnnnnnden"* that first opened my heart to the idea that we should all be in a conversation together. By "we" I refer to the potential America, the America that has expanded significantly since the late eighteenth century away from that small group of white men who were the original "we" in "we the people."

When I first went to California to study performance and look for whatever carcasses were left of the "revolution," I thought I was actually in search of the authentic. It came as no surprise to me that the study of acting in the 1970s was about getting "real."

This went hand in hand with what the short-lived "revolution" had in mind. Here we were, in that odd time in the seventies before Nixon was threatened with impeachment—standing in the sawdust of something being constructed. In my college years I thought we were taking apart the throne upon which the white male patriarch had comfortably been perched. The drama of burning bras, the Panthers' guns, Woodstock, et cetera, may have been short-lived. However, a conversation reverberated for three decades in schools and universities and popular culture about who could speak for whom. Women wanted to speak for themselves, people of color wanted to speak for themselves, et cetera.

In this cacophony of sound, where does "we" come from? That's what we're still working on in 2000.

2000

We are in a communications revolution. Yet, as the great Americanist Studs Terkel tells us, "We're more and more into communications and less and less into communication." In this time of a global economy and business mergers happening as often as sunrise and sunset, where is the human merger? Where is real human engagement?

The theater was where I started my quest for the "we" of the new "we the people" the sixties had promised. I soon saw that the theater would be a resource for my quest but that it had serious limitations. It's a business. It's the business of representation, and the people who make all productions "possible" are the same white men in bow ties and women with Chanel bags who have always run "the arts." In thirty years the theater itself has not made very many strides toward creating a bigger "we." It struggles with how to engage younger, diverse audiences, and it has very little to show in terms of a diverse working community. This is how the theater in the year 2000 defines its dilemma: It is worried about its relevance. Yet, in 1973, while I was in school, I had that very question. The theater had been a door into "getting real." Yet it was only that, a door, and only one door, and luckily a kind of revolving door. I would move in the theater and out. I would move in academia and out.

Academia has been a wonderful storehouse of information during the culture wars of the last thirty years. It has pushed itself to be more porous, more absorbent of the world around it. To some extent it was successful, and to some extent it was not. The very schools that had begun to collect and teach information about "us," a bigger "us," struggle with the problem of tenuring sufficient numbers of women and people of color, and of treating them respectfully once they are appointed. Academia too was a revolving door. I would need to find many doors if my goal was to absorb my culture in its moment of promising to find a bigger "we."

To me, the most important doorway into the soul of a person is her or his words, or any other external communication device. I am a student of words. The theater gave me Shakespeare, Molière, Adrienne Kennedy, Sam Shepard. Life would give me other kinds of characters, nestled in the speakings and misspeakings of the people I met in all walks of life. I supposed that words could also be the doorway into the soul of a culture.

I set out across America, on a search for American character. My search was specifically to find America in its language. I interview people and communities about the events of our time, in the hope that I will be able to absorb America. I use the interviews as texts in one-person shows, in which I perform the people I have interviewed. This is a country of many tongues, even if we stick to English. Placing myself in other people's words, as in placing myself in other people's shoes, has given me the opportunity to get below the surface—to get "real."

After almost twenty-five years of my journey, I went to Washington, D.C., with my tape recorder. It was my objective to capture the American presidency in its words. The words of the American presidency are now, more than ever, mediated by the press. For this reason, I determined to look at the relationship of the press to the presidency. I knew that I knew nothing about the president, or any public figure for that matter, that the press didn't tell me. I would have to look at the press too.

WASHINGTON, D.C.

ARRIVED IN WASHINGTON, D.C., ON THE DAY OF THE OJ VERDICT, in the fall of 1995. I was to live in a town house in Georgetown that was a part of a two-house complex. My hosts were Congressman Amory Houghton from Corning, New York, and his wife, Priscilla Dewey Houghton. Priscilla is a lover of the theater, and when they heard that I, a theater artist, needed someplace to sleep and pile my books, she and Amo generously offered an entire empty town house in Georgetown for my use for the five years I would be in and out of Washington. The house itself was the Theresa Fenwick House, a historic monument built in 1826.

When I arrived, workmen were cutting down a two-hundred-year-old cherry tree in the backyard. (Because it was dead, dead on the inside.) My hosts, whom I had yet to meet, were in Corning, the district of the congressman. They were doing exactly what I was doing when I arrived, except miles away—watching the OJ verdict.

The garden and backyard were between the two houses. The kitchen, which served both houses, was on the ground floor of the house I lived in. There was a bumper sticker in the kitchen that said, "The road to hell is lined with Republicans." In Priscilla's handwriting was added, "Except for Amo." Amo is a Republican. Priscilla is a liberal Democrat. She was a Bostonian, and a descendant of abolitionists. Amo's great-grandfather was a glassblower who made Thomas Edison's lightbulbs. The place was grounded in history and current events. In the living room was a photograph, prominently placed, of Amo and George Bush. Not fully nonpartisan upon arrival, I was made instantly nervous by that picture—nervous about meeting Amo, who, at the time, was still only a name to me. But so much for looking at pictures of the past. Current events awaited upstairs, within moments. I went to look for my assistant.

Marcos Najera had gotten to town a day or so before me, from Arizona, where he lived. He was at the top of the house, on the third floor, unpacking my books and converting the space into an office. The doorbell rang. Segrario, the housekeeper, went to answer it. A thin woman with a face lined with character, she was from Spain and had a very thick accent. She came upstairs with a man from the phone company in tow. He was a tall, very well built black man with a West Indian accent. What would Theresa Fenwick think of us all?

"What time is it?"

"The verdict!" somebody said.

We all ran down a flight of stairs to the "red room," a sitting room with a rather large television. We turned on the television. The man from the phone company, who had arrived just seconds before, joined us.

I sat next to Marcos on the couch. The man from the telephone company stood in the doorway. My heart started beating really fast, and it was hard to catch my breath. I surveyed the room through squinted eyes, as if squinting my eyes would protect me from seeing something I didn't really want to see. It was like waiting for something nearly violent to happen.

FALL 1991
CAMBRIDGE, MASSACHUSETTS

I was at Harvard on a fellowship.

Who could possibly forget Anita Hill weekend? We sat in front of our televisions watching an amazing parade. It's difficult to believe that it was only one weekend, the event stayed so imprinted on many of our minds. I did not have a television and had to watch what I could in hallways and lobbies.

On the night of Clarence Thomas's testimony, I was to have dinner with the preeminent teacher of voice for American actors. Her name is Kristin Linklater. She wrote a very important book called *The Thinking Voice*. She has trained many people in her technique and has disciples well placed in schools all over the country. Even as people teach a variety of techniques, it's rare to find someone who did not cross the path of Kristin Linklater, her disciples, or the influence of the notion of a "thinking voice."

At this time, I didn't know her. I knew only of her eminence. I was prepared, and rather nervous about meeting "the master." The plan had been to meet in a restaurant in Boston.

When I called to make last-minute arrangements, she was watching the Hill-Thomas hearings, and she said, "I can't pull myself away from this. Let's meet at my place, watch this, and then decide what to do for dinner." My guess was that people were changing plans all over the country.

We watched the testimony. She was, of course, appalled by the entire display. Her ears were attuned to lies and truths. We were both screaming at the television, using all we had gathered over the years about authentic voice, true-seeming feelings, and grounded speaking.

We sat with our brows furrowed, and with our mouths hanging open. To some extent we were both like impatient teachers. She was the master, I was still in development. We were both appalled at the complete and total lack of authenticity.

All that I had learned about acting from my own work, and from watching my students since the seventies, came to bear as I watched for these intense hours. She, who was the eminence of voice, had a lot to say. What an amazing tutorial I had as we watched this political drama unfold.

"Oh—my—God!" became our descant. Often we would get as far as "Oh, my . . ." and something else would happen that would make us lose words completely. Perhaps we would simply slap our thighs or shake our heads.

Before our very eyes there was a wide display of patriarchal Washington, many of its members speaking to Anita Hill in condescending tones. One among them even inquired, with accusatory tones, why she was not eager to go out with Clarence Thomas. The presumed entitlement took our breath away—but not completely away. We certainly had enough breath to roar at the TV in unison, "Because she didn't *like* him!"

"Oh—my—*God!*"

It was one of those moments when the truth of the matter comes pouring down from heaven. Men and women live in different universes. Washington and the rest of us live in different universes.

I was so amazed by what I had watched that the next morning I took the T across Boston to a discount center and bought a television, so as not to miss a moment. Friends of mine were visiting from out of town. We huddled around my small color TV and hung on every word. No one could decide what was true or not. It didn't matter.

When the decision came down, many of us were stunned that Thomas was to be appointed after all. How could this *be*? I felt completely disconnected. Where does one go in such a civic moment? You would think there would be halls we could go to, even coffeehouses, someplace for *us* to talk. The pundits talked, and I suppose one could have called in to a talk show. But where could *we* go? Those of *us* who were not linked to any community organization or club? And how many of those clubs and organizations exist? Wouldn't it be wonderful if we had civic organizations where *we* could go and talk about any manner of things in any town? Perhaps these could be as available as, say, AA meetings. I knew of a poetry reading being given in Cambridge by Adrienne Rich. Perhaps this could be the antidote to such an intense feeling of disconnectedness. That is where I went. There was no conversation. I just thought that the safest place to be was in the presence of a poet.

FALL 1995
THERESA FENWICK HOUSE
WASHINGTON, D.C.

As the moments ticked away in the red room, I grabbed on to Marcos as if I were in a horror movie. Lance Ito had forbidden noises of any kind in the courtroom. We watched every gesture. Of OJ, of Cochran, whom I had once interviewed—every blink of every eye. The public spectacle.

As the nation waited, what was it that they wanted? OJ to hang? To hear him confess? To have him repent? As on the scaffold? Most people would say they wanted justice done, but justice being done has become such a spectacle. Democracy and the justice system are owned by television ratings.

I flashed back to a dinner I had in Beverly Hills with a woman who had helped OJ select his "spring palette." Here was a man who may have been on his way to the gallows, selecting the color of his suits. Everything was so overdetermined, everything was based on a guess about "our gaze"—what we would be watching, and how we would feel about what we watched. The jury vote was really supposed to be a sequestered affair, but no one believed it was. There's no privacy in our culture.

I had gone to Los Angeles several months before the trial started. I was given a tour of the media villages being created in and around the courthouse. My guide walked me around a parking lot that was showing the earliest signs of what it was going to become. A few trailers were already there, and equipment from the networks was being piled into them. Then she took me across to the courthouse, and upstairs to a floor that had once had offices. I had visited it when I attended the so-called Rodney King trial—the federal trial that President Bush had ordered after the first trial had brought back all not-guilty verdicts on the cops, and a subsequent riot. The entire floor was in the process of being turned into media central. There were wires and boxes everywhere.

"There's no going back now," she said. And this was months before the coverage started. I did not want it to be true. This structure of exposition is now ready for any event—whether the event warrants it or not—and it's so huge that it kills the character of the event. It promises to bring us closer, but, like overbearing parents, it alienates us from the event. It's like a huge scaffold.

In 1996, when I went to the Republican convention, pundit Jeff Greenfield took me for a walk along a row of trailers that were all electrical wires, machines, and manners of connection. There looked to be enough wiring and enough whirring of electricity to hook the convention to the moon. Yet the Republican convention was so overhooked, it unhooked itself from the public's interest. All the wattage in the world doesn't make us watch if we're not already connected.

And to think that Thomas Edison had gone to my host's great-grandfather to ask him to make lightbulbs.

The verdict was announced. Johnnie Cochran wimpered, just for a split second. He covered his mouth like a Cub Scout and had to stop himself from cheering, it seemed. And then the sobbing started. It was Kim Goldman, Ron Goldman's sister.

No one among us screamed out for joy, even though our group, with two blacks, one Latino, statistically would have been expected to do so.

The verdict was like the Winslow Homer painting of soldiers coming home after the Civil War. All three of us likely had less than cozy relationships with police. Nonetheless, there was something like a deflated balloon about the atmosphere in the room. The press had built a huge scaffold. I don't think they'd built a scaffold like that in a long time, if ever. The scaffold, in the middle of the square. All around America, instant community was created around those few moments.

"Well, we'll never know," one among us said.

How could that be? That we would never know? Wasn't all that exposure, all that talk, all that information, all those testimonies, all of the articles, all of the money, all of the commentators, every kind of expert, the birth of the expert on the air from USC, UCLA, everywhere else, all of this expertise, wasn't it about knowing? How could we not know? "We'll never know." My colleague at Stanford, a biologist named Marcus Felman, warned me several years ago that there is no proof that knowledge would make us a better species, that is to say, no proof that knowledge in and of itself will save us from extinction. There's a lot of money spent, a lot of time spent, a lot of smart and talented people giving over their talents to this enterprise of all news all the time, of telling us all . . . and . . . we'll never know? Evidence wasn't enough? There wasn't enough evidence? Well then, why were so many hours spent?

The man from the phone company stood at the door, shaking his head.

"What do you think of this?" I asked him.

"Look like if you got the money you get away wid anyting. If he didn't have dat money he wouldn't have gotten away wid it."

He looked as if he were at a loss. Segrario wasn't happy with the verdict either. What was it that we wanted? Did we want blood drawn? I wonder. Is there something deep inside of human beings that longs for the scaffold in the middle of the square, where the body is displayed and tortured? Was this what the media were banking on when they built their structures of display? They could never really follow through. Supposedly, we were anticipating truth. On the other hand, we didn't think it was possible.

The two-hundred-year-old cherry tree was being buzz-sawed outside as the four of us talked about the fairs and unfairs of the OJ verdict. We all felt disconnected from the justice system. I was grateful that this time, unlike when the Anita Hill–Thomas hearing came to a close with news of Thomas's appointment, I was in the company of others. At the time the verdict came down, that day I arrived in Washington—did I think that the OJ verdict had anything to do with the president of the United States? No. But I didn't know at the time that a scaffold would also be built for the president.

When the president was finally acquitted, two days before Valentine's Day 1999, the nation did not hold its breath. When I had gone to see the House take their impeachment vote, near Christmas 1998, it was anti-climactic. People roamed around the gallery, chatting as though it were just another day. "Order" was called constantly, to no avail. And as for the rest of the nation, it was Christmas shopping, disconnected from it all.

The phone man asked: "You want how many lines?"

"She needs four," Marcos called out.

"Four?"

"Two phone lines, one for fax, one for e-mail."

He headed into the bedroom. The phone man's job was to connect me, and everybody else, up to the world. All communication is possible.

Television, the Internet, all of the descendants of the lightbulb, and the telephone promise to connect us up like we've never been connected before. Yet connection is much more than spectatorship.

It seems that, since the OJ trial, the courtroom has become ever more present in our lives. The courtroom and the media stand as the places where we resolve our differences—in public. Are the courts, together with the media, a collaborative scaffold building? Isn't there some way other than to immediately head to court that we can work out differences? It gets more and more difficult to negotiate fairness without the aid of the legal system.

"Do you want two lines in the bedroom, or one?"

"Uh . . ." I headed down the steps. On the way down, I heard a crash.

"Oh no." (Marcos.)

There was a long pause, in which I could hear the saw outside, still hacking away at the two-hundred-year-old cherry tree. I stopped dead in my tracks on the steps. Marcos came out.

"We broke a mirror," he said. "We" was kind, because it was actually the man from the phone company who, while moving a dresser to look for a phone jack, caused a mirror to fall.

"Has this mirror been here since 1826 too?" Marcos continued.

"If it's an antique, we're dead," I mumbled. I hadn't even met my hosts yet, and I had bad news to report.

"Seven years bad luck," Marcos called.

By now the phone man was ready with an energetically stated alibi: the mirror was shaky in the first place—it wasn't his fault, it was the mirror's. The truth is always mitigated.

What a way to start a journey into the jungle of Washington. The OJ verdict, a saw whirring outside as the two-hundred-year-old cherry tree, dead, dead on the inside, hit the ground, and "we" broke a mirror.

HELEN THOMAS

WHITE HOUSE PRESS CORPS

"Little Match Girl"

My interest in secrets?
You mean why I have been uh
so nosy?
All I know
is
when I was five years old
a lovely woman came to visit our home.
She was a sort of distant relative
very beautiful clothes on and I kept asking her all these questions
and she
turned to me and she said "You're so inquisitive"
and I ran to my sister and said
"What does *inquisitive* mean?"
And I was just, ya know.
So my nosiness has always been—
I have a curiosity
and uh

it could be called nosiness.
I like to think, I like to know a lot of things.
I like to know everything I could possibly know.
I don't like secrecy.
I think it could be detrimental to democracy
and I don't think we should have secrecies
except for maybe the extreme
national security propositions
but otherwise I think we should have an open society and I don't
    believe in secrecy at all.
I think secrecy is uh
I think it's very hurtful to the American people.
I don't think it's necessary.
I think it's fantastic to have the privilege of covering the White
    House because this is where it all happens in terms of our
    country, in terms of the world.
We're the only superpower in the world.
We are the leaders of the world, and so I
I am able to see someone operating
And this office is the center.
You know, so when you're watching them, you feel very lucky.
Watching history every day in the making.
I mean I don't, I'm not personally affected by it because I always
    consider myself the match girl with her nose against the
    windowpane.
And, and I'm an outsider and I want to be that way.
And I'm an observer.
I'm not part of the inside.

CULTURE SHOCK

GETTING READY FOR
THE JOURNEY

ANY ANTHROPOLOGIST HAS RULES, LESSONS, SURVIVAL TECHNIQUES for moving where you don't normally move, in fact, moving where you don't belong. The need for a sense of smell, the need for a sense of humor—whether in a "rough" neighborhood or in finer circles. These are the kinds of things I have been told in the past. I try to take lessons and apply them wherever I am going. I try to pinpoint what sorts of transformations I need in order to "cross the lines." I normally take advice wherever I can, and try to follow it. I had to take information from all sources to get ready for Washington.

As I sat forward at a visiting-room table inside a prison near Washington, a compulsive thief taught me how to dress and fit into a "street environment": "To be honest, in an all-black neighborhood, a lot of people may not know that you're [black]. Maybe you need to change your lipstick to a darker color, like plum."

Later, in a tony restaurant, an anonymous Washington insider advised me, "It's a very tight, Wasp environment, it is a very tubular, closed environment. Your costume designer is going to have to go really to Pappagallo! It's as if they got their stuff at um, at um *Loehmann's*."

I figured what the prisoner had to say would be helpful in establishment Washington too. A little plum lipstick, a little Loehmann's. I wore the same outfits to visit the prison outside Washington as I wore to visit the White House.

COMPOSING LESSONS LEARNED FROM PAST

INCIDENTS OF CROSSING LINES AND

WEATHERING CULTURE SHOCK, 1959–2000

I am constantly in a state of being, to borrow a phrase from the cultural theorist Homi Bhabha, "almost, but not quite." It's actually not a bad state to be in. It might just be the best state in which to find oneself during the twenty-first century, as our culture wars continue and identity politics moves into its next phase. At such a time as this, it would be useful, I think, to have at least a cadre of people who were willing to move between cultural lines and across social strata. Globalism will require it, so we may as well practice our moves.

I am prepared for difference, live in difference. My pursuit of American character is, basically, a pursuit of difference. Character lives in that which is unique. What is unique about America is the extent to which it does, from time to time, pull off being a merged culture. Finding American character is a process of looking at fragments, of looking at the *un*merged. One has to do the footwork, one has to move from place to place, one has to stand outside. It's not easy, and the danger is that, when you stand outside, you could end up undocumented.

When I visited Thomas Jefferson's home and farm, Monticello, I went on a tour of the site of the slave quarters, which is currently part of an archaeological dig. The archaeologist was named John Meeks. I asked him what the difference would be if an archaeologist, five centuries from now, did a further dig of Jefferson's house and the slave site. He said, "There's going to be no guesswork when you run into the walls of [Jefferson's house]. It's a very substantial house type. Here [at the slave site] we have to really coax the evidence. We have nothing that marks the outside of the house. Just nails, and all outside. Which goes to what we know about slave housing. The activity took place outside the house, not inside."

The most comfortable place to live is inside of what I call one's safe house of identity. I have observed that this is where most people live. Even if they leave a previous identity to enter another identity of choice, they often end up in another safe house, and leave behind any ambiguity that met them as they went from one house to the other. I tend to be more interested in the unsettled part of us.

I am continually leaving safe houses of identity. When you leave the house of what is familiar to you—your family, your race, your social class, your nation, your professional area of expertise—it is not likely that you will find another house that will welcome you with open arms. When you leave your safe house, you will end up standing someplace in the road. I would call these places that are without houses crossroads of ambiguity. On the one hand, they are not comfortable places. On the other hand, in them one acquires the freedom to move. In my work I have moved across many cultural boundaries. For this reason I do not suffer culture shock often. I've developed a lot of stamina for being where I don't "belong."

My journey to Washington showed me that I had less stamina than I thought.

I come from a matriarchy. Pearl Banks Young, my maternal grandmother, told me many stories about her mother, and also about the woman who raised her after her mother died. The woman who raised her was called Sister Annie. She was the Grand Matron of the Eastern Star, the female counterpart to the Masons.

Grandma's subtle power was all too obvious. She was a very small woman, with a high forehead and a warm smile. She automatically engendered trust, not fear. Until the day she died, this rather short woman with a very sweet face had moral authority over all of her eight children and their children. She walked the streets of Baltimore and took buses to take care of her grandchildren. Never one to waste, she would collect pennies dropped on the floors of the homes of her grandchildren. At the end of the year, she would present us each with our pennies rolled in bank paper so that we could turn them in for dollars that we otherwise would not have had. She was a major source of nourishment in all ways. She cooked. She told me stories.

I often accompanied her around the city. We walked and took buses around Baltimore together. Since we had the same type of hair, we would regularly meet to get our hair done in an all-white salon. This in itself felt like a move into a house where I didn't belong. The salon was very different from the black salon I was used to: the smells, the colors, the clientele. Wherever we went, either to a fancy salon such as that one, or to

East Baltimore, where the poverty seemed to me to have its own smell, she would take Kleenex in her pocket in case there was a child with a runny nose.

She was a member of the Harriet Tubman Club. The Harriet Tubman Club was a club of black women, all about Grandma's age. She went on a regular basis, by foot, to pay her dues to the treasurer of the club. I often accompanied her on these occasions. As the treasurer was a short, stocky, brown-skinned woman with a wonderful smile, and as her hallway was cool and dark, and as we never ventured past the hallway, I always thought that Harriet Tubman was being kept alive in some mystical tribal way. I always thought that the club was about action, and not much talk. Grandma never told me about the club meetings or what went on there, she just paid her dues.

In my formative years I experienced a long line of matriarchs, a long line of women, tough and with their feet firmly on the ground, in power. Nothing that I learned from being in a matriarchy prepared me for Washington. Nothing that I learned from walking the varied areas of Baltimore with my grandmother, even as I can remember the determined fearlessness of her stride, or the charm of her warm smile, prepared me for Washington.

I also had a patriarchal side to my worldview. I am coming to believe that the black patriarch is significantly different from the white patriarch. There's a difference in reach. On my father's side, there was a patriarchal culture. The paternal side of my family was drenched in American history. I don't know my "roots," so to speak, but my father's aunts and uncles represented to me, as a child, American history. They looked like they had been here a long time, and many Sundays and holidays were spent visiting my Aunt Hannah in Gettysburg, and playing in the battlefield.

My paternal grandfather was a patriarch. He was called "Pop." He was tall, thin, and aristocratic looking, and had ruled, I am told, with an iron rod. He had an eighth-grade education, started a coffee and tea business with a pushcart in the early part of the twentieth century, and put all six of his children through college. He and I were good friends, because he liked to talk, and I liked to listen. He is the one who taught me the kernel of all that I understand about acting. "If you say a word often enough it becomes you" is what he said.

If Grandma showed me the world on my feet, with few words, and lots of action, Grandpop showed me the world in conversation. When he came to dinner he dominated the conversation. But even after my having grown up with our version of the patriarchy, my education in that matter was completely insufficient for the patriarchy that I met in Washington.

In my adult life I moved in the culture of the arts, which has all manner of behaviors, gracious and supremely ungracious, humanitarian, yet sometimes racist and elitist enough to take your breath away. We are in the business of representation. We are humanitarians, those who study mankind. Yet our world in art is not a diverse world. The hallways of theaters, museums, and other arts institutions are surprisingly empty of people of color (unless those people are sweeping the floors, guarding the doorways, or serving food).

When I got out of acting school, I went to my first meeting with an agent. She had a British accent. All of my classmates came back with tales from similar meetings. My meeting was one of the briefer ones. She quickly, and with no expression on her face, looked at my résumé. She turned it over and glanced at my black-and-white glossy. "I can't possibly send you out to auditions," she said. "I wouldn't want to antagonize my clients."

"Antagonize them?" I asked politely.

"Yes. You don't look like anything. You don't look black. You don't look white."

That was the end of the meeting.

My career was a long series of such meetings, and rejections. Still, none of those interactions prepared me for Washington.

An artist brings to the table, by necessity, a personal voice, a cultural voice, which is organic to where he or she once was. But once these wares are brought to market, the shock, the culture shock, is sharp, and stark. The upside of this rather downbeat tale is that in the arts one develops techniques for developing intimacies with strangers quickly. The most obvious intimacy is that with the audience. You might find yourself baring your soul or your body to complete strangers, either live or on film, an anonymous crowd who sit in the dark.

Being vulnerable in public is a way of life for artists. Yet in Washington I saw public figures being shamed publicly, and wondered at how they would ever recover. At least a movie star has the cover of persona. Politicians pretend not to have a persona. Yet both politicians and movie stars have to deal with a myriad of projections that are cast upon them, and, when they are hit hard in public, they have to survive. It was Raquel Welch who I remember hitting the first warning bell, in a droning voice, seated like a queen, on the Dick Cavett show: "They're treating politicians the way they used to treat movie stars." (She meant poorly, and with scandal lurking.)

That was in 1980. Now, I would imagine, she would say they treat them worse. I am reminded of a story about Marilyn Monroe. The studio didn't want to give her a proper dressing room when she was shooting *Gentlemen Prefer Blondes*. They said this was because she was not the star. Since the star was a brunette, Monroe's response was "I may not be a star, but I am the blonde, and this movie is called *Gentlemen Prefer Blondes*." Dignity does not come without a fight in public life.

The stakes are higher, and there is the added factor of morality in Washington. People in Washington are expected to behave in a "moral" way. Whereas artists have always been thought, if unfairly, to be degenerates. In the arts, there is a rejection process, which is humiliating. In Washington, there is a public shaming process.

NEW YORK–LOS ANGELES
1991–1992

I visited two race riots. One was in Brooklyn between blacks and Jews. The other was the Los Angeles riot in 1992. In Brooklyn I went through the war-torn streets alone, afraid only that my tape recorder, which was my most valuable possession, would be stolen. As for Los Angeles, I went to Watts, to Beverly Hills, to Simi Valley, where an all-white jury had come back with a verdict of not guilty on the videotaped beating of Rodney King, a black man, by four police officers. I went to Koreatown, where so many businesses had burned. I was more afraid in Washington than I was in the embered streets of race riots.

I am an academic and academia has all manners of behavior. Collegiality can be rewarding. Yet all the adages about the atmosphere of backstabbing and petty politics for low wages are true. We're in an era when students come to us to prepare themselves by and large for the marketplace. In the nineties, they were much more likely to gobble up answers than to see education as a process for finding the right questions. I worried that we were allowing them to be so smart, they were not wise. Academia, with all its provosts, deans, presidents, and white-haired emeriti, its colors and processions, offered a smattering of experiences, but they were not the patriarchy in its pure form.

Yet the promise and the disillusion in academia, the complex loyalties, and the quiet brutalities that sometimes appeared, did not prepare me for what I saw in Washington.

WASHINGTON
1995

Washington once sat on a swamp. Now it sits, I think, upon the patriarchy. It is the grandest of patriarchal structures. I learned that popular culture and its few stabs at making the illusion of a multicultural society could not fool me, where gender and race politics are moving, slowly, but are nonetheless moving. We're not so far along as I thought.

Ideally, Washington would be the place from which our national dialogue would emerge. I am told that in FDR's time, you could walk down a street and hear radios sending out his fireside chats. People would gather around radios of neighbors if they did not own radios themselves. Now, most of us have our own home entertainment centers. Even in a South African township, I entered a very small two-room home dominated by an enormous television from which blasted an American soap opera. Hollywood seems to hold the voices and bodies that want to talk to us, not Washington. In Washington they are talking to each other.

Is this because they can't figure out how to talk to a diverse society? What has happened that keeps us from talking to one another, even as we have so much equipment, so much technology to help us do that? Some say that the spirit of Washington is not quite right. That cynicism has overtaken the streets there. People cite Watergate as the beginning of that cynicism. They credit Woodward and Bernstein. Younger journalists seem on the prowl for that story that will land them a town house like the one Woodward has, or a movie deal. On the prowl for a story at any cost. More than a story, they want a coup. If they smell the blood, any blood, of a president, they circle. Others cite Vietnam as a turning point.

THE MADISON HOTEL
WASHINGTON, D.C.
DECEMBER 1995

Early on during my stay in Washington, I met with David Broder for breakfast:

"Vietnam."

"Oh, right."

"I mean you can go back to the battle over the United Nations, after World War I, when the Senate defied the president. But in the time I've worked here, it really turned around with Vietnam. That's when Congress stood up on its hind legs and said, No we don't support what the president's doing."

"I had thought that Watergate was sort of a point for the beginning of what people call the cynicism of our time."

"I think that a man named Murray Marder was the first to use the term *credibility gap*. And he was talking about Johnson and Vietnam."

It was the point when mistrust was bred, when many thought that the patriarchy could not be trusted after all. Perhaps, in terms of credibility, Washington is still on a swamp. Yet for all the mistrust, people still cling to and long for that patriarchal model.

We have from all fronts, for the last thirty years, questioned the moral authority and the intellectual authority of the white male as great explainer. Even as we suspect that the soul of America lives in our diversity, and even as different intellectual and cultural factions have voice, the persona of the white patriarch still thrives. We have challenged it, but it holds on to its chair with ease. We know there is no great explainer—his explanations were shown as false. And we have witnessed the power of divisive forces. David Broder continued:

"It's much, much harder for this generation to build trust for themselves, because the forces that shaped them were divisive forces within the country, not unifying forces. I mean the people who are part of that generation, the biggest things that have occurred in their lives were the civil rights struggle, the women's rights struggle, the battle over abortion, both pro and anti. And most important of all, of course, Vietnam."

It was beginning to make sense to me that the other explanation that I had been given, that is, the Watergate explanation, was too simple.

"We have yet to find among all of these enormously gifted and well-educated men and women anybody who, for very long, has been able to build a real bond of trust with the American people. And somewhere they have to find that in themselves, or it's going to be a really rough passage for the country."

No wonder Washington felt more dangerous than a race riot. It's a bigger, more complicated powder keg that holds among other things the potential for race riots . . . and wars and more. On the other hand, it holds the potential for something remarkable as well.

The language of Washington is in disrepair. Americans don't believe the language that comes out of there. Is it because that credibility gap born nearly forty years ago has never been repaired? To repair it would take more than the patriarchal voice. Perhaps the repair could be helped along by the diversity that we have, by the new canons that have been built, by the stronger, more literate, more articulate populace that we have.

MARK FABIANI

FORMER CLINTON STAFFER

"What Do They Want You For?"

We moved to Washington.
In the first year it was great because it was different from L.A.,
and the seasons
and we were about to go see all of the museums
and the sights and everything.
But after that it became appalling
appalling in its
insularity
appalling in its

strict hierarchy
appalling in its
oneness.
It is a one,
and this is not an original thought,
but it sure is true,
it's a one-company town.
Everybody works for the company,
lives off the company,
attacks the company,
lobbies the company.
You go to a party and,
if you're somebody who works at the White House,
people want to talk to you.
If you're someone who has a business—a really interesting
      business—
Yeah—
unless you're Kevin Costner or somebody
you know
it's like
well, who do you work for?
You don't work on the hill?
You don't work in the White House?
You start.
People look over your shoulder.
I think if people were exposed to it,
they would think even less of Washington than they do already.
I think that if the common person were really exposed to what—
I mean they've heard about it,
and they've read about it,
and they've seen spoofs of it on TV.
But I mean if they really saw it
they would be appalled,
I think.
Appalled!
The pomposity of the
of the whole thing.

Oh yeah.

It's unbelievable.

I mean a relatively mediocre level of talent taking itself seriously.

This is a surreal experience.

The day Hillary was in the grand jury, which was a horrendous
week.

It was a Friday.

Late that Friday night when I was going home, I took the metro.

I got mugged.

It's like dealing with reporters!

You try to develop a rapport.

I mean you try to treat people with some respect.

I had spent a lot of time in L.A. with young black kids and you
know

kids with problems,

and he was looking to be treated with respect.

He was looking for someone to take his threats seriously,

but also to treat him honorably in that,

if you did what he wanted you to do, he would do

what you wanted done.

So if I did everything, you know, he would live up to his part of the
bargain.

He would let me go.

We lived up near the top of King Street in Alexandria.

So I was just walking up to my house.

It was late.

It was like 11:30 on a Friday

or 10:30 on a Friday night.

He turned me around, walked me over to his car with his friend.

Drove around for a couple of hours in Southeast.

Visited ATM machines.

You know I mean he could have

Well he got like sixteen hundred dollars, which I think was more
than he expected to get.

Because one of my credit cards had cash access in addition to the
ATM card.

I don't know what would have happened if he had only gotten the
    four hundred dollars that you get from an ATM card, but he
those things usually don't end that way.
So whatever you can say about the guy, he didn't do what he could
    have done, or what most people would.
I mean when they found who this guy was, I punched him up on
    Lexis-Nexis [when] they arrested him.
It was a really sad story.
He was a former first-round draft pick in the NBA, a big college
star in North Carolina State, and a high school star at DeMatha in
    Washington.
he pled guilty—
Oh he blew out his knee when he was first-year pro from Kansas
    City
and actually had quite a life.
He adopted kids in their teenage years and tried
to help them out, even after he had blown out his knee, and his
    career was over.
But then he fell on hard times and ran out of money
and started using crack, and it was a terrible story.
It was a very sad story.
So later it was a couple—it was a month or two later
and the FBI, early Saturday morning,
had asked me to go out and walk the scene for them.
And it was like freezing cold,
and I'm going out there.
I'm trying to walk up this hill, in this slush and rain
and my beeper goes off.
And I look at it, and it's the first lady calling me.
So I rush to the phone and I say I'm sorry there
was a delay in getting back to you,
I was with the FBI.
She said as cool, as calm as could be
"What do they want you for?"
That put it in perspective for me.
And I waited for her to laugh

or something.

And then she—she—"What do they want you for?"

[He explodes into laughter]

I said "Well Mrs. Clinton, they didn't want me for anything, I'm just
    helping them with the investigation of this thing."

She goes "Oh, oh oh, oh, okay."

I'm thinking this has become such a commonplace part of their lives

that someone who has, you know,

no connection to much of this at all . . .

It was a great moment.

I'll never forget the tone of her voice.

"Oh, what do they want you for?"

I'll never forget when Hillary said "What do they want you for?"

[He keeps laughing]

A TROCHEE IN THE
SECOND BEAT

MY PURSUIT OF THE AUTHENTIC WITH THE USE OF ACTING AS A frame was not entirely fearless. I was afraid of many things. I was afraid of heights. Circus class was a terrifying prospect once we moved from juggling socks to juggling balls and then clubs. The next step was the trapeze. Then came the day that we all had to hang upside down on the trapeze. I had no choice but to confess my fear. My circus teacher, much to my surprise, looked me straight in the eye, and said, "I understand fear." She still made me hang upside down on the trapeze, but at least I knew that she had heard me, and I heard her. We had communicated; this alone made the task seem doable.

But nothing matched my fear of Shakespeare. This seemed to be an overwhelming task—to speak in Shakespeare, that thick, antiquated language that seemed totally irrelevant to the world around me. Yet it was learning to speak Shakespeare that would catapult me into the quest, into the search, that I am now pursuing with the same vigor that I had all those years ago.

Our Shakespeare teacher was like a racehorse waiting at the gate. Whenever we entered class, she was waiting for us, impatiently drumming her fingers on her leg, or on a table. She was originally from Appalachia. I suspect that she came, like I did, from an oral tradition, only a white one.

She told us on the first day about trochees. Most of us had heard of iambic pentameter: BuhDUH buh DUHbuh DUHbuhDUHbuhDUH.

"Okay?"

"Yes," we mumbled in unison.

"Now, a trochee," she explained, "happens when the iamb goes upside down. So that instead of Buh DUH, you get BUH duh."

She maintained that if you got a trochee in the second beat, a character was really "losing it" psychologically, and this "loss" made it possible for you to really know something about that character, if you wore his or her words.

Losing it is a good thing in that it is a defeat of an imposed rhythmic structure.

The classic example of everything falling to pieces rhythmically as an indicator of a character's psychological state is King Lear, who says at one point, "Never, never, never, never, never!"

Which is all trochees.

From this idea, I began to see Shakespeare in general as not so frightening at all. I began to perceive him as a jazz musician, who was doing jazz with the given rhythms of his time.

Character, then, seemed to me to be an improvisation on given rhythms. The more successful you were at improvising on language, the more jazz you have, the more likely you could be found in your language, that is, if you wanted to be found in your language. Some people use language as a mask. And some want to create designed language that appears to reveal them but does not. Yet from time to time we are betrayed by language, if not in the words themselves, in the rhythm with which we deliver our words. Over time, I would learn to listen for those wonderful moments when people spoke a kind of personal music, which left a rhythmic architecture of who they were. I would be much more interested in those rhythmic architectures than in the information they might or might not reveal.

Our Shakespeare teacher then gave us an assignment: "Go home, take fourteen lines of Shakespeare, and say them over and over again, until something happens."

That's all she said. Now, in 2000, when my students pay as much as thirty thousand dollars a year for an education, I find that they have little tolerance for metaphor and usually want more from me than those kinds of instructions. Even in the openness of the seventies, some among us did grumble. I was intrigued by the instruction, and was determined to do exactly as she asked.

I went to the Tenderloin, where the down-and-outers were. There were a number of used-book stores there. As Shakespeare was not a hot ticket in that neighborhood, I had my pick of volumes. I found one that was wonderfully well worn. It was red, beat-up, and looked a bit like a Bible. I paid five dollars for it, which at the time seemed like a fortune.

I chose a speech from *Richard III*. I had no scientific way of choosing a speech, I simply turned pages until I found fourteen lines. I chose Queen Margaret. She was speaking of Richard III to his mother in this way:

That dog, that had his teeth before his eyes,
To worry lambs, and lap their gentle blood . . .
Thy womb let loose, to chase us to our graves.

I said these words, as instructed, over and over again "until something happened." Everything happened. Not only did I feel as though I had "become" Queen Margaret, but I had what in the seventies we would have called a "transcendental experience," fully unaided by chemical substances of any kind. I, in fact, "saw" Queen Margaret—she was a small vision, standing in my apartment. She came from the same place that the tooth fairy came from when I was a child. She came from my imagination. She was concocted somehow from the words. Words, it seemed to me, from then on were truly magical, not only by their meaning but by the way we say them, how we manipulate them.

My paternal grandfather had told me when I was a child, "If you say a word often enough, it *becomes* you."

What has happened to the manipulation of words in public speech? Imagine the potential of the magic of words—to communicate, to intoxicate, to *sway* a crowd. To concoct a vision? Without language there is no vision.

We sit and watch our politicians speak, and we change the channel. There seems to be no place for swaying with words.

I was teaching freshmen. These were people who were born in 1981. Nonetheless, I decided to try some old-fashioned oratory on them. I had a videotape of Bobby Kennedy on the occasion of the death of Martin Luther King, in Indiana, and I had a tape of Barbara Jordan, the congresswoman from Texas, during the Nixon impeachment hearings. I played for them Kennedy's speech.

"Could you lower those signs please?" RFK began. "I have some very sad news for all of you and that is that Martin Luther King was shot and killed tonight in Memphis, Tennessee." He quoted Aeschylus. He said that he could understand that people may want to give up on race relations because Martin Luther King had been killed "by a white man." And from the looks of things, it really didn't look very good for race relations. Then he paused. And he said that a member of his family . . . And he paused again and said that a member of his family had been killed (pause) by a "white man."

I sat in the back of the room; the students huddled around the video. I was worried that they would find no connection with the speech. Not so. There was something riveting about this speech, which Kennedy made without notes—and what was riveting, according to the students, was his vulnerability.

Acting, the study of the authentic, puts a high premium on vulnerability. When there is vulnerability there is a greater possibility that something will actually happen. Seated in the back of the darkened room as I was, even having watched this speech a number of times before, I was arrested by Bobby Kennedy's openness about race. Few politicians since have spoken as openly as he did. Race is a particular issue that calls for covered, coded, euphemistic language. Even my students in 1999 found his references to race to be surprisingly "honest." "You don't hear that type of talk now," one of them said. Then what have we been doing all these years? I thought. Yet Kennedy's job was in part to plead for nonviolence. Apparently the city from which he spoke was one of the few that did not burst into riot.

Later in that same session, I ran the tape of Barbara Jordan for them. She held forth with planned cadences—all iambic pentameters, really, but with such clarity, and such courage, and then, quite unexpectedly, as she spoke about the Constitution, in one alarming moment, a trochee appeared; she said, almost in another register, that if the Constitution were to mean nothing, then it might as well be relegated to a "twentieth-century paper shredder." She had been speaking so carefully, so deliberately, naming herself as a person who had not been adequately protected by the Constitution, moving inch by inch over slavery and right up to the present moment, when Nixon had not honored the honorable document, which she herself honored. She reminded me of Queen Margaret. In iambic beat, she spoke to a hushed and attentive audience. She spoke of "ob-fus-cations." She enunciated every consonant, every vowel. And yet it was not stiff, it was music. Why was it music? Because, underneath, one could hear all that was *not said*.

The not-said is as important as the said. Yet not saying is not the same as lying, it is not the same as covering. In authentic speech, it is what is felt that is transmitted. We live in a time when what is felt personally is at a premium, but when what is felt civically is not. We live in a time of coined phrases (phrases that are designed to move like currency) and studied nonchalance.

I asked the freshmen for the most memorable moment in the speech. Knowing nothing about trochees, and very little about Nixon and Watergate, and having been born nearly a decade after, they selected the "twentieth-century paper shredder."

Speaking calls for risk, speaking calls for a sense of what one has to lose. Not just what one has to gain. Clearly for Barbara Jordan, the Constitution in the paper shredder would be a significant, if not earth-shattering loss. Speaking calls for heart.

It seems very hard to find this kind of speaking in public life now. It's not only because of the speakers, the leaders. It's also because the audience doesn't want this type of passionate earnestness, or at least that's what we are told. The public does not trust words. People seem to be looking beyond the spoken word. The word is not enough. When was the last time any of us accepted a person's "word"? We need contracts, we need laws, we need evidence. We need much more than verbal promises.

Perhaps this is why political life is now cluttered with pictures rather than words—photo ops, which make things seem more "real" perhaps. Our "word" is not enough. We need evidence.

Why is it so difficult to find public speech that has trochees in the second beat—or trochees at all? I would have to look for the answer to this as I went on my search to "find" American character in the presidency.

Character depends a great deal on trochees. We must wear our language, the language must not wear us. Language is a dance between you and the other, it is not meant to be camouflage, or cover. The dance of language is not the same as the confessional, which has also permeated our culture.

There is so much talk after all—talk shows, talk therapies—to some extent we are talking ourselves to death. But it's just like food—we can eat junk food, or we can be nourished. And it's not necessary to have volume; birds, after all, fly with only seeds and water. The question is, does the talk make anything happen—or is all our public talk only connected somehow to the marketplace? Is it just one more thing that we consume?

I believe that talk comes from a rather divine place, and that the real conversations are the ones that cause change. I am fully aware that this is not a modern way to think. Yet language is part of what makes us human. We humans are linguistic animals.

1996
SAN FRANCISCO

I was speaking with a scholar of rhetoric, Hayden White, from the University of California at Santa Cruz.

He is more jaded than I about that possibility of an authentic voice. He thought that the power of rhetoric in modern life is that it makes connections that aren't even true.

He is midspeech in a restaurant at the Fairmont Hotel: "So that when I teach ideology . . . you have to ask the question of why it is that so many people who are otherwise quite—may be quite nice people, like people of goodwill . . ."

"Wow."

"Christians and so forth and yet they're still racists—right?"

"Right."

"They seem to think that that's justified."

"Right."

"Or if people who identify democracy with the free market."

"Uh-huh."

"The assumption is that the free market and democracy go hand in hand. If you buy into the free market, you have to take a certain amount of unemployment, a certain amount of exploitation, a certain amount of corruption, and so forth. It has nothing to do with democracy."

"Oh? Yeah."

"So, I mean, that's been the greatest triumph of Western capitalism—it's been to identify democracy . . ."

"Uh-huh."

". . . with the free market."

Our modern American problem is not a lack of communication. The problem is a disconnect between the heart of a voice and the purpose that the voice is meant to serve. The public voice repeats the status quo. And most voices that we hear have been adjusted by the time they get to us. We rely so much on mass communication, and mass communication controls so much of what gets to us. It's very hard to hear an original voice. We are very far from the personal, the one-to-one, the human touch.

Shakespeare's technology was very simple. A printing press, and accepted poetic rhythms of the time. It broke through accepted rhythms. He proved that accepted rhythms were too restrictive to hold humanity. He brought us human character that has lasted centuries. What would it take now to bring across some trochees in the second beat? We have studied nonchalance—the rhythms of distance and coolness—as our iambic pentameter. And, as we are in an age of incredible discovery in the communications field, I wouldn't dare to define what is as prolific as the printing press. Who knows, it's possible that by next year even the e-mail by which I send this to my editor will be replaced by something else.

When I told Hayden White that I believed in authentic voice, it was as if I told him I still believed in Santa Claus. He laughed, and looked at me with both a sparkle, and pity, in his eyes.

STUDS TERKEL

AMERICANIST

"Defining Moment in American History"

Defining moment in American history
I don't think there's one
you can't say Hiroshima.
That's a big moment.
I don't think there's any one.
I can't pick out any one.
It's a combination of many.
I can't think of any one moment I'd say is the defining moment.
But the gradual slippage—
slippage is the word used by Jeb Magruder
one of Nixon's boys that went to jail—during Watergate—
moral slippage.
We accept it daily now more and more.
It happens bit by bit and drop by drop.
It's a gradual kind of thing.
A combination of things.
The funny thing is you see we also have
the technology.
I say less and less the human touch
so I can tell you of another funny
playlet.
The Atlanta airport is a modern airport
and as you leave the gate
there are these trains
that take you to the
uh
concourse
and out to a destination.

You go on these trains
and they're smooth and
quiet and efficient and there's a voice you hear on the train
the voice you know was a human voice—
See in the old days you had robots
the robots imitated humans.
Now you have humans, imitating robots!
So you got this voice
on this train
"Concourse One
Dallas
Fort Worth
Concourse Two
Omaha
Lincoln"
Same voice.
Just!
as the train is about to go
a young couple
rush in
and they're just about to close the pneumatic doors?
And-that-voice
without-losing-a-beat-says
"Because-of-late-entry-we're-delayed-thirty-seconds."
Just then
everybody is looking at this couple
with hateful eyes
the couple is going like this shrinkin'
and [I]
said "Oh my God."
I'd happened to have had a few drinks
before boarding
I do that
to steel my nerves.
And so
I
imitate a train call

holding my hand
over my heart
"George Orwell,
your time has come."
Everybody laughs when I say that
but not on that train!
Silence!
And they're lookin' at me
And so suddenly I'm shrinkin'!
So there I am with the couple
the three of us
at the foot of Calvary
about to be upped you know.
Just then I see a baby
a little baby in the lap of a mother—
I know it's Hispanic cause she's speakin'
Spanish
to her companion—
about a year old
a little baby with a round little face ya know
and so I'm going to talk to the baby
so I say to the baby—
holding my hand over my mouth cause
my breath may be a hundred proof!—
So I say to the baby
"Sir or madam
What is your considered opinion
of the human species?"
And the baby looks
you know the way babies look at ya
clearly
and starts laughing
busting out with a crazy little laugh
and I say
"Thank God
for a human reaction!
We haven't lost yet!"

And so there we have it!
But the human touch
that's disappearing you see.
So we talk about defin—
There ain't no defining moment
for me.
All moments are defining and add up.
There's an accretion of movement that leads to where we are now
when trivia becomes news.
When more and more less and less awareness
of pain of the other.
So this is an interesting dilemma with which we are faced.
I don't know if a used this or not
I was quoting Wright Morris
this writer from Nebraska, who says
"We're more and more into communications and less and less
into communication!"

THE THREE QUESTIONS

1981

MANHATTAN

JIMMY CARTER WAS PRESIDENT AT THE TIME. I HAD LEFT MY TENURE-track job at Carnegie Mellon University, much to the surprise of my parents and others. Thinking I was simply not cut out for university life, I decided to go to New York, and walk dogs if I had to. Which is what I did. Interestingly enough, I walked the dog of a woman who coached newscasters, some highly public figures—including presidential candidates. She was teaching them to be "natural." I typed her notes to them. The notes, without divulging anything specific, were often about what tie they should wear, or how they could improve their enunciation, or reminders to keep breathing. It was really good old-fashioned common sense. It was easy to observe, at the time, that people were still so enamored of the camera—as if the camera was going to catch something mysterious about them that they themselves weren't fully conscious of. Her work was to firmly plant them in the moment. The moment of who they really "were." The idea being, of course, that the camera sees all, and that what it really wants is who you "are"—who you *really* are. She was kind enough to give me a free lesson one day. It's hard. To be "yourself" in front of the camera. Really hard.

Two of her clients at the time were George and Barbara Bush. I became fascinated with what it meant to groom public figures. It seemed to me that public figures were as interested in authenticity as actors were. Or at least they wanted the *benefits* of authenticity. Yet none of them would have given over three years of their lives, as most actors in training do. It takes at least three intense years in a conservatory to become a transformative being. It was clear that her clients wanted the instant "result" of that training. That result being "presence." In fact, presence can most likely not be taught.

My boss had herself been a student of one of the most important teachers of acting—when everyone was teaching "the method." If you would like a crash course on the method, take a look at Marlon Brando in *On the Waterfront,* particularly that scene in the back of the car, when he says, "I coulda been a contender." It's a cliché now, but it is also startling in its "realness." This idea of performing "realness" is what seems to permeate political and public life now.

The dog walking lasted until I got cast in a couple of plays. Such a windfall of work for an actor is enough to make you believe you *are,* after all, an actor. When that windfall of luck fizzled out, I found myself, once again, at the mercy of the winds of chance.

I worked doing very low-level secretarial jobs out of a temp agency and going to auditions whenever I could. I also had, by now, collected some students here and there, and did private coaching.

Then came the whiff of a turning point, but it was not the type of turning point a careerist would imagine. One of the numerous low-level secretarial jobs I had was in the dimly lit offices of J. P. Stevens. I sat next to a woman called Julia, who had been a secretary there for quite some time. She was, for all intents and purposes, my "boss." I did photocopying and such, she did the heavy lifting. Julia was a very dark-skinned black woman with flawless skin and life pouring out of every pore in her body despite the horrifying lighting and low ceilings of the office. There was more light coming out of Julia's eyes, and her occasional smile, than on the whole floor. Thank God they could afford Julia, because clearly they couldn't afford Con Ed.

At first Julia was rather lukewarm toward me. But I was determined to get her to talk. I would catch her eye and smile whenever I could. I knew that under that layer of professionalism was someone who was full of stories, stories with wonderful rhythms, stories with wonderful performances. I was right. She could barely get through a story without a giggle.

Dismal as the place was, I preferred working there to working in some of the tonier law firms I'd been to, with their sleek wood, fine furniture, and the occasional salacious comment from one man or another who was not the stereotypical geezer you would imagine but rather someone who looked like he was still in junior high, with no hair on his face, a crisp white shirt, and a tie that was too big for his neck. You were also apt to land a boss who was (Gloria Steinem, forgive me for saying this) one of those humorless women in a headband, obsessed with exactly how sharp you had managed to get her pencils. Undoubtedly these women saw through my obedient secretarial manner, to see that I (or any other artist who might cross their path) was likely nearly as educated as they were. And these were always the most disturbing moments. I kept thinking that the women's movement would have not only succeeded at placing women, like this one, in positions that were formerly meant only for men, but also made headway in ensuring that women would be comrades—comrades across race and hierarchies. Not so.

Not to put the women all in one category.

This cast of characters, the women with bluntly clipped hair and the men with ties too big for their necks, would be a descant throughout my working life, and they would show up again in Washington. It's not the ties or the haircuts, it's the lack of light in their eyes that characterizes them.

One advantage to acting is that you move up and down and all across the social circles of our country. You never know what your status will be, and so you understand that status is man-made. It's not written in stone. I've now met with presidents and prisoners. I've been on death row, I've spoken to the nation's best chefs, I've been behind closed doors at Monticello after the place was closed down for the day. I'm a visitor, and from this vantage point I have ever more difficulty understanding the lines that mark us one human—away—from the other.

Jean-Paul Sartre, in an essay on actors, gives the following picture: An actor is on the bus reading the financial pages. If you look closely, you see that the pages are upside down. We should see that the pages could work just as well for the study of humanity if they were upside down. But actors today are more likely to have the financial pages right side up. And perhaps, in this activity, we give over part of what is most useful about us. We're all taking ourselves awfully seriously in America right now. Even the clowns have mortgages.

I certainly preferred working for Julia to working for the associates with whom I was often placed in law firms. Slowly but surely I got her to talk to me. I learned about her circle of friends—I learned about the zany events that had happened to her on her bus rides from her home in New Jersey to work. I saw how easy it was to get people to talk. It could start out as a nearly subversive act, whisperings over workstations—and it could land finally in a full interview over dinner after work.

In the midst of my temp jobs, an unexpected thing happened. I came down with a terrible case of mononucleosis. I had no health insurance and no money.

Then came my big break. I landed a low-level secretarial job at KLM Airlines. I was working for the complaint department. All day long I read complaint letters. These were wide-ranging. There was the man who was outraged about a flight with a drunken soccer team that ended with lost luggage—luggage that had his glaucoma medicine in it. Then there was the woman whose eighty-five-year-old mother had flown in from Egypt to Dulles Airport. KLM was to have provided an escort, as the mother knew nothing about Washington, had never been to the United States, and spoke no English. They failed to send the escort, and so the mother, somehow, ended up in a cab in Washington, D.C., driving around all night, with no idea of where she was and no ability to tell anyone where she needed to be. I loved my job—I laughed out loud from time to time.

I could not have been given a clearer counterpoint to the job I had done previously. Then I had spent a year typing up letters to newscasters and presidential candidates about how to get it "right," how to sound "perfect" for the audience. Now I was reading letters about how very wrong a large airline had been. These letters were *from* the people. The notes to the newscasters were about how to *approach* the people. The letters of complaint were much less inhibited than the notes to newscasters.

I began to see that there was a theater project in this. What exactly it was I didn't know. I wanted to know the relationship of character to language—and, to be even more scientific about it, I wanted to know, What is the relationship of language to *identity*? What does language, the way we render language, tell us about who we are? What does it tell us on an individual level? What does it tell us on a societal level?

So, basically, in the offices of KLM Airlines my project "On the Road: A Search for American Character," which had many sources, began to gel. Everything I read seemed to offer a clue. I had come across something that the writer Eudora Welty had said about her childhood. She would sit in the hallway outside the room where all the adults were talking, and her ears would "open up like morning glories."

My colleagues from KLM were from all over the world. Perched as I was in my little corner, behind a divider, in the complaint department, I read complaints, and listened listened listened to a wide variety of vocal tones that spanned from Holland to the Caribbean, Brooklyn, and onward.

I loved what I was hearing and wanted to hear more of it. How could I hear people authoring their speech, putting themselves in their speech? How could I study speech as a design around identity? How could I study speech as *betrayal*? When does it betray, when does it cooperate? When is it powerful enough to cause action? The wonderful thing about dramatic speech is that it is built to *cause action*.

If I were to go around and listen listen listen to Americans, would I end up with some kind of a composite that would tell me more about America than what is *evidently* there? How could I get underneath the surfaces? I could tell that speech would *have* to be a resource. Look at the way people can dive and dip and breathe and exclaim and come up with all manner of sounds in the course of saying a word. No one among us talks like anyone else.

How could I learn more about those powerful moments when people speak their speech, speak a moment in their lives until the music of the moment overpowers the information they are trying to communicate? I found a key, by sheer luck. I was at a party, in New York, I cannot remember who gave the party or why I was there. But I do remember meeting a linguist. She was not an invited guest, as I recall. She was the date of somebody. Most likely I was the date of somebody myself. It was not an actors' party, it was fancier, which is what leads me to believe this was sort of outside my normal circle.

I don't remember her name. We struck up a conversation. I told her some of the things I was learning in the complaint department and a few of my theories on acting. I told her about my dismay with the "self" technique of most acting teachers. I was on my own for all intents and purposes—for finding even a way to continue the study of acting for myself, let alone my students. At the time it was getting harder and harder to find the difference between psychotherapy and acting in New York. I just couldn't sit in another class and see someone brought to tears by a coach. I had sworn not to go to another one of those kinds of teachers who did psychoanalysis as acting teaching. She understood what I was stumbling around to find—or at least part of it. I told her, in essence, that I wanted to get people to talk to me, in a true way. Not true in the sense of spilling their guts. Not true in the sense of the difference between truth and lies. I wanted to hear—well—authentic speech, speech that you could dance to, speech that had the possibility of breaking through the walls of the listener, speech that could get to your heart, and beyond that to someplace else in your consciousness.

I knew enough to know that this quest was not only about the development of my voice as an artist. To develop a voice, I told her, "I need to develop an ear." She told me she could describe to me how to get people to talk, to really talk to me. She gave me her phone number and told me to call.

It was a Saturday when I called her. I told her more about what I understood. I told her that this "thing" I was after had another tangible sign. I didn't tape-record the conversation, but I can remember and imagine that it sounded something like this, although possibly less coherent or more coherent. It went something like this:

"When they're talking that way, their syntax starts to fall apart, their grammar starts to fumble, they lose words, sometimes they go off words, sometimes they make sounds that have nothing to do with words."

She agreed with me enthusiastically.

"See the thing is," I continued, "it's like jazz. They start out singing a familiar song, with a predictable pattern. If I listen for, say, five minutes, I can tell what that pattern is. They might talk for an entire hour in that pattern. It might be a pattern that they learned from their mother or father or friends or on television. . . ."

We agreed.

"It's usually a composite pattern of, say, their years of hearing and talking."

This was obvious.

"But what I want to do is get them to break that pattern while they're talking to me, because when they break it, they do things that are so specific to them and only them. And if I can take those few moments—it might be only three seconds, it might be a full minute—if I can get a hold of those moments, and reproduce them—then I will seem to be just *like* them."

She thought that was interesting.

"I was a mimic when I was a kid."

She thought that was interesting.

"I'm not interested in mimicry the way an impressionist is on a talk show. You see, I want to use my ability to mimic to sort of get at those moments when people are themselves, becoming themselves in language. I believe identity is a process and that we are every moment making an adjustment, and sometimes those moments happen while we're talking—I mean, people use language to get married, to come to the realization that they're dying. I mean it happens—right—in the words."

I could tell I was making a good impression.

"And, look, this neighborhood where I'm living in Manhattan—it's changing overnight. Every bit of individuality is disappearing. Amsterdam Avenue, where I live, and Columbus Avenue, which is a block away, used to be the service streets for Broadway and Central Park West. But look what's happening. There's no more baker, no more candlestick maker; the shoe-maker is closing down, and these huge franchises are moving in. I want to chronicle this disappearance of individual effort, and its replacement with franchised life, in language. We're all going to talk like each other before we know it. In the end, I believe it can be seen, like fossils, in what we say and how we say it to one another."

The vibes were good. She seemed to be with me.

"If I can do this, I can avoid a lot of the so-called psycho technique. I'm talking about an acting technique that was developed by a man named Konstantin Stanislavsky in the last century in Russia. The goal was to have stage behavior look real. This entire century has been smitten with the same idea. That we should look real on stage. It's become almost a religion. The thought was that realness on the outside would flow naturally from realness on the inside. In other words, if, as an actor, you took the time to think and feel like a real person, the result would be that the actor would seem to be acting, externally, like a real person. Think of it, we like performances in movies that seem 'real.' So this was a powerful technique that he had. It has many heirs and has lasted a long time."

She thought this was interesting.

"He did this work during the same era in which Freud was writing. I think that we have other ways of studying and replicating human behavior now. He wanted to rid the stage of stiff, histrionic acting. But we are getting to the point now where we think people act the way they seem to act in television and movies, but the problem is, we often act like what we see in television and movies in real life! I want to find other ways of getting to the inside of a person. I don't think I should base my idea of another person all on my own feelings, which is what Stanislavsky was after." Ultimately I was to believe that the Stanislavsky technique, for all its undeniable success, was a spiritual dead end.

"I'm not the other and can never be the other," I continued. "I can only try to bridge the gap, and I'm looking for ways to bridge the gap."

I hunkered down, and drove on to my ultimate goal—my experiment. "I think we can learn a lot about a person in the very moment that language fails them. In the very moment that they have to be more creative than they would have imagined in order to communicate. It's the very moment that they have to dig deeper than the surface to find words, and at the same time, it's a moment when they want to communicate very badly. They're digging deep and projecting out at the same time."

She was following me.

"The traditional acting technique wants to know who I am in the character. Perhaps it's based on a very humanitarian assumption that we are all the same underneath. I don't believe that. I'm interested in difference. I want to know who the character is, not who I am. Somewhere in all of it, I may learn who I am, too, but that's not the goal. It's in language that I think I can find the other. If I can get people to that moment that they're digging deep, and then I repeat what they have done, I should actually end up seeming quite like them."

She was intrigued.

"And we're in a moment when technology can support what I am doing. Stanislavsky did not have the tape recorder. I do. I am able to study a person's language and breaths very carefully, because I can record it, and listen to it over and over again. I think it's about finding that moment when syntax changes, when grammar breaks down. Those are the moments I should study, if I want to know who a person is."

She thought this was interesting.

"So the idea is that the psychology of people is going to live right inside those moments when their grammar falls apart and, like being in a shipwreck, they are on their own to make it all work out. I mean, I'm talking about something that lasts a few seconds, it's not a catastrophe, and it is seldom frightening or anything like that. Although I suspect there would be circumstances where it *could* be frightening. It could also be joyous, like when you tell someone you love them."

I went on to ask about the variety of situations that leave us putting our words together on our own.

If I simply say those moments as specifically as I possibly can, I am going to know a heck of a lot about who *they* are. If I could wear them in those kinds of moments, I could seem to *be* them. But it's all about finding that moment when syntax changes."

She agreed.

"How much time do you have?" she said.

"You mean now?"

"When you do an interview, how much time do you have?"

I thought about the reality of my life at the time, which was if I could get an interview it was usually over lunchtime.

"Oh, I don't know, about an hour, or forty-five minutes. Seldom more than an hour."

"I can give you three questions that will ensure that their syntax will change in the course of an hour." She had one of those wonderfully efficient and confident vocal tones that people like linguists and anthropologists have. Sometimes they are as direct as accountants are.

I, of course, will never forget this part of the conversation. She stated the questions, quickly. I was writing as fast as I could.

"One is, Have you ever come close to death?"

"Okay."

"Another is, Do you know the circumstances of your birth?"

"Interesting."

"The third is, Have you ever been accused of something that you did not do?"

She went on to say that sometimes asking people about their first day of school is a good one too.

These three questions became the spine of all of my work for the next several years. I had a Panasonic tape recorder that was about eight inches long and five inches wide. I took it to talk to anyone who would talk to me—the lady in the clothing store up the street, the lifeguard at the YMCA pool where I swam, people I met at parties. At the time I had a small group of actors who were working with me, people I had met in different schools and studios.

I would simply walk up to a person and say, "I know an actor who looks like you. If you give me an hour of your time, I will invite you to see yourself performed."

Somewhere in that hour, I would ask those three questions. The result was a performance that I produced myself in a loft in Lower Manhattan, with twenty actors and twenty real people who came with their friends. I played Julia.

I don't ask those questions anymore, but they taught me how to listen—because after I asked the questions, I would listen like I had never listened before for people to begin to sing to me. That singing was the moment when they were really talking.

I've taken that tape recorder, which has now become a Sony professional, and sometimes a DAT recorder, from place to place all over America since the early eighties. I took it finally to Washington, D.C., and listened as hard as I could for the talk, the talk of the big talkers, to turn, if only for a moment, into a song that they and only they can sing.

ALEXIS HERMAN

U.S. SECRETARY OF LABOR

You know, my daddy was very active during his life.
You know
he was the first black to sue the Democratic Party because they
    wouldn't give him an absentee ballot.
He just didn't take no for answers, you know.
He wasn't a fiery man; he was just steady and persistent, you
    know?
But he had this quiet way
of getting people out of trouble, you know,
in the South when they would get arrested or folk would end up in
    jail in the middle of the night or these—we call it police
    brutality now; I don't know what the name was for it then.

So

and on Christmas Eve, we always took these rides out, you know,
    and that's how he would put me to sleep and bring me back
    home.
So that's kind of what I did with him.
And this one Christmas Eve night we were going over the bay
to Father Warren, he's a priest, and—
And we went for our ride
and he went to one of his meetings over the bay.
My daddy had a silver pistol with a pearl handle,
and he was a peaceful man. I never heard my daddy curse or raise
    his voice a day in his life.
He kept his gun right here in the front of his old DeSoto.
Green and white.
We had lots of DeSotos [but] ours was green and white. But
    whenever there was trouble,
you know,
something was going on,
the gun came out from under here,
and he would always put it by his side.
Now, I used to like to sit up under my daddy when we would be
    riding
and sometimes, you know how daddies put you in their laps and let
    you steer the wheel.
But if the gun was on the seat, then I knew that there was a
    problem.
I was scared of that gun.
I was scared of that gun
you know. I didn't like that gun because it just was a symbol of
    tension and something was wrong, and my daddy could be
    hurt.
I didn't want anybody messing with my daddy.
So this particular night the gun is out
we go over the bay
we go over to Father Warren's,
and they were all in their meeting.

And we get back in the car.

In those days, over the bay, dark roads, dirt roads, no lights, the
church is way back off the road.

And we're coming back from the meeting that night

and

you know

the cars and the lights had come behind us

and my daddy starts driving fast

and we're trying to get around these cars

and they're, you know, pushing us off the side of the road with the
cars, and he's having—

It's the Klan, yeah.

He pulled over

just stopped

and he said, you know, he said, Poppy's got to get out of this car

and he says, I'm going to put this gun in your hand, and I want you
to get right down there

and he pointed, like, under the dashboard. And he said

You get down there

and Poppy's going to put this gun in your hand.

And he says, I'm going to have to get out of this car, and I'm going
to lock this door.

He said, If anybody opens that door

I want you to pull that trigger.

And he took my finger and he put it right on that trigger and he put
that gun in my hand and I had it just like this and I was down
under the dashboard.

Oh, yeah. I was tiny.

I was always a small child.

And that's where I got.

I got down on the floor underneath the dashboard by the seat with
the gun in my hand, and he got out and locked the door, and
he just started walking to face the Klan.

And he told me don't raise my head

don't look up

don't look out.

You know, I could hear them, you know.
I could hear them.
You know
you could see the car lights and stuff
but mostly I could hear them.
What I remember more than anything were these sounds, you
    know. Yelling, names, and shouting.
I remember that more than anything.
That's why for years I didn't talk about this because I could hear
    those sounds.
"Nigger"
you know
"Get him"
"Kill him"
"Beat him"
you know
just, just sounds.
I just remember—I remember "nigger" more than anything.
What I remember more than anything was just the word "nigger."
    "Get that nigger."
"Here comes that nigger," you know.
So, anyway, I just remember "nigger" more than anything.
So it seemed like forever.
I really don't know how long it was, but it felt like forever that I was
    down there with this gun, and eventually I heard Father
    Warren's voice saying
Alexis, it's all right.
It's all right.
I'm coming to the car.
Don't do anything.
Don't do anything.
It's Father Warren.
It's Father Warren.
I'm coming to the car. I'm coming to the car.
This night they had made a decision to follow Poppy
so they followed,
and luckily they did.

His shirt was torn off.
I remember—because my daddy was a neat man, too.
That was the other thing
and I think, for a child's impression
to see my daddy's white shirt torn off of him
and he had straight black hair that he wore back, and it was, like,
    hanging all down around
you know.
[Pause]
Unfortunately, I think what we've evolved to is not having
quite frankly
almost the absence of the visible and the tangible leaves the
    impression that the problem isn't there
that the issues are not there
you know.
And so I think what you have is this false sense
really
now
that everything is okay
you know
because you don't have the Klan.
So the flip side of that is this immediate conclusion that it's no
    longer a problem
when it still is.
And so I'm trying to figure how to say my feelings of it.
[Pause]
Oh, I can't say this on tape.

TALKING TO JESUS

IN THE BEGINNING WAS THE WORD, AND THE
WORD WAS WITH GOD, AND THE WORD WAS GOD.
THE SAME WAS IN THE BEGINNING WITH GOD.

—*The Gospel According to St. John 1:1–2*

AND THE WORD WAS MADE FLESH, AND DWELT
AMONG US . . . FULL OF GRACE AND TRUTH.

—*The Gospel According to St. John 1:14*

THE WORD WAS MADE FLESH AND DWELT AMONG US. A PERSON? WAS the word? That huge big Bible that loomed out over the pulpit at Union Memorial Methodist Church was said to carry the *word* of the Lord.

There were the black poets, and we knew them because one good thing about segregation was black pride, such pride for all the people of letters—James Weldon Johnson, Paul Laurence Dunbar. And I learned from those poems not to be timid about big sounds—such an extroverted idea of language they had, such a love of sound:

> 'Lias! 'Lias! Bless de Lawd!
> Don' you know de day's erbroad?
> —"In the Morning," Paul Laurence Dunbar

I listened with rapture whenever my paternal grandfather opened his mouth. I asked him to tell the same stories over and over. I would listen to story after story on the porch of Miss Johnson (always Miss although she was married, widowed, a mother and a grandmother). Miss Johnson weighed at the very least four hundred pounds. She couldn't move much further than to a house or two up or down from hers for that reason. She'd call me over, and I would listen, or go down to the store to buy her fatback. She also baby-sat for us from time to time, and would iron. I would sit by the ironing board and listen. I would request her stories as if they were songs or concerts.

The other place for oratory, of course, was the pulpit. Reverend Carrington was the pastor of my church and had been since I was a little girl. His father had been white and British, his mother black. I didn't always pay attention to what was said from the pulpit when Reverend Carrington spoke, even though I was afraid I would go to hell if I didn't. The drone of the ladies in the choir at Union Memorial Methodist Church sounded like a wail:

> What a friend we have in
> Jeeeee-uh-suuus
> All our griefs [quick stop hard on the fs]
> and sins to bear
> What a priv-e-lage to caaauh-ry
> every-
> thing
> to God in prayer!

And the piano and the organ, and the preacher, Reverend Carrington, a slender, shortish man with a neat mustache, light skin, and glasses, sitting in profile, so that we couldn't really see how he might respond to the music.

> Oh
> what peace we often for-
> feit
> Oh what needless pain
> we bear
> All because we do not caaaaa-uh-ry
> every-
> thing to God in prayer.

This was a pulpit that became political in the nineteen sixties. Black men running for city offices came to talk. We were urged to vote for certain white candidates and not others.

Mrs. Green, somehow Mrs. not Miss, rarely dressed up as the others did. She didn't always wear a hat. Sometimes she wore a scarf. I have a dim memory of her in bedroom slippers. She looked as though she came to church exactly as she was, the way we were told that God was prepared to receive us. She was the only member in the entire church who "got the Holy Spirit." Being of a moderately logical mind, I tried for years to figure out what triggered it. I had to accept the fact that it might happen at any time, that it was unpredictable.

"Yes, Jesus. Thank you, Jesus."

Sometimes she would outcry the wail of the choir. And sometimes these two sounds would go together.

Have we tria-als and tempta-aaay-tions
Is there trouble anywhere
We should never be discouraged
Take it to the Lord in prayer.

Can we find a friend so faithful

"Thankyou Jesus yes Jesus, thank you Jesus yes yes yes thank you Jesus"

And sometimes she would sit and weep while they sang on.

Who will all our sorrows share
Jesus knows our every weakness
Take it to the Lord in prayer.

It seemed that Mrs. Green was the only person with a telephone line to the Lord, because she was the only one who dared call out his name and, in fact, would stop the service to have a conversation in our presence. Well why shouldn't she, if she had that line, why shouldn't she?

We thought this was very funny.

"Don't laugh," my mother said.

"But why does Mrs. Green do that?"

"She believes in Jesus and sometimes that happens. It's called the Holy Spirit."

"Do you get the Holy Spirit?"

Silence.

"Well don't you believe in Jesus?"

"Yes I do."

"Well why don't you do that?"

"Different people believe in Jesus different ways. Different people get the Holy Spirit in different ways."

Are we weak and heavy laden
cumbered with a load of care
Precious Savior still our re-eh-fuge
Take it to the Lord in prayer.

"Well what about Grandma? Doesn't Grandma believe in Jesus?" (Our maternal grandmother, my mother's mother, would by contemporary standards be considered "born again.")

"If you sit next to Grandma in church sometimes you'll see a tear come out of her eye. That means Grandma is getting the Holy Spirit."

"The Holy Spirit is—"

"Yes Jesus Thank you Jesus yes Lord thank you Lord"

"Well how come Grandma doesn't—"

"I said Grandma cries when she—"

"Well then what about you? How come you don't—"

"Ssssh."

She probably thrust a hymnal in our hands by this point.

Do thy friends despise, forsaaakke theee?

The words were sometimes disturbing, but the music was soothing.

Take it to the Lord in prayer
In his arms he'll take and shield thee
Thou—wilt—find—a—solace—there.

Ahhhhhmen.

So there was Mrs. Green, who seemed to have a faster train to Jesus than the preacher himself, because the preacher in our church did not talk to Jesus, he talked to us. When he talked to the Lord, he did so silently, with his hand on his forehead and his face tilted down. Mrs. Green subsided in her experience, talking to Jesus, by walking sometimes up and down the aisle, sometimes sitting with her head bowed in an intense prayer, sometimes crying or moaning. I always wished she'd talk to us. She wasn't interested in talking to us. She had bigger fish to fry.

Since that time, in my travels, I've visited churches where the Mrs. Greens of the world are not so rare. Reverend Carrington wasn't the only one with a through line to God. But the only person in that whole church who seemed to work as hard as Reverend Carrington, or who came prepared to work as hard, was Mrs. Green. She didn't need a uniform, she wore no robes, she wore no ribbons, she came and sat on the outskirts. She didn't come to socialize. She didn't come to join the auxiliary, but she came to work in our community in another way. She came to work in a spiritual way.

Maybe our leaders aren't the only ones who hold the Gospel of America inside of them. Maybe they need some help to release that gospel. They need another kind of partner. I see this in many ways. Reverend Carrington was very educated, and he had been educated to have command of the word. Mrs. Green was not in words at all. She was the perfect partner for Reverend Carrington. She was not a part of the political structure of his church, but her presence was critical. We are a very material culture, with little room for those things that do not add up in numbers. Many participating elements in democracy are managed. Mrs. Green was anything but managed, yet she had something important to offer.

Maybe the very help that politics needs can come from someplace other than the halls of Congress or the desktops of punditry. Maybe our leaders need more voices from the outside. Maybe the voice of a nation lives in the fragmented voices of its people, even the less articulate ones. Maybe the voice of the nation is not so much the leader's plea to the people but the people's plea to the leader, and to something beyond the leader. Maybe the voice of a nation is the plea of the people to the idea of the nation, the plea to make the idea come alive. Perhaps the voice of a nation should be an incantation to the spirit of the nation rather than to a single man.

PEGGY NOONAN

"And Make the Crazy People Cry"

You know what [the press]
is the opposite of, in a way?
You remember in the eighteenth century in
the
in the eighteenth and nineteenth centuries
in the finer and more refined circles in England
It became the habit to go to um
homes for the mentally ill and go see the people there
and be very *moved* by their predicament?
It was a weird
sort of thing.
You wanted to go see the mad people
and then feel.
And almost show all your friends
see how compassionate I am.
I'm deeply moved by
the misery
I'm deeply moved by the misery around me.
But then again I've always been very sensitive.
The *press* is the exact opposite of that
They
they don't
They wanna go to the insane asylum
and make the crazy people cry
[she laughs, fully delighted]
They wanna go to the insane asylum with a fork
and say, "Hey, how'd ya like that Dole?"
"Hey Clinton, what did you mean about Susan MacDougal and her
    legal bills?"
Nyerrrn!

I mean I love to see old 1930s films the 1930s old
tape of the great
ocean liner
landing in New York
and Greta Garbo gets off and you know
says hello to her fans
you know
you know those old
arrival shipping news videos from Movietone?
Do you remember the one with the queen and king of England
coming down the plank?
And some of the photographers start yelling
"Hey, Queen, this way!"
That's what journalism is
at its worst and still at its best
"Hey-Queen-look-this-way"
"Hey King over here"
Click click.

SEGREGATION

IT WAS THE GRIDIRON DINNER IN 1998. THE GRIDIRON DINNER IS A time when the press spoofs the president. There was mild questioning about whether or not the president would come. Yet it was determined that it would be a mistake for him not to come. Monica Lewinsky was on the tip of everyone's tongue. The room of people dressed in white-tie attire was all abuzz with how the president would get through the evening.

Newt Gingrich stood up to make remarks. He was notably somber. He said that even as it was hard sometimes to read the paper in the morning, he was moved to look around the room and be grateful that he was in "the center of intellectual and political life in America."

I was stunned.

The Gridiron Dinner is not a huge affair. True, there are a lot of people, but they all fit into a fairly normal-sized hotel ballroom. It is not as extensive as, for example, the White House Correspondents' dinner. The room is large, but you could probably see someone at the opposite end of the room without binoculars. And when the president speaks, or the "skit" is done, there's no need for video projection. It was a room, not a football field. Yet Gingrich felt secure to say that the "center of intellectual and political life of America" was represented inside those four walls.

BROWN V. BOARD OF EDUCATION

I grew up in segregation. Although *Brown v. Board of Education* came down when I was four years old, it took until I was a teenager before I actually sat in a classroom with white students or had a white teacher. My world as a young person was a world of almost all black people, except for when we had to go downtown to "take care of business," as my mother would say. There was something intimidating about the big buildings where business was "taken care of." The stores were segregated, so even if we got into a store, we couldn't take the escalator or try on clothes. We only went to black doctors and dentists, unless something was very wrong with us, something Dr. Wooldridge couldn't take care of. Going into white territory gave me butterflies in my stomach.

1998
WASHINGTON, D.C.

By the time I went to Washington, I had traveled to many places in the world. I had met, dined with, even lived among the rich and the poor, the famous and the most unfamous. I had faced large and small audiences, baring my soul to strangers in the dark, never knowing who was there or what they thought. I had survived the ego-battering process of pounding the pavements as an actress, hearing all manner of things, swallowing rejection like the one cup of deli coffee per day that my budget allowed. I had survived the tenure process, with its scary balding white men in suits or in cotton short-sleeved shirts and pen guards, women in Hush Puppies and no-nonsense plaid wool suits, or later hip-looking, sighing, never-to-be-impressed, seen-it-all-heard-it-all men and women with expensive haircuts, designer eyeglasses, and multiracial backgrounds, its football teams and covertible cars, its floats and entourages of deans and provosts and chairmen. I had gasped out loud on several occasions, in my case and the cases of friends, at how closely and blatantly, elusively and subtly, but how oh so real-ly racism and sexism lurked in the halls of ivy, threatening at every turn to force you to sue, make a case, or run. This racism and sexism lurked *even* as these universities were in the process of questioning the canon, and stocking their curricula and libraries with information that would be, we were all told, the antidote to racism in the late twenti-eth and early twenty-first centuries. And anyone could be the culprit, a secretary (or even a student!), perhaps, who just didn't get "diversity," or a chairman who was outright capricious and nasty, causing you to remem-ber everything you ever learned about the unfair practices of segregation in the old days. After nearly dying on my sword as a young professor at one university, whose name will go unmentioned, I landed somehow on my feet, at a nice and rather fancy place: Stanford, and almost uneventfully made my way into the ranks, but still. It had been rough.

Given that I had been through many culture-inspired wars, I was surprised to feel the return of those same butterflies from the segregation of my youth when I was in Washington, D.C. It is a feeling that something could go wrong, something could go wrong, and you wouldn't have the power to make it right. Why should you have that feeling when you're merely trying to find out something about the place that is said to be a bedrock of where you live? Perhaps I was, as an actress, empathizing at large with those around me.

I think the butterflies came back because of the way people in Washington tend to look at a newcomer. Suspicion, mostly. This is truer of the media's gaze than of the gaze of those in the White House. Perhaps the media has no guards but itself. The White House, after all, has armed services, Secret Service, metal detectors, and an intricate process for finding out who you are before they admit you to the gate. The media, I suppose, has to be its own guard, reporter by reporter, editor by editor, producer by producer, columnist by columnist. Perhaps this is what gives them that scrutinous gaze, that quick look up and down, with their arms across the chest, the head tilted back, and perhaps even a look away, or an actual wander away, when you are introduced. Or perhaps those in the White House are simply better at charm, at least if you are of the same party as the man who captured the place.

1958

BALTIMORE

In segregation, it was not as if we were totally cut off from the white world. Many of our parents and relatives worked for white people, in their homes, in their clubs, in their businesses. We had the opportunity to learn many things about them, because we watched them. They did not work in our houses, or for our businesses, so they never had the opportunity to learn about us the way we learned about them. It would seem, on the face of things, that this would make them less culturally literate. Yet in the year 2000, in our society, cultural literacy is only an idea, and not valued enough to really become an issue. And yet these people, who don't know us or anything about us, although we are constantly learning about them, affect every aspect of our lives. They make decisions about our education, they are our surgeons, they are often our lawyers, our teachers, they edit the major papers (and there's not much of a black press to speak of now, or at least it isn't what it used to be), they hire us (or not) in major corporations. In short, they create our realities in body and mind. The end of segregation helped position people in places they hadn't been before, but it didn't make things go both ways. And they still don't know so much about us. Not that knowing is enough of a solution, as we would see in the nineties.

We believe we know about public figures. They broadcast what they think, and sometimes they broadcast what they feel. Sometimes public figures, and not so public figures, seem to be speaking to us very personally about intimate details of their love lives, their sexual lives, their financial lives, their family lives. Indeed, the president was caused to speak in a taped grand jury testimony that we can all watch about very intimate details of his relationship with his lover. When I watched the grand jury testimony, I was very surprised at the questions the interviewer asked, and the tone with which he asked them. "Did you tell Monica Lewinsky that you were going to leave Mrs. Clinton after you left the White House . . . ?" It was as if Jack Nicholson in *Carnal Knowledge* suddenly turned into a prosecutor as he asked Art Garfunkel about his first sexual experience with Candice Bergen. Those of us who were black in segregation learned some very profound things about the dangers of believing in the false intimacies that television can create. Psychiatrists believed that these types of false intimacies that we made with television were very bad for the health of our identities.

Television was a way that we, as black people, learned about white people. In my generation, it was less likely that we would have the kinds of intimacies that our parents and grandparents had had with whites. It was becoming less likely that we would wash their floors, or wash their clothes, or serve them their food, or take care of their children. Less likely that we would be "living in" with them. Less likely that we would be in their homes. This was in part because of education. We would go "beyond" those jobs. At the time, most of us did not have the foresight to see that the people who did not go beyond those jobs would be replaced in those jobs by members of immigrant groups of other colors. And we certainly couldn't have projected that many of us, men and, more shockingly, women, would not be having those jobs because we would be incarcerated.

Television was not a communicator about everybody. It was peopled with white people. When I turned on the television, except for Amos and Andy, everything I saw was white. I *identified* with white people, but I didn't know very many. In other words, I was brought up identifying with something that was really strange. I was brought up with a false intimacy with people who had nothing to do with me. I was brought up identifying with their world, the problems and joys they had, and the products that they were selling. The downside of this is that white people were not brought up to identify with us. It took us black folk until the nineteen sixties, and the late sixties at that, to publicly question that, and to publicly rally around an idea that we needed to see on television, in jobs, in positions of authority, people who we could *identify* with. Psychiatrists said that black children had a problem because they had no one to identify with, and in particular we had no role models. The fact is, we didn't have any trouble identifying with the other in the first place. My grandmother, a devout Christian woman, had no trouble identifying with the people on her "story" as she called it, her "soap opera."

I don't think the problem was that we had no one to identify with. There were plenty of white people that we did identify with. We cried about *Old Yeller, Bambi, West Side Story, Love Story,* all the sad stories, just like everybody else did. Our overidentification with white people was ultimately analyzed as a problem. But was that the problem? An ability to identify with the other is called empathy. That empathy is a proof of humanity, it is a proof that we don't all stop at the front and back doors, the floors and the ceilings of our physical selves. Empathy and the ability to identify with the other is proof that our color, our gender, our height, our weight is only a frame of something else called the soul. And politically, of course, that proof is the very ingredient we need to get to "we," to get to move from "me" to "us."

So I don't think, in retrospect, that the problem was so simple as we had no one to identify with. I would say, rather, the problem was that white people only had *themselves* to identify with. If it had gone both ways, we would have a different situation. This is what I see in Washington in 2000. The people there have themselves to identify with. Their daily lives do not give them the opportunity to identify with us. We learn about them. We are beginning to know a lot about the pundits and newscasters who tell us the story of our world. Our "hosts" are themselves becoming the subject. But they are not learning about us. The vestiges of segregation are all around us. We do not have our own talk shows in which we simply blast off our ideas to them. The technology is here, or nearly here, for us to do that. The question is, once the technology is here for us, "we the people," to let them know what we're doing—will they be interested to watch? I wonder if, five years from now, I might find "the people" talking—"community people" talking on shows that are not orchestrated by major network programming. That is, community punditry. But pundits are the dominant culture, and the dominant culture is, still, very self-interested.

The desegregation of schools was really the gateway, in my life, for a beginning of an understanding that the world should be larger than those black kids I sat next to during reading, and played with on the playground. People were being shot and jailed in order to get the right to vote or to sit at a lunch counter. Although I was too young for that, I was aware, in my "experimental school," that something was afoot about where I was going to go to school, and who I was going to go to school with. My school was given many of the same privileges as a white school across town. This must have been a part of trying to bring people around to seeing that we weren't simply of inferior intelligence, and I'm sure there were other more complicated political agendas. It played out in a very strange way, because my class was the actual subject population for that experiment.

At various times a year from third grade on, my mother would dress me up, straighten my hair, and send me off for what was a special day. The people from Twenty-fifth Street were coming. Twenty-fifth Street was the Board of Education. We would go to school, seeming to have a perfectly normal lesson. It of course had been rehearsed. There was a crowd of white people sitting in the back watching us learn. We were literally asked to perform the fact that we were learning, as if our tests weren't performance enough. I don't know if those presentations encouraged the white administrators to identify with us. The sum total of all those presentations, in my child's mind, was that I ended up in an integrated junior high.

2000

We like to think that education is the route to learning how to be together. We know that education alone is not the answer because, in part, once we got to the schools we still stayed among ourselves. We stayed well nestled in safe houses of identity. The assumption was that knowledge was the key to getting rid of racism, and knowledge was the key to encouraging us all to live together in that way that Martin Luther King suggested we live together. Many schools, or societies, are still segregated, not by law, but by choice.

I have met many people who know a lot. They aren't necessarily the same as people who move across cultural lines at all, they don't move at all toward that Martin Luther King image of the little black kids and little white kids being together. Not at all. And Washington is full of people whose business it is to know everything. What they lack is the ability to identify with anyone, other than those just like themselves.

Whatever happened to the idea that the media, for example, would "afflict the comfortable, and comfort the afflicted"? They themselves are comfortable. They are living in a highly wired, every day more wired cocoon.

I was looking at *Brown v. Board of Education:*

We come then to the question presented: Does segregation of children in public schools solely on the basis of race, even though the physical facilities and other "tangible factors" may be equal, deprive the children of the minority group of equal educational opportunities? We believe it does. In finding that a segregated law school for Negroes could not provide them equal educational opportunities, this Court relied in large part on those qualities which are incapable of objective measurement but which make for greatness in a law school. In requiring that a Negro admitted to a white graduate school be treated like all other students, we again resorted to intangible considerations, his ability to study, to engage in discussions, and exchange views with other students, in general to learn his profession. Such considerations apply with added force to children in grade and high schools. To separate them from others of a similar age and qualifications solely because of their race generates a feeling of inferiority as to their status in the community that may affect their hearts and minds in a way unlikely ever to be undone.

I would think that segregation would keep *any* of us from learning our profession, particularly if that profession has to do with society, and society's idea of itself, and society's idea of the other. How can the people who serve us, and the people who write about us, put us on the air, be so distant, so self-contained, so segregated from us, and do a responsible job? And if they are relying on communications technology to bring them closer to us, or us to them, that may be shortsighted. Again, I ask, in an age of global mergers, where are our human mergers?

I was speaking with someone working in a corporation, struggling with how to be a whole person in an environment that causes him and his colleagues every day to make "small compromises." He said, "People want to do good, but they don't believe they can. They believe they will be punished for being good, so they repress all that and get on with the job." In every area of American work life we will find this conflict. The desire to "do good" gets more and more repressed, less and less visible, and takes the form of cynicism.

The world of inside Washington, with its politicians and pundits, and the chorus of media, is a place where people do not look for the good very much anymore, they assume they are only looking at the bad. They honor truth, yet they are not looking for truth, they are looking for lies. There is a difference.

Washington has made it clear in the last several years that, even when people go there to try to contribute something good, they may very well be punished, exposed, humiliated. It looks like a very inhospitable place.

Fewer and fewer people want to go there to make contributions to our society. As a black woman, I am particularly sensitive to how it has chewed up and roughed up and sometimes spat out, in a very public way, other black women—Anita Hill, Lani Guinier, Maggie Williams, Alexis Herman.

"We" the people. In the beginning, "we" was a small "we," that "we" was a small community of white men. During the last two centuries, people have slowly, and sometimes in fits and starts, tried to make that "we" seem bigger. We have been trying to make that "we" a "we" that allows more people to have a voice in saying who "we" are. And then we had that one particular forefather who put in our minds an idea—and it's probably a good thing that he did—one particular forefather put on the record the idea that "all men are created equal." As Americans, deep down we have tried, at least, to absorb and to behave as if we believe that. And yet we're still confused. I believe we're confused because that very forefather was confused. Thomas Jefferson wrote "all Men are created equal [and] they are endowed by their Creator with certain unalienable Rights, that among these are Life, Liberty, and the Pursuit of Happiness." It is significant, I am told, that he chose to write the word *happiness* rather than the word *property*. But this same man had slaves. Around 130 of them.

Something I heard from a tour guide at Monticello always rings in my head: "And another thing Thomas Jefferson said about slavery, he said 'Justice is in one scale, self-preservation in the other.' "

America was not a very hospitable place for many people in the beginning. Presumably we are more civilized now. We keep trying, on paper, to make the place healthier for more people. And yet the bloodless assassinations of character that take place every day in the name of keeping the place clean create an atmosphere that is not clean, or healthy, or nurturing to "we the people" at all. People are speaking to us in such planned, designed language that a free flow of ideas is harder and harder to find. We are being given packaged discourse. Even the mainstream seems frozen; there's not enough movement.

But this move toward segregated circles of decision makers, segregated circles of expertise, is not limited to Washington. People stick with their own kind.

The assumption in *Brown v. Board of Education* is that the black kids lose out, and come away from all of this with a feeling of inferiority. What about the white kids? Don't they lose something too? Why do we not all feel inferior, when in fact what we are all losing out on is the opportunity to identify, to know, to be with the other? We are losing out on the wealth of exchange, the wealth inherent in that *human* merger. Separation is how things work, as I saw dramatically in our nation's capital.

The state of separation is what is expected. To move out of your separate place, your safe house of identity, is hard work. You have to be prepared. Because remember the lesson from segregation. The side of power will not be as invested in learning about you as you are in learning about them. It will be hard to find dialogue. You have to simply get inside the circle, be as inconspicuous as possible, get what you need, and get out. But as for really engaging? It rarely happens. And people think the answer to racial strife is demographics? I refer you to Newt Gingrich's comment. In that one ballroom, he said, was "the center of intellectual and political life." It'll be a long time before demographics change that center.

A NONREADER

1997
THE BRONX

My mother had dedicated most of her early teaching career to proving there was no such thing as a nonreader. This was before the days of dyslexia and defined learning disabilities. There would often be a very large boy at our house after school whom she was teaching to read.

During one of the summers that I was doing this project, I met with a boy who lived in the Bronx named Dennis. I spent an afternoon talking to him and to his father. Dennis was not able to read and had been simply graduated to push him on. He had five or six siblings. His father, Dennis Sr., was a single father. Dennis's mother was a drug addict who was suffering from AIDS and who lived under the 125th Street Bridge. When I tried to get Dennis to talk to me about his mother, he said to me very directly, "I don't want to talk about her."

I didn't ask him again.

After having spent quite a while with them, I was most disturbed by the casualness with which the schools dealt with the problem, and the fact that the father had nearly had to sue the school system to get his child tested. He took out a very neat box of all the letters he had written, and all the documents he had collected, while simply trying to get a test. He had even written a letter to the president.

His father told me that one of the teachers at his son's school had simply said to him, "You may as well get used to it, your boy is either going to end up in jail or end up in the graveyard."

Why can't we do anything about these stories? The fact is we can. Why aren't we doing more? What's inhibiting us from looking further than our own immediate circle?

PENNY KISER

MONTICELLO TOUR GUIDE

"Jefferson's Nailery Boys"

Now the boys' incentive in the nailery
was if you
and boy those records were strict but if you were the best producer
then you would get a
new suit of clothes a red suit or a blue suit
and remember great George?
His son Isaac often won that prize in fact at the age of sixteen if
you'd done a good job Thomas Jefferson allowed you to learn
a trade and he took Isaac to Philadelphia where he learned to
be a tinsmith.
If you didn't do a good job where do you think you'd end up?
Yeah, in the fields
it's called going into the ground
and that would be your job you would go into the ground.
Same with the girls

who worked in the textile industry
and we know that
there was a young boy who worked here and his name was Carey
and we don't know the circumstances
but we know that one day Carey comes to work it's probably hot
    and sticky and they're
working over these fires.
He takes his hammer and he hits the boy next to him, Brown,
on the head, he cracks his head wide open
and the overseer
who I think might have been Mr. Bacon at that
time thought that
Brown might die
so
he's in a total panic 'cause he thinks all these young boys might
    take their hammers and
we're gonna have a riot here.
So he takes Carey and he puts him in jail.
Now Thomas Jefferson is in Washington.
And he has to write Thomas Jefferson to find out what the
    punishment might be.
Now Thomas Jefferson always said that
he loved industry
industry or hard work.
He abhorred or hated severity.
And the overseer said when Thomas Jefferson was here on the
    plantation that that whip
was put away as much as possible.
So when he writes Thomas Jefferson
Jefferson writes back and he says we must give Carey the worst
    punishment
he has to be an example to these
boys.
What do you think the worst thing could happen to you if you were
    a slave?
Death would be pretty bad wouldn't it?
That would kind of be the end of you.

But you know what?
If Thomas Jefferson had you killed, every slave is worth money so
    he's kind of losing
money if he does that
he's got to think of something else where he doesn't lose money.
Sell him to the worst . . .
Yeah,
okay what did he do?
He writes back and he says take Carey and sell him
so far away that his parents will think he's dead,
all the boys around him will think he's dead.
You can imagine
if you don't own anything
think how important your family is
so that's what happens to Carey we think he probably ended up in
    Georgia
say in the cotton fields
we do know—
I have read that if you ever ended up down in the sugarcane
    plantations
on one of those plantations say in the West Indies?
Your life expectancy was only five years.

GARRISON JUNIOR
HIGH SCHOOL
BALTIMORE, MARYLAND,
1961

TRAVEL IN PURSUIT OF LANGUAGE. MY TAPE RECORDER IS MY CAMERA. Here I am, two decades into my journey, and I find myself worrying about the future of language, or at least language in America. I have heard about a culture in Cameroon where they have a language with only five hundred words:

> My grandmother she still lives in Central Africa
> And she speaks a language called Sango
> Which has only five hundred words.
> I mean, five hundred? Five hundred?
> It's "I'm hungry." "I'm hot." "How are you?"
> That's it!
> That's it!
> But every time I go back to Africa
> It brings me down on earth.

Imagine. There are people who live in minimal language. We have so many words. Does it change what a human being is, as a species? That woman and I are of the same species, even as we stand thousands and thousands and thousands of words apart.

* * *

IT MAY BE THAT CULTURES WITH FEWER WORDS ARE IN LESS DANGER than we are. So many of our words are being contorted, mangled, stretched, distorted in public life. I'm surprised they survive. I'm surprised they mean anything.

So suspicious is the ear. Its structure has changed. We sit with only one ear toward the speaker, and the other is tuned to the nonexistent next beat. In Washington, I found many people who were watching the world from over their shoulders, like smokers, who stand with their heads away to keep from blowing smoke in your face; we are addicted to another direction, to any direction other than straightforward contact.

BEING A NEGRO GIRL FROM BALTIMORE RAISED IN SEGREGATION, INtegrated into "it all" when I was eleven, and newly in junior high school, I was terrified of white kids. We outgrow these things, of course, as Jacob Lawrence, the great painter, told me when I went to visit him in Seattle. "Well it's scary, talking about how brutal it was, the brutality of people being burned and hung by trees. It was scary, frightening. So much so that if you'd walk down the street or you'd see a person, a Caucasian, you would immediately think, Oh this man was a lyncher. I guess as a young person your imagination is very fertile. It's very—you know, it's like seeing goblins. It's like it doesn't take much, but as you develop your experience broadens. So you don't have the same kind of apprehension." History always lurks, changing reality into shadowed moments that are haunted by a past.

And the gorgeous reality of American culture is that our diversity breeds for us a smorgasbord of nightmares, fantasies, justified fears, and unjustified fears. It might seem strange that as a child Jacob Lawrence thought every white person was a lyncher, but think of how many adults think that any black man on a dark street is a thief, a mugger, or a rapist. And so for me, somehow, my fear started with a girl with red hair. Her name was Nancy, and she was in my homeroom class in seventh grade.

She was very mean in the classroom. I don't know much about how she was on the playground, because I didn't have the opportunity to watch her there. We didn't play together on the playground, whites and blacks, Jews and gentiles. We had to go to school together, but no one could tell us how to play at lunchtime. I have been surprised to learn that, more than thirty years later, in many junior and senior highs in this integrated country, students still prefer to sit with their own kind.

Whites didn't play with blacks, or Jews, for that matter, and Reform Jews didn't play with Orthodox Jews, and Orthodox Jews didn't play with Jews fresh from Europe who didn't speak English. Even Jews made fun of a Jewish girl with a Russian accent who brought sandwiches made of meat with a strong smell and purple horseradish, despised her for being so not "of it."

Nancy was quite popular in seventh grade. She had a thick head of hair and freckles, and she sat somewhere near the front of the room in class 7-7. There had been no girl quite as mean as Nancy in James Mosher Elementary School—an all-black school. We had boys who were bullies, and girls who were goody-goodies, but the room was dominated by either a bully on the playground or a teacher's pet in the classroom. So a white girl bully in the classroom was a novel idea.

Nancy sat second from the front in French class, and always seemed to be the first one there. She was not attractive by any stretch of the imagination. Perhaps her brutishness was a compensation for that. She didn't suck up to the teachers enough to be considered a "good student," but she ran the room, with the threat that at any moment her mean spirit would lash out in the form of ridicule. She never said anything racist, as far as I can remember, but there seemed to be the possibility or the threat that she would, since we were on borrowed territory and for some reason the territory seemed to be hers.

Nancy. This is where I began to learn that bullies weren't just the big guys who hid behind buildings and sprang out to steal your lunch money or beat you up. Nancy was never hidden; she was always quite apparent. She sat very tall, very proudly, with her not yet breasts supported by a straight back. In fact, she seemed to like people to see her. She made us all very uneasy, very uncomfortable, because we never quite knew what she'd do, what she'd say.

Stranger still was what happened to Lila. It was the one occasion that we did not need Nancy to exploit our unspoken hostility for us. The entire class came forward with their own individual meannesses. I'll never forget when the whole homeroom class took it upon themselves to beat up Lila. Not physically. There were surely fights, but at least among the girls those fights tended to stay within racial lines. Perhaps we were a little too civilized.

Perhaps beatings are subverted when "shoulds" appear in a group. Those subverted headings transform into another type of hostility. Baltimore, like Washington, is neither North nor South. It wouldn't have been right to behave like southerners. Our situation was not overt. I didn't hear much "nigger" calling. Most of the integration in housing and education happened with the Jews. Perhaps their own situation caused them to be silent about their thoughts. But underneath the silence was contorted aggression.

Lila was beat up with humiliation. The class was predominantly Jewish, at a time when many Jews in Baltimore were not entirely assimilated. My father would drive us across town to the Jewish neighborhoods on Sunday to buy things, since they had celebrated the Sabbath already. Our neighborhoods were quiet; most of the businesses were closed on Sundays, and theirs were wide awake. There were no boyfriends and girlfriends across racial lines, or religious lines. All Jewish holidays were observed. I didn't know why they made us come to school on the High Holy Days, because there was no one there. Our teachers never taught on those days; the eight, or ten, or sometimes as few as three or four of us would simply sit in empty classroom after empty classroom until the end of the day.

Our homeroom teacher was a black woman who was not particularly popular. She was also our science teacher. She had to fight to get control of the room. I can only imagine what it was for her, too, to be in integration for the first time, probably having been educated in segregation (I know, for example, that she had gone to a black college) and now having to teach in this "loaded" integrated school. By Christmastime, we calmed down. She "proved" herself to us and we actually felt warmly toward her. The class decided to buy her a Christmas present. A rumor started that Lila, who was the quietest person in the room, Lila, who never ever had to be told to sit down, to be quiet, to do anything, Lila, who simply came to school and went home, who never seemed to socialize with anyone . . . Lila was not going to chip in for the Christmas present. Her parents wouldn't allow it. This became our headline for two weeks or so: what we were going to do about it, how we were going to vote in terms of ostracizing Lila.

A tall, beautiful black girl (who was pregnant and would soon be forced to leave school) began some of the mockery toward Lila. I remember that it pained me. I also remember how surprised I was that the Jewish kids (again, the predominant population) began to turn against Lila too. What had started as a sort of 50–50 vote about whether to buy a Christmas present at all, now turned into 99 percent for the present, and Lila on her own. No one took her to the schoolyard and threatened to beat her up, no one stuck her head down the toilet, but the daily vote would be taken, the vote toward unanimous for buying the present or not, and as the days went on Lila became stronger and stronger in her position. The teacher would be out of the room. The tall, beautiful black girl would take the vote.

Every day Lila would sit with no expression on her face as we lifted our hands. Her hands stayed firmly planted on the desk. Her parents did not celebrate Christmas, and they would not allow her to buy a present for the teacher. I did not know if the fact of the teacher being black complicated it on another level. Lila never cried, she simply sat quietly as all kinds of things were said, and she never explained anything further. In fact, I don't remember her ever saying anything—it was simply known she would not be chipping in for the gift.

Finally, the teacher got wind of the whole thing and shamed us all by saying, as she should have, that in this spirit she didn't really want a Christmas present, and that Lila should not be forced to participate if her religion wouldn't allow it. I remember this story because it was the first time I saw that a beating—even a public beating—could happen without anyone so much as striking a blow.

WALTER SHAPIRO

COLUMNIST

"Loaded for Bear"

Also the Bush campaign reporters came in,
some of whom
worshiped at the shrine of Marlin Fitzwater,
some of whom
thought that
Bush had gotten an unfair deal in the '92 campaign.
And Bush did.
The press was unbelievably sycophantic on the way up
and too cruel on the way down,
and while I've only read excerpts from Fitzwater's
memoirs
he probably captures
correctly
the unfairness on the way down
and probably glosses over
the gushy excesses on the way up.
Most of the Bush reporters
and these are the Brit Humes of the world—
the Andrea Mitchells have now gone on to the State Department—
the Tom Friedmans, the Ann Devroys felt that their counterparts had
    been too soft on Clinton
so they showed up in Little Rock
loaded for bear.
They were going to show him
what a real press corps was like
not like those sycophants on the plane.
What happened is
Clinton,

who had
loved the press
learned to hate the press during Gennifer Flowers and the draft
     letter
for some cause,
was getting back
to his comfort level with the press in the last three weeks of the
     campaign—
revealing himself in useful ways—
without feeling like that anybody's gonna do a gotcha on him?
You know
coming back and sort of schmoozing in the corridors at two in the
     morning on a campaign plane on a Wednesday night sort of
     half off the record half on the record
not talking about anything newsy?
Reminiscing about odd things
you know but these are little moments where you can get a sense of
     who Bill Clinton is.
Yeah, yeah.
He was beginning to do this again.
Ya know it's like that old
poster for *Jaws*—
Just when you were
Just when you were willing to go back into the water
you know, for *Jaws Four*.
For Clinton—
Just when you thought that you can be seminatural with the press
the guard changed.
Everybody thought Bush was the winner
so their best—both their White House reporters
and the reporters who had been promised the White House in the
     future—had been given
the Bush campaign to cover.
Clinton was seen as the likely loser.
For a lot of news organizations
their wrong reporters had covered the victorious president.
So what happened is

after the election
two-thirds of the people who covered the Clinton campaign
were ordered back to Washington and in their place were the
    people who covered the Bush campaign.
And this had nothing to do with Clinton.
This had to do with lots of assignment editors
and vice presidents for news
had gambled on a Bush victory, and staffed the campaigns
    accordingly.
For lots of the White House reporters
who'd been covering the White House for ten years
fifteen years.
Major temper tantrum if you're pulled off the White House
even if it looks like your guy's gonna lose.
It *is* the White House.

THE EAST COAST
CORRIDOR

I HAVE BEEN TRAVELING UP AND DOWN THE EAST COAST CORRIDOR all my life. First in a car, and when I went to college, in a train. In the five years that I was trying to understand Washington, I traveled the corridor all the time, by Delta or USAir shuttle.

The "corridor" was fun when we took the train. When I was younger, it was significant that the train station was a place where people gathered across class lines and racial lines. I often wish that the theater, onstage and in the audience, would look like Pennsylvania Train Station in Baltimore looked in the nineteen fifties and sixties. But the theater still does not look like that. Neither does the academy, and neither does Congress or most institutions. The message was clear: If people want to move, they have to at least all meet at the train station. (Even in the case of Jim Crow, which I never experienced, you'd have to sit in a special car, but you'd have to gather at the station.) So a train station, for me, was always a good metaphor for a place that was big enough, structurally, for all of us. This kind of a place required a big booming voice, and very clear speech. I loved those voices.

As a ritual, we would go to the train station following the Thanksgiving Day Parade. Every year, my mother said the exact same thing about the drum majorettes: "I feel so sorry for those drum majorettes. Their little legs were so cold, they didn't even have on stockings. Now you know their legs were cold. Those white legs. They were completely red." At the time there were no black drum majorettes. After the parade my brothers liked to watch the trains. I liked to hear the announcements and watch the arrivals and departures of the people. I loved the stories that were told in those arrivals and departures, although I couldn't hear the words. I would stare at the groupings of people in conversation.

"Don't stare," my mother would say.

The voice that announced the trains was usually male in those days, deep and authoritative.

"Announcing
on track num-ber
two
the arrival
of the Silver Constitution
from Washing-*ton,*
going to
Phila-del-phia
Wil-ming-ton
Delaware
Tren-ton
Newark
New York City
New Haven, Con-nec-ticut
And
Bos-ton
Massachusetts!
Alllllllllllll Aboaaarrrrrrrruhhdd!!!!!!!"

During my college years, the sounds caused quite a bit of adrenaline and hurry when all four of my siblings, my parents, and sometimes my grandfather would come to the train station to say good-bye. They would run, even if we had plenty of time, as if I were going to miss the train. My little sisters, who were only seven and eight years old at the time, would be, of course, nearly beside themselves with the excitement of the flurry of motion and the echoes all over the very tall, stone train station. People even dressed to travel then. The sound of the announcement signaled a flurry of activity: luggage moving, porters moving, high heels clicking on the stone floor, whisks of perfume flashing by; in the winter, it was still politically all right to wear fur. All social classes convened at the train station, and across these lines you saw kisses, hugs, last-minute mementos and gifts, dollars, being handed off. As you ran to your train, out of the corner of your eye you might even catch a sob here and there, or the last moments of an argument. My brother Deaver and I *always* fought before I left, so my brother Maurice, the younger of the two of them, was inevitably left to pull the bags along, while Deaver sulked. You were leaving. And each time you left there was less and less certainty that you would be the same when you came back again, or that *they* would be the same.

The conductor's and the announcer's voices had a mild kind of grandeur that was a cousin to the vocal tones I had heard at funerals—"Ashes—to—ashes"—and at christenings and weddings. These are words that have been said many times, but the person who speaks them understands that each time it must be said as if it matters because it does matter, and we never know what lies ahead, and we never know what just happened, and all words must house respect of those two unknowns.

We are relatively calm about arrivals and departures now. And the way we deal with it is very low-key. We've seen it all before, heard it all before. Airports are the major gateways. You often have to travel very long distances across the airport, taking trains and shuttles and long walkways. It's less about your departure, and more about "getting there," wherever "there" is. There are a series of "theres"—the ticket counter, the gate, and the variety of lounges.

Recently I was in San Francisco, and went to the so-called Red Carpet lounge to speed up my check-in process. The line was all the way out the door. Businessmen and some women with suitcases on wheels were everywhere, it seemed. I remembered that I am a so-called 1K Traveler, which means I can go to an even more exclusive lounge. I went to the 1K lounge and there was a line there too. Then a concierge came over and told me about yet another lounge, across from the 1K lounge, that I might like to know about. I realized that the most efficient place for me to be may be back at the ticket counter in the front, given the fact that everyone is fleeing to the other "special lounges." Maybe the least average thing to be now is "average." If everyone is "special," then what's the point? I was sitting next to a man on a plane who told me that he and his colleagues were so fed up with the airlines they were going to chip in and get their own plane. "I guess somebody will make something like FedEx for air travel," I said.

Sometimes, those who accompany you to major airports cannot go with you past security. The only place I see a mass of human emotion in an airport comparable to what I used to see in the train station is in the arrivals area after an international flight. There, after all the business has been done, all security, all customs, all government affairs are finally over, as you exit, behind a rope you will see clusters of people of all nationalities holding signs, placards, balloons. And speckled between the relatives and lovers, daughters, sons, mothers, fathers are members of that club of mostly colored men from Africa, the Middle East, Latin America waiting with their car service signs to pick up people that they do not know.

Years later, in my time trying to "capture American character in Washington, D.C.," I would fly up and down the eastern corridor to New York and Boston. I became a regular customer on USAir and Delta. Sometimes it was so frequent I felt as if they were tantamount to a subway. In contrast to those old conductors, the flight attendants never enunciate ending consonants, and they have the most peculiar rhythm pattern. We were told in acting school that if we want to take full advantage of getting a message across, we must stress operative words, usually verbs, and never stress prepositions. I marvel each time I hear a flight attendant announcement at their affinity for stressing prepositions, their resistance to elongating vowels, and their tendency to simply let the breath run out at the end of a phrase so that the last word sounds like a motor winding down. Their speaking and breathing patterns have absolutely nothing to do with the thought they are transmitting. So, given that big companies like airlines are sure to instruct people down to the last detail about how to behave on the job, one can only imagine that there is some corporate reason that they do not want us to pay full attention to these messages, or to really listen to them each time they are said.

"WELcomdoDeldairlinesairflightnummertwoeighdynineWITHzerviz-toWashingdnNatshnulairporrrrrd.KINDLYreadtheinstructshunsINtheseat-poggetinFRONTufyoooooou.ForTHOSEpassengersittinginandemergenzy-exitrows(BREATH)bewarethatfederalregulationsDOrequirethatyoubeable-toassistothersINtheeventofanemergencylandinnnnng."

On a graph this would look like the flat line in the intensive-care unit. The speech, unlike the conductor's speech, is often associated with women, because although there are male flight attendants, one normally thinks of that job as a woman's job, and if anything it is a job that men have entered into later than women. What I don't understand is why the flight attendants aren't able to give that speech as if they are thinking about what they are saying. When the pilots speak to us, their manner is, by contrast, quite "normal," and lifelike. Especially if they have to bring disappointing news. That news, if anything, is told with a certain amount of charm, and the sound that "we're all in this together." It often starts with the word *Folks,* and if the pilot is particularly good at this, he will sigh after he says "Folks," to lead you to believe that he's peeved a little bit, too. He *wants* to identify with you.

"Folks, this is your captain again. I'm sorry to have to tell you this, but we're going to have to go back to the gate. We're gonna let you off the plane, then we're gonna let you back on the plane, and we'll sit on the runway. We don't know how long that will be. But there's weather at La Guardia and . . ."

The moans of the passengers usually overwhelm the rest of the speech, and the flurry to get on cell phones to call offices and find alternate modes of travel or, in the worst-case scenario, find places other than the lobby of the airport to spend the night.

Notice the safety announcements never start with the word *Folks.* The safety announcer does not want to identify with you. If there is ever a moment when we're all "folks," it would be the moment when we all need those safety instructions.

I was on one commuter plane from Pittsburgh to New York. It was the first time I had ever (and I have sometimes had to travel as much as three times a week) heard the safety announcement make sense. I was so shocked, at how serious the announcement really is, that I struck up a conversation with the flight attendant. She told me that she used to be a police officer, in an urban area. "I'm not foolin' around," she said. I asked her if she had practiced the speech. "Absolutely," she said. "I practice it all the time. It's important. Your safety is important."

She told me that there was a man who wouldn't fasten his seat belt. She went over to him to instruct him to do so. "I take this flight all the time," he mumbled and put his head back into *The New York Times, The Wall Street Journal,* or whatever he was reading. She leaned over, put her finger right in front of his face, and said, "I don't care if you are president of the airline, you're fastening your seat belt."

He fastened it.

Who's listening anymore? What does it take to get people to listen? When do people feel they need to listen? When do they feel they *have* to listen? Only for the banker, the lawyer, the doctor, or the police?

We get so used to hearing things that they have no meaning. And there is, of course, the chance that one day those safety instructions will have meaning. Then it will be stark raving clear. Until that time we live in the expectation of a verbal flat line, a verbal minimum. We live with the expectation that words mean very little, because we have seen it all before, heard it all before. And that is why I find myself going on a quest down memory lane for a time when words meant something in my family, in my church, in my city, in my world.

MIKE McCURRY

FORMER PRESS SECRETARY TO PRESIDENT CLINTON

"A Troubling Time"

We're coming into a domain in which there may be questions that
    in the past never even would have been contemplated here uh
    that are now
you know
asked all the time.
We had [a nominee for a cabinet department post]
withdraw his nomination uh, today
because he is accused of sexual impropriety, and as near as I can
    figure it, it amounts to he had, he made an improp——
    improper, is alleged to have made an improper advance on a
    woman, she complained, it was looked into, the process by
    which it was looked into within the department was irregular,
    the irregularity of that was going to become a big controversy,

the Senate was going to haul everyone up and have open
testimony next week, embarrass this man and his wife, make
his life miserable, and he said screw it I'm just not going to take
the job.
And so the the the boundary of questions that never were asked in
the past
the bar, the threshold
has been lowered and lowered and lowered.
And we, we came very close in the last week for, to a point where I
thought I was going to get asked about what kind of erections
the president has.
I mean quite seriously.
There was and, and that was, and this actually happened on the
trip to Latin America which was great so that we didn't get too
deeply into the subject but there was sort of a collective
judgment made that that was off-limits.
So it's a, it's weird.
It's kind of this merging of our popular culture and tabloid mentality
and the evening shows,
that sort of the tabloid television shows at night
and it's kind of this morphing of what we consider, you know,
civil discourse
and ah so it's it's it's a troubling time.

THEATER AND POLITICS

I. THE PRESIDENT

WINTER 1992
CAMBRIDGE, MASSACHUSETTS

WAS AT HARVARD ON A FELLOWSHIP. ANOTHER FELLOW IN THE SAME program was the former governor of Vermont Madeleine Kunin. We were living in the same apartment building. One day I was coming in as she was rushing out.

"Have to go to New Hampshire and help Bill Clinton! We've got to do everything we can!" she hollered as she took off down the street. She said "we" in a way that made "we" seem like it included me too, and like I and everybody else should follow her wherever she was going. From the freedom in her wave, and the glee in her voice, it certainly seemed that wherever she was going was the right way to go. Political people do seem to have that talent.

SPRING 1992
NEW YORK CITY

Clinton was in the midst of his first campaign for president when my career, or rather my language work, "took off." I was in New York preparing my play *Fires in the Mirror,* about riots between Jews and blacks in Crown Heights, Brooklyn. The riots began when a young black boy was killed by a car in the entourage of the leader (the Grand Rebbe) of the sect of Lubavitcher Jews. In retaliation some young black men killed a Hasidic scholar from Australia. Riots broke out, and police occupied the neighborhood for several days. I created a one-woman performance piece out of the stories I gathered from the people who had witnessed the events.

When I took the Crown Heights text to begin working on it in a theater in New York, one of the designers told me that "no one would care about this. People don't care about these things," she said. Everyone at the table, except for one other designer, agreed. "People in New York just don't care about this stuff." "This stuff" meaning race relations. Race as a concern, as "matter," is like fog in our country, or like floating anxiety. One moment we rest on our laurels—that things are better—after all, people aren't still being chased by dogs as they try to go to school. The next moment it's the most "serious problem our nation has to face."

Given that the eighties had not yielded much conversation on race, I assumed the design team was right. The theater has perhaps not been very hospitable to race issues. Unlike academia, where people can "study" blacks or other ethnicities, and never actually talk about race, in the theater we must embody the material. In academia, professors can glide right over the students' complicated feelings or their own complicated feelings about the subject with the excuse that they have to "cover the material." In the theater we can't simply "cover the material"; we "become the material." In fact our job is to *un*cover the material. So perhaps it makes sense that the theater is about a decade, or perhaps two decades, behind academia (which is not necessarily a bastion of progressive attitudes) in terms of its ability to articulate difference and its ability to think through issues that have to do with representation and identity in an ever more complex society.

April 30, 1992, was the scheduled first performance of my play. On April 29, a jury of all whites in Simi Valley, California, came back with a verdict of not guilty on four police officers who had beaten a black man. The videotape had been seen by most Americans. Few people could believe the verdict. Least of all the young blacks who lived in South-Central L.A. By now, everyone knows the story of what happened.

I knew nothing of what was going on in Los Angeles until I got home that night from dress rehearsal and "tech." Tech is the most insular time in the theater. You live in a world away from everything. When I got home there were a number of messages on my answering machine. All the voices were worried. One was in tears. "Anna, I know you don't usually watch TV—you need to turn it on tonight. You won't believe what is happening." Flames exploded across the screen.

I returned to the theater the next day for what should have been the continuation of "tech" time. It's the time when everyone is pushing ahead in the tunnel to bring the show to its opening. Designers, director, in my case, since there's only one actress (me), the crew, the stage manager. It's a very focused time, which has to last through many adjustments until another crew of people—the critics—come and take their turn at what you've done. Then everyone leaves, and you are left, each night, to your own devices with a crowd of interesting people—most of whom you do not know—who are sitting in the dark. But on good nights you find times in the course of the evening when all of you are apparently there for the same reason—to wonder, to laugh, to cry, to ache about something in the human condition.

This was my New York debut, I was nervous, in fact beyond nervous. The audience, the critics, were all a sea of strangers, scary strangers, and judging from what the designers had said to me on the first day, there was a chance that they "would not care" about the material. There did seem to be something just a little out of kilter about our huffing and puffing to put final touches on a play about a riot when a real riot was going on full force in another city.

This particular day, the day after the riot, was the first preview. The general manager was a woman. She came in with a scowl. "This theater," she said, "is closed." A lot of buildings in New York had closed because New Yorkers were frightened that their city would also burst into flames—a memory I suppose of the multiple riots that rocked the country when Martin Luther King was murdered.

"This theater is closed." She looked braced for an argument.

No one argued.

I decided to go to Times Square to the demonstration that was taking place. The director and costume designer joined me.

The riot was one of those events that cause the public to think, as they do from time to time, that race is one of the most important issues our country has to face. As it turned out, given these circumstances, people not only cared about the subject of the play, they came in droves. In that period, I felt each night as if there were a force pulling me downtown to the theater. There was a real urgency, a real purpose. For the first time in my career, I needed vocal coaching every day. It was because it was the first time I had something to say, and the first time I had a public that consciously knew they needed to hear it.

I finished my run in New York and went immediately to Los Angeles to study that riot. Again, the text was rich. I spoke with 280 people, all of whom would have, like those I spoke with in Crown Heights, gone to the highest mountain to tell their stories to anyone in the world who would listen. The two hardest people to perform were actually those who were in charge, the chief of police, Daryl Gates, and the mayor, Tom Bradley. Strangely enough they were also in better physical shape than anyone else I talked to (other than Anjelica Huston and Charlton Heston).

I then wrote and performed a play about the Los Angeles riots called *Twilight: Los Angeles, 1992.*

For all the entertainment quality to politics, it doesn't seem like too much fun these days. The challenge is you have to run to keep up with those who control the dialogue. So many people have given up on that chase. Perhaps it's because there are so many other things to chase. Or is there something about the barrage of media that feels like an assault? I am reminded of a friend who told me about training to be a tennis star with his father. He had to train even on Christmas Day, in the rain. His father was barraging him with tennis balls. My friend threw down his racquet and walked off the court, but his father kept hitting balls at his back until he was out of view. His father's aim and stroke were so good, he managed to get him squarely in the back each time.

We are running in different directions. We pay taxes, but we don't vote, and they say we don't watch political television unless there's a scandal.

1993
LOS ANGELES

I had created fifteen theater pieces with my method of looking for trochees in everyday speech. Two of them got national recognition. Both of the two recognized ones were about race riots.

I was performing my show about the Los Angeles riots when Lani Guinier was being tossed around by the process.

I met with Lani about what happened. I was surprised at how little help she had been given to move in that enormous Washington machine. When I asked Kweisi Mfume, then the head of the Congressional Black Caucus, why no one had helped Lani, but many people had clearly helped Clarence Thomas, he paused and chuckled as he said good-naturedly, "I think everybody thought she'd be fine. Nobody thought she needed help. It was clear he did."

I then spoke with the person in the Bush administration who was "in charge" of "Anita Hill Weekend." At the time this person, like many people who leave politics, was working in the entertainment industry. In our reflecting back on that period with Clarence Thomas and why it was possible to push that nomination through, I was told, "It just shows you what the power of the presidency can do, okay?"

Both Lani's story and Anita Hill's story smoke-signaled to me that you cannot be in Washington, D.C., without a patron, without a chaperone. You must have someone there who can walk you through what is now an incredibly complicated process. Although we have free speech, and are supposedly expected as citizens to come forward and "do our part," only a few get to do "parts."

Lani developed quite an audience as a result of what had happened to her. I asked her in a public interview, "When you go out and you speak about what happened to you in Washington, who do you think you are talking to?" Her answer took my breath away: "I think I'm talking to the president. I half-expect to come home and find a message on my answering machine saying, 'That was interesting what you said tonight.' "

Politics also seemed to be a place where losing your friends could be par for the course.

FEBRUARY 1994
WASHINGTON, D.C.

I met Clinton for the first time at a dinner at the White House during Black History Month. I was seated at Hillary Clinton's table. I understand that it means a lot to people to be invited to these events, but it felt less like a dinner party and more like an awards ceremony at high school. You were there because you were being recognized for having done well at something—or, as was my case, you were the guest of someone who had done well at something. At the conclusion of the meal, Mrs. Clinton said to all of us at her table, "Would anyone like to dance?" We rose. Only one couple danced.

At the end of the evening Clinton shook hands with each one of us as we left. If you had something to say to the president, it was best to have thought of it in advance. Economy was necessary. I didn't say anything other than "Hello." It was something to call home about.

II. THE PRESS

FALL 1993
WASHINGTON, D.C.

The following fall, while performing *Fires in the Mirror,* my play about the Crown Heights riots, in Washington, I was asked by the artistic director of the theater that presented me—the Arena Theater—if I might like to do a play about Washington. I was asked this question as we were driving. I remember looking at a view of monuments as I said, "How about if I do something on the president?"

"What about him?" he said.

"He has to be in the press so much. I wonder how he has time to do his work."

As I looked at the city around me, I was sure there were a million stories. And many of those stories were totally disconnected from this inner circle of monuments and government buildings.

I said, "If I'm really doing a 'Search for American Character,' sooner or later I should look at the president.

"But you know what?" I said. "I know nothing about the president that the press doesn't tell me. I can't really look at the president without looking at the press."

The press are as present with the president as we know him as the Secret Service are. Even more present. The Secret Service are only really visible if you see the president live. Most of us view the president as a product of a camera lens.

FALL 1995
WASHINGTON, D.C.

One of my first meetings in Washington was with Bob Kaiser, managing editor of *The Washington Post*. He had responded immediately to my call for a meeting. Everything about Kaiser is done with great dispatch. His secretary signed a variety of notes he sent me from time to time with her name "to avoid delay." He has a pocket watch, which he carries in the breast pocket of his jacket. As he pulls it out, he explains it away as his "one affectation. Everyone deserves one affectation."

I think one reason for Kaiser's immediate response had to do with a rendition I had done of his colleague Shelby Coffey of the *Los Angeles Times*—Shelby having been a character in my play *Twilight*, about the Los Angeles riots.

We sat in Kaiser's office at the *Post*. "The first thing you have to understand about this town," he said, "is that there are different ways to talk to the press. There's on the record, off the record, background, and deep background."

He looked to see if I was following him. "This conversation is on deep background."

He paused again. "My wife tells me I needed to get that clear with you, because I didn't want to end up like my friend Shelby Coffey."

He made it exceedingly clear that under no circumstances did he want to see himself being performed onstage, by me.

And so that first conversation remains in deep background. It was deep background, although I wasn't talking to the press, the press was talking to me. Nonetheless, I abided by their rules.

The delineation of on the record, off the record, background, deep background would be one of many delineations that would be made from time to time as I tried to understand the world of "the press." If you say the word *press*, members of the press will immediately ask for attention to diversity. *The New York Times* is not going to want to be categorized in the same breath as a tabloid. And, who knows? Perhaps a tabloid doesn't want to be mentioned in the same breath as *The New York Times*. *The Washington Post* is not even going to want to be considered in the same breath as ABC News.

People speak with great concern about the degree to which political journalism is a part of the entertainment media. Yet I learned in my journey that this is not new.

1997

MONTICELLO

It was through my researchers, and their dealings with Monticello, the home of Thomas Jefferson, that I began to become more and more interested in a journalist in Jefferson's day. His name was James Callender.

Callender had written volumes of letters to Jefferson. First, he was looking to Jefferson for patronage and sent him his writings. Jefferson frequently wrote back to him, commending him on the ideas put forth. Callender was from Scotland, well-read, and had the gift of being able to turn a phrase with wit. To make a long story short, Callender went to jail for his writings against John Adams, who was Jefferson's opponent in a presidential election. From jail, he wrote time and time again, asking Jefferson for money and, finally, when Jefferson became president, for a job as postmaster. Jefferson clearly wanted to distance himself from this man, and he wrote as much in a letter to a friend. When Callender got out of jail he went, enraged, to one of Jefferson's associates, demanding his "hush money."

Callender was also a racist. It happened that he was in jail at the same time as a number of slaves who had taken part in a well-known outbreak called Gabriel's Rebellion. His distaste for black people was palpable.

Failing to get the post or the money he wanted, Callender spent a great deal of time exposing his claim that Sally Hemings and Thomas Jefferson had been sexually involved. In fact, Callender is known better now because he is said to have "broken the Sally Hemings story," that is, the now well-known story of Jefferson's supposed fathering of the children of a slave woman, who was a quadroon. She was one-quarter black and was in fact the sister of Jefferson's late wife. So if slaves were "in law," they would have been in-laws.

What amazes me is the time and imagination Callender spent turning this story into entertainment. I am also amazed at how much he did to make an image of Sally that could only be distorted. She was very vulnerable to his pen's distortion; Jefferson was not nearly as vulnerable in that way.

Callender wrote, for example, a very racist takeoff on Hogarth's *Rake's Progress* that was about Jefferson and Sally. He wrote numerous articles and ditties. This one, about Sally Hemings, was sung to the tune of "Yankee Doodle":

> *Of all the damsels in the green*
> *on mountain or in valley*
> *A lass so luscious ne'er was seen*
> *As Monticellan Sally.*
>
> *Thick pouting lips! How sweet their grace!*
> *When passion fires to kiss them!*
> *Wide spreading over half the face,*
> *Impossible to miss them.*
>
> *In glaring red and chalky white*
> *Let others beauty see*
> *Me no such tawdry tints delight*
> *No Black's the hue for me!!!!!*
>
> *What though my Sally's nose be flat*
> *'Tis harder then to break it*
> *Her skin is sable what of that*
> *'Tis smooth as oil can make it.*
>
> *If down her neck no ringlets flow*
> *A fleece adorns her head*
> *If on her lips no rubies glow*
> *Their thickness serves instead.*

This reminds me of the way Monica Lewinsky and all of the women revolving around that story, Linda Tripp included, got "beaten up" in the media. They were categorized, across the "media"—from tabloids through Jay Leno to the op-ed pages of *The New York Times*—in ways that were disrespectful in terms of physical appearance. I wonder when people look back on those writings generations from now if they will be as horrified as I was when I read some of Callender's writings.

Callender never got what he wanted from Jefferson. He was an alcoholic and died by drowning in the Potomac River. There will be no monument built to James Callender; however, he probably caused quite a headache for Jefferson in his time. Then, and now, his diversions could also divert the public from other matters at hand.

I am not the first to marvel at how much of the public's imagination was taken up by the Monica Lewinsky scandal.

The press are thinking people, many of whom have Ivy League educations, some of whom might be found quoting T. S. Eliot, or waxing poetic about having the opportunity to reread Plato, or any of those "men" from the "canon." But when does being a thinking person become merely being a clever person? Sometimes, tucked into that "cleverness," are troublesome thoughts that we'd best not glide past too quickly. Callender's cleverness could allow his audience to glide over their racist feelings.

After having been in Washington for a while, and having interviewed a few hundred people, I began to long for an interviewee who lacked reverence. Even as most of the press people I interviewed had enormous disdain for Bill Clinton, they still had quite a bit of reverence for the process they themselves were in. It was hard to find anyone who had not bought into the process lock, stock, and barrel. I was looking for a modern-day James Callender. It would be too obvious to go for the stand-up comics—this needed to be someone who was playing even harder than they were.

The press for all their war with those in power, and their charge to reveal any misuse of power, are very much the status quo. They are very middle-class. I found my modern-day Callender in Christopher Hitchens. I was amazed at his likeness with James Callender. Callender was Scottish; Hitchens, English. Both were irreverent. Both felt they had nothing to lose in terms of moving against the grain of the status quo.

We met in Washington on a sunny day at the height of the impeachment proceedings.

FEBRUARY 1999
WASHINGTON, D.C.

Hitchens at the time that I met him had just stepped "out of bounds" by raising questions about Sidney Blumenthal, a Clinton staffer, and doing so in a way that disturbed even Hitchens's closest colleagues. At lunch, amidst a passionate telling of his drama with Sidney Blumenthal, he broke into an account about Clinton's response to Gennifer Flowers's having come forward during the '92 campaign: "Because from the love nest with [the] blonde—who, by the way, you're content to libel and slander—someone who loved you—and say she's a lying minx; she's done it for money—later, and only under oath say, 'Yeah, well, maybe once I did fuck her,' but everyone knows incidentally, should know, it's quite bad manners to screw someone only once. The rudest thing you can do, I would think—one of the rudest things you could do. . . . I think it's very nasty to say, 'Well, I'll fuck you once and not call you again.' I have a good reason to think that was also a lie and why he thinks it would make it better. Yeah, once. What a vulgar thing to say. What a revolting thing to say."

The press gather the information. But they do a lot more than gather and disseminate information. At their best moments, they use their wit to make us question power in a way that we may not have. And they must get our attention in the first place. They have to creep into the brains of the readers, or listeners, and alter the flow of our ideas.

So if I'm listening along, as I was to Hitchens, about an issue that most of us have heard quite a bit about—Gennifer Flowers—I might think I've heard it all before, until he offers up: " 'Well, maybe once I did fuck her,' but everyone knows incidentally, should know, it's quite bad manners to screw someone only once. The rudest thing you can do."

That's a trochee in the second beat. It's not where he seemed to be going. The last thing I expected from him was his way of looking at the situation from a woman's point of view. Normally the women in these accounts become, by association, sluts.

The problem is, politicians are not *allowed* trochees in the second beat. They're scared stiff into iambs. It's the columnists like Hitchens and others, and talk-show hosts, and radio hosts, and comics in this mélange of press/media/entertainment et cetera, who have the trochees.

What would we as a public have to do to give our leaders the courage to take back the trochees—to speak originally—to stop our trains of thought, just when we think we've heard it all before, seen it all before? To get our attention again, they must.

When I met the president the first time, I called home to tell my mother and father. I suppose I called because the president is a powerful man. I didn't call them as I met members of the press. Yet the press represent another kind of power. They have power as a team—they accumulate power with all the words they put forward day after day. It's like a constant drip that affects the way we think, and the way we see the world. They can change us without our full awareness. It happens slowly, bit by bit, that we take on attitudes that are perpetuated in the media. How can we as a public regain control of words?

TODD PURDUM

THE NEW YORK TIMES

"Surf and Turf"

You see, the big thing
this is the other thing—
it's better to be on the press charter,
because the press charter is all first-class seats.
Air Force One has first class seats, too
but it's much roomier,
and it's all designed to compensate the press.
But, um, you know, they try, they do the best they can.
But the network people are particularly—
cushy.
And they have minions to carry their things around,
and we're just all there
but they have burdens we don't have, too.
They have to look great on the tarmac or whatever.
They have to stand up and talk sense off the top of their heads,
whereas we have,
basically always, hours to futz around.
And the two sort of cardinal rules are
if you have an opportunity to eat or go to the
bathroom, you should do either one,
because you do them when you have the chance because
you never know when you'll next have the chance.
But what happens is you keep having food put in front of you,

and I've been on trips where you eat five meals a day.
Literally,
once,
we were coming back from someplace—
Wyoming—Montana, Montana
at two in the morning,
and they served us sort of surf and turf on the plane
—steak and shrimp or lobster.
And we all ate it.
We all ate it all.

ORIENTATION: DINNERS AND LUNCHES

HAD A LOT OF MEALS IN WASHINGTON. PEOPLE GAVE ME QUITE A bit of orientation and advice for the price of lunch, dinner, or breakfast, as their schedules would have it.

FALL 1993
BREAKFAST WITH HELEN THOMAS
ANA HOTEL
WASHINGTON, D.C.

Any sitting president is only visiting. Early on I had breakfast with Helen Thomas from UPI, the woman who is the first to stand in a press conference and ask a question of "Mr. President." She told me that there was nothing like seeing a president the moment he leaves office. The power is so great that, as he passes the mantle, you can actually see him decrease in size. Obviously this mantle, or this cloak as I have heard it called, is borrowed property. Supposedly, we the public lend that mantle. It is in part a mantle of our trust.

FEBRUARY 1995
DINNER
MORTONS, BEVERLY HILLS, CALIFORNIA

I was filming the movie *The American President*, with Michael Douglas and Annette Bening, directed by Rob Reiner. I was playing the press secretary to the president. By an inexplicable confluence of events, the first major grant for the project on the press and the presidency came through just weeks before I met with Rob and he cast me in the movie. I had done quite a bit of research on the role, and it fed right into what I would be spending the next five years on.

One night I was invited to have dinner with Robert Sheer and Narda Zacchino of the *Los Angeles Times*, along with George Stephanopoulos and his brother. I sat next to George. He gave me one of my first lessons in how stories are created about our times and about the people who lead us:

"Clinton's gonna win in '96 because that's the best narrative."

To me, it seemed early to predict such a thing, but I was all ears.

"A narrative about a guy who is falling and pulls himself up is a good narrative. What the press wants is the most interesting narrative."

I had never thought that our reality was so dependent on narratives. I was hoping that who won had to do with voters. But given that there aren't so many voters, it may be that we need narratives to create a certain fiction.

SPRING 1995
DINNER AT RITA BEAMISH AND PAUL COSTELLO'S HOUSE
WASHINGTON, D.C.

I was going to Washington as a guest of *Newsweek* to attend my first White House Correspondents' dinner. It would be the first of a few.

Rita Beamish, who was an AP correspondent at the time, and her husband, Paul Costello, hosted a small dinner party for me. Among the guests were Andy Rosenthal, from the Washington Bureau of *The New York Times*, his wife, and other journalists. Paul Costello had worked in the Carter administration.

As the evening progressed, there was an enthusiastic and generous indoctrination into this place I was about to study. It was stranger than other places I had been, and I could tell the preparation was going to have to be significant. I was faced with an absolute tumble of words at that dinner party, unlike anywhere else I had been. It was a cacophony of voices—long tones, short clipped tones, but all relatively loud and excited. The one with longer tones in his voice took on the role of translating, or filling out the shorthand. The conversation went something like this.

"He's the one who wrote such-and-such about so-and-so."

"Oh, no no, tell her about ———"

There would be a guffaw and then an explanation.

And there were moments that were not so funny. I didn't know the difference, so I could only watch the room as though everyone were speaking Turkish. If they smiled I smiled, if they looked serious, I looked serious. At best I was a mirror of their roller coaster of enthusiasms and feelings.

"Well, that was the grocery store scanner scandal."

"Marlin—Fitzwater . . . ," the one with longer tones started out. He was cut off.

"You know Marlin?"

"I don't know anybody," I said.

"He's great. . . ."

"Well . . . ," someone droned.

"No, he's a sweet man. . . ."

"George Bush and I used to jog together."

Bush jogged with members of the press? I thought.

And there was some pontificating:

"Now you have to understand this. Watergate—changed—everything. You see before that tiiiiiime . . . ," the one with longer tones expounded.

"You need to meet Bob Woodward."

"You think he would talk to me?" I said in partial disbelief.

"Oh surrrre."

"Have you met Jane Mayer?"

"Uh, did she write the book about Anita H———"

"Oh, tell her 'bout Naomi. . . ."

And everyone sort of howled in unison.

"Naomi."

"Naomi Novis . . . a woman who . . . ," one of the ones with longer tones explained.

"Who does she work for?"

"I don't think anybody knows."

"Oh come on, don't say that, she's looking for real information."

"Anyway, one time we were leaving a hotel, and she—"

Someone howled.

"She had *emptied* the minibar!"

"Into her suitcase, see."

"She thought it was *free!*"

And they howled about how someone came after her from the hotel with a huge bill, and she opened up her suitcase and gave all the booze back. Right then and there, maybe even on the bus or on the sidewalk just outside the hotel. . . .

These people live with each other on the road, I thought to myself.

"Oh! Judy Woodruff and Al Hunt. . . ."

"They are the classic, inside-the-beltway couple."

"You know who you should contact," the one with longer tones said thoughtfully, "Jody Powell, who was press secretary to Carter. . . ."

"Well, he's with Powell Tate now . . ."

"That's what I was going to say. . . . He has a consultancy. . . ."

Everybody, it seemed, left Washington and had a consultancy, or went to Hollywood. In the course of being in Hollywood to do *The American President,* I had already come across former politicos.

There was some ground being covered by nods. Sentences being finished with laughs or gestures. Oh, this is going to be one tough study. It'll take me a year just to bone up, I thought.

"You're definitely going to travel on the campaign trail, right?"

"That's the plan."

"I can jot all this down for you later if you like. . . ."

The one with longer tones was the most helpful in the bunch.

Then someone suggested emphatically, "You *have* to get on Air Force One."

"I heard it's really expensive."

"You *have* to . . ."

"I heard it was first class and a half."

"Well the *press* plane is first class and a half, that's what you pay."

"But the press plane is not the same as Air Force One."

"Oh no?"

"No."

"It's not the same as Air Force One."

"And by the way, the press plane is not first-class, that's what you pay, or rather what the news organization pays, but it's not first-class."

"Well, for some of the major networks . . ."

"*New York Times, Washington Post,* ABC, NBC, CBS, they all go first-class."

"But Air Force One is a different story."

"You have to be in a news organization. The pool travels on Air Force One. You know what the pool is?"

"Unless you have friends in high places . . ."

"You must know someone who could get you on Air Force One."

"See, the pool is . . ." the one with longer tones began to explain.

They started to brainstorm about how I might do that. No one came up with any solution, just the suggestion.

"Anybody know where I can find a good gym?" I asked.

A good gym turned out to be *the* hardest thing to find. It was easier in the long run getting in to see Clinton than it was finding a good gym.

Washington is, in every way, an *un*body experience.

I wouldn't know for quite some time just how much conflict there is in that town about the body.

For all the talk of Evian and jogging having replaced booze and smoke-filled rooms, the inside-the-beltway crowd seemed to like to down a healthy amount of booze, eat hearty, and talk up a storm. The first thing I would need is a grant to take care of the lunches, breakfasts, and dinners of my subjects. They liked to meet in fancy places.

FALL 1995
LUNCH WITH GEORGE STEPHANOPOULOS
THE OVAL ROOM
WASHINGTON, D.C.

One of the many people I took to lunch that first fall in Washington was George Stephanopoulos. He told me stories of glory and horror. Of talking to the president about his draft scandal in a men's room on the road, during the campaign. Of how the president in his big health care speech went out to face the nation on television only to find the wrong speech on the TelePrompTer, and of how he, George, had to leave his seat and run to the back to where the technical guy was trying to fix it.

"So he had to give the speech with no text?" I said.

"It's worse than no text. A hundred sixty million people . . . okay, let's not exaggerate, are watching you, and what you're seeing on your Tele-PrompTer is another speech text scrolling by at quadruple speed because the way the guy got through it was to go through the state of the union to get to the health care speech. So he's got two TelePrompTers, one with the state of the union at quadruple speed, while he is extemporaneously giving the health care speech."

I gathered that the first term was full of such escapades.

George is a very personable, charismatic guy. It struck me as we talked that he might know something about Air Force One, if it was really some sort of major sign of the culture, and if so how I should go about getting on it.

"People tell me I should try to get on Air Force One as a part of my research."

"That's true, you should," he said, as we were moving from lunch to espressos.

"Any advice on how to do that?"

"How many big donors do you know?"

BEN BRADLEE

FORMER EDITOR, *THE WASHINGTON POST*

"Off the Stage"

Well, it started with television, right?
It started with television.
These guys, uh—they were really performers long before the,

uh, the press was of the, the scribes.

The scriveners were—uh, uh,

Brinkley—uh,

Cronkite,

Sevareid.

These were performers

and uh, uh, it, it got so that what they said was less important than how they said it and

the authority that they could, uh, force the public to believe they had.

And then as we got used to this, as this became part of our culture, they ceased to be reporters of any kind.

They're not.

I mean, they love to think of themselves as reporters and occasionally they still can report, but in this wonderful time when we were downstairs in the city room when Hoffman was here, Dustin.

And he was absorbing and trying to learn how we all talked and what the culture of—and, you know, not unlike what, I guess, what you're doing

and we got the word that there was a jumper.

A jumper means that somebody has gone out a window and is threatening to jump into the street and off himself.

I said to Dustin,

Would you—yeah, you want to see this?

This is a, uh, a kind of a, uh, ritual story.

Happens twice a year and happens to almost all reporters.

They get to cover it.

So, we went down and walked and it was right around the corner.

We walked a block and a half.

And, you know, everybody's looking up this way and a few people say, Jump, jump. But mostly just looking.

Then they spotted Hoffman

and the whole audience turned around and looked at us.

Just they all looked at *Hoffman*!

Now, if, if, uh, Dan *Rather* did that, he went to cover a jump, they'd do the same thing.

They *intrude*—upon the event—and this is why the smart editors
    who taught us wanted us off the stage
because,
uh, uh, you *changed* the event by your presence if you're really a
    performer.
It's a cheap thrill for uh—
I mean, I don't suppose that was such a cheap thrill for Hoffman.
He's been seen a thousand times and oohed and aahed over,
but it sure changed it for the poor bastard who was jumping and—
    he didn't jump.
But—uh, they very seldom jump.
But—and, you know, there's a principle in physics—I have the
    book.
I bought this huge physics book, which is so unusual for me—
called the Heisenberg principle, and—
and that is, if you, if you, uh, split an atom,
you don't end up with two half atoms; you end up with two
    different things.
Observing the phenomenon changes the phenomenon.

A BRIEFING

FALL 1995
WASHINGTON, D.C.

THE BRIEFING ROOM COULD REMIND YOU OF A CLASSROOM OF VERY smart, very aggressive kids—waving their hands, having the right answer. In this case, they are raising their hands to ask the right question, which in Washington is tantamount to the right answer, because the question inscribes an idea in the public's mind regardless of the response. "Mr. President, isn't it true that . . . ?"

It's a little like the day that a substitute is there, or a new teacher, or a student teacher. It isn't like a scene with a substitute in the ghetto. It's like a substitute teacher in Scarsdale or a community like that. The aggression on the part of the kids would never be physical. No one would turn over a desk, or moon the teacher, or throw chalk, or write graffiti, or spit, or do something sexual, or any of those kinds of things. The aggression would be in the form of the fifth-graders proving, and some of them can pull this off, that they are in fact smarter than whoever is in authority in their normal teacher's absence. And if it's a dynamic with the normal teacher, then they're smarter than the normal teacher is, because the kids are actually spokespeople for their *parents*. The normal teacher is the president, the substitute is the press secretary.

In actuality, the press see a lot more of the press secretary than they do of the president. The press secretary briefs daily, sometimes more than once a day. This is even the case on the road, where they make a makeshift briefing situation by putting together a makeshift podium with appropriate signage. I suppose Christianity was like this in the days of colonialism. Missionaries could do their work anywhere. So this religion of getting and delivering information happens under all conditions. The same is true of "filing." The press get the story in the way the postal service gets the mail through all conditions. I was told that in the old days they had to file over the phone, word by word. Now, computers make this quite simple, but also, they make it dangerously fast. We can get information transmitted faster than we can digest what we've just heard.

Mike McCurry was press secretary when I saw my first briefing. A briefing is not a conversation. It's almost athletic. It's a kind of badminton or tennis. There's a team of thirty against one. They are serving—Mike McCurry, who doesn't have a racquet, either ducks or easily hits the birdie or the ball back with his hand. Six to ten serves come on the same subject matter. At my first briefing, Mike had done ten ducks and hits, and suddenly, from another room entirely, came a voice; it was Brit Hume.

"Oh—come—on—Mike!" he yelled, in a rhythm that sounded like a windup for a Sousa march. He yelled this and came storming in. The briefing room of the White House is a little like a den in a basement. It doesn't have a very firm feel, so when Brit Hume stormed in, the floor and the windows shook.

DEE DEE MYERS

FORMER PRESS SECRETARY TO PRESIDENT CLINTON

"The President's Haircut"

Uhm,
we were in L.A.
and the president uh was previously scheduled to get a
haircut
and rather than go
to

uhm a hotel
or
he couldn't go to a salon
but we decided that we would do it on Air Force One save some
time.
So we got to the airport and he got on the plane
he got his haircut.
We were on the tarmac for quite a while but
when the president
you know then everybody,
Christophe got off
buttoned up the plane
and Clinton did something that he almost never does
which is he walked back
to the press section of the plane.
He almost never does it.
And of course one of the women
because
men would never notice this kind of thing
said
"He got his hair cut!
when did he get his hair cut?"
and um you know I, I, I uh think I, I, I, I can remember just
thinking Oh God I—he got his hair cut yes it was obvious—I
didn't deny that yes he did but I didn't want to get into the
details of who had cut it
but somebody else had seen
him and somebody goes, "Oh yeah I saw that guy. Who's that guy
with the long hair, getting off the plane?" At that point I was
running to the front of the airplane.
Well what really there was a little chirping about it and I
think there was a little item on
one of the reporters there put a little item on the wire,
President Clinton got his hair cut onboard Air Force One blah
blah blah
well then somebody from the FAA told
somebody that

while the president sat there and got his hair cut by this
guy Christophe
that it had delayed air traffic.
So we went back and checked with
they checked with the FAA.
It was a blind quote.
Um
one woman had said that delayed air traffic
we checked with the Secret Service
they said no
um and Christophe is um a Beverly Hills coiffeur, he charges
two hundred dollars for a haircut normally of course
the president
wasn't paying two hundred dollars
but that for some the story got out that all these commuter
planes around the country were you know backed up while the
    president was leisurely getting his hair cut.
So
uh
the next day when I went out to brief
you know you can sometimes sense the uh building momentum of
a bad story.
Um
so I walked out there
and I remember I have to look at the transcript
but I can remember Brit Hume
from
ABC News being very obnoxious and saying
"What is this about Clinton getting his hair cut?"
it may have even been the first question I don't really
remember
and then he started this
with "Monsieur *Christophe!*"

LOCKED UP

FROM TIME TO TIME WHILE I WAS IN WASHINGTON, I WENT TO VISIT women at the Maryland Correctional Institute for Women. I had first learned about MCIW when I went there to research an article for *The New Yorker* in their special "women's issue." Frankly, it was a verbal vacation. The language of the inmates was so much more energized and varied than the language of the status quo in Washington. The prison was also a strange relief from the intense masculinity of Washington.

But the prison was a very sad place. The number of incarcerated women has increased exponentially over the last fifteen years. The majority of the women in the prison were black. Many of them were from Baltimore, where I grew up. As they told me about the crimes they had committed, the streets of Baltimore came alive in a new way.

I met a woman who was eighteen who had been imprisoned a year before for murder. She had shot someone nine times, as she told me, "once in the head, and the rest in the chest." Most of the women were there for violent crimes, and most of them had been abused or had violence committed against them. One woman had raped another woman. I was stunned by her logic: "What I wanna rape a old woman for, that woman 'bout fifty years old. What I wanna rape a old woman for? When I got my own girl?" I met a very tight-lipped woman who was in for life. She wouldn't tell me why, but she spoke poetically of how she stopped taking the drugs they gave her and woke up to hear the birds every morning and how she was committed to making this her life. She knew it was her life, such as it is. And I was mindful of the extent to which they had no controls, none at all. Their mail, their gifts would be returned if they weren't sent in the exact regulated way. The warden explained to me how frequently people tried to take advantage of things. I learned the multitudes of ways that drugs made it into the jail, cocaine being "passed," for example, in a balloon, through a kiss. A balloon of cocaine swallowed and eventually defecated out of the body.

What strikes me most about the prison mentality is the degree to which both the jailed and the jailers are incarcerated. The warden and I talked at length. He kept emphasizing how strong the guards had to be. It seems that some of them ended up committing crimes while on the job. They were caught bringing drugs into the jail, having sexual interactions with inmates, doing illegal things in collaboration with people "on the outside" for inmates.

I had been told that the relationship of the president to the press was one of captives. They are captives of each other. I know now that that is probably not an appropriate metaphor. The fact of the situation for those who are incarcerated is that there's almost no way out.

I met eighteen-year-old girls who will spend most of their lives in jail. Lives ruined. I saw the dramatic role play that was going on—of girls who really looked like boys or men. One guard in a San Francisco jail explained to me that, for incarcerated men, sex and sexuality was really about "getting off," and that most of these men on the outside were straight. The women, by contrast, were more interested in creating families, staged families, in which someone was the father, someone was the mother, and someone was the child.

What does this darker side of our society tell us about ourselves? It tells me that, as much as we seem to be addicted to hope, we also give up on people if they are truly on the margins. I once asked a psychiatrist if he knew of anyone doing psychoanalysis in the jails. He explained to me that it was problematic. "Who's the client?" "Who's the client?" comes down to "Who's paying?"

I often thought about the prison when the Clintons became more and more criminalized. I thought about the prison when the Monica Lewinsky story broke. For all the talk of this being a "relationship" or an "affair," it seemed to me to live in the same sort of distorted shadows that housed these "relationships" in prisons. Everything fast, furtive, with the possibility of captivity, entrapment, being caught right there. Sexual encounters in a gym, in the laundry room, the kitchen, or sometimes a female guard backing up to the bars and having sex with a male prisoner. Our president was spoken about in the same way. His every move dissected. The press, like the prison warden, gleeful about the captive. Ken Starr gleeful about the captive. Caught in the act. The graphic act. What did it mean that our president was seen in such a shadow—and seen there in a way that could only be interpreted as pathology?

What was the difference between the guard who made me empty my purse at the prison and the guards who made me empty my purse at the White House? What was the difference between clearance at the prison and clearance at the White House? In the case of the prison, it once took the lieutenant governor of Maryland. In the case of the White House, it always took someone on the inside, who cleared the way. Access on the "bottom" was as tough as access at the "top."

HOMI BHABHA

CULTURAL THEORIST

"Sucking the Toe"

The way in which the clothes of leaders
of public leaders in democratic societies
now
you know let's think of all the stuff you hear
even today about Clinton's hairdress——
you know hairdresser in Los Angeles airport
yeah
I think it's part of this general system
and I want, I want to just give a range of examples that are
absolutely crucially important in the public view of
leadership.

Jacqueline Kennedy
um um uh of course Princess Diana's
uh vestments
(1997)
so what I'm saying this is not some little airy-fairy idea
but, but in a way
now that we do not mark authority so obviously by clothes and
clothes were the way, the way in which the king's body or the
    despot's body was, was
marked out
we mark it
you know
we, we mark it in terms of fashion
and then the other big thing at the moment
is the enormous interest in the unclothed body
sex
lust
I mean I sincerely believe
that the day well
I half-sincerely believe
that the day in which uh Fer——
Princess D——
Whatever her name is Ferg——
Fergie
you know
the day in which her nipples were actually shown in the press
you know photographs of herself naked
sucking the toe of this American boyfriend of hers
uh that was a major major day there was almost nothing then
in royal authority that was enigmatic or charismatic
but on the other—
so things like a haircut are completely quotidian
every day
it allows for this identification, this immediate
identification
and you know the haircut—
Why has the interest in the body of authority and those who

embody authority lasted so long?
You know the thing about the common person, is uh everyday
life, the details they're just next to you
they could be you?
It could've been you instead of Clinton—
It's, it's your, it's your neighbor
it's the boy or the girl next door
uhm uh and so forth right?
that's the everyday
that's the kind of why
President Clinton's hair or Princess Diana's tampon becomes
so interesting.

THE POWER OF

MUTENESS

HAD BEEN IN WASHINGTON FOR FOUR MONTHS. I WAS IN NEW YORK for a weekend, and I was having my hair and makeup done for an event I had to attend. The person helping me was in the world of fashion but had gotten some Washington insiders ready for photo shoots. She had also coiffed many a newscaster. (I wonder if Huntley and Brinkley had stylists?) Glamour hits Washington too.

I told her about my project—

"Well, you have to talk to [she named a prominent woman newscaster]."

"She refused to give me an interview."

She continued blow-drying my hair. Then she turned off the dryer.

"Oh, what about [she named another one]?"

"She refused to give me an interview."

"You're kidding."

She turned the dryer back on. Then she shut it off.

"Well, of course you've talked to ————"

"She doesn't want to do an interview."

I looked at my stylist. Suddenly I said, "Oh my God. . . . I just realized something. You're naming all white women."

I thought for a minute. A number of the white women I had approached for interviews either would not talk to me or, after they had talked to me, decided they wanted to be off the record, or at least that I could not perform them in a "show."

"I don't even want to think about this," I said.

"No," the stylist said. "Don't go there."

She proceeded with drying my hair. I lifted my hand. She stopped.

I had an awful memory, and thought twice about sharing it, but decided I would.

The person who scheduled my interviews had gotten into a tangle with one well-known radio correspondent. She said she was not interested in meeting with me and wanted to know who had agreed to meet with me. He named the names of a few people. Two of them were women, and both friends of hers. She said she couldn't believe they had agreed and was going to call them up herself, because she couldn't imagine they would have consented to do this.

We were alarmed when this happened. Even given the task of calling movie stars as well as people who toted guns in Los Angeles during the riots, I hadn't had this particular type of problem. I had always had challenges when it came to gaining access, but I hadn't yet had the problem of women calling their friends and saying, "Don't talk to her." Apparently the decision of this correspondent and her colleague was based on something they had *heard* I said when I gave a (free) brown-bag-lunch talk at National Public Radio a year or so before. Very frightening. I had happily spoken at the brown bag for no fee—it was an honor to have been invited—and I was paying a price.

For my work in the theater, I often use release forms. We had to get a special release form created just for Washington. I still wince about the legal fees.

It's expensive to get people to talk to you in Washington.

The guy in our office who did all the calls felt pretty bad about this and other snafus. We decided that this was not as simple as calling up people as we had in Los Angeles and other places to get interviews.

We ended up having to hire a consulting firm to schedule the interviews! It was clear that we did not know what we were doing, in this very peculiar world. We winced about the consultancy fees. Luckily a firm called Powell-Tate was kind enough and generous enough to take us on for just a nominal amount of money. Sheila Tate and her colleagues generously opened doors that would have otherwise remained shut.

Theaters, which often do plays by dead white men, are not prepared for these kinds of expenses, or this type of risk. This is what happens when you dare to move out of the margins and into another place. I was stunned at my sudden realization that women had been the instigators of this falling apart.

Having been educated at a women's college and an all-girls high school, and being a product of feminism, I was confused by this. I was disappointed.

On the face of it, one might expect that the white women in Washington, and white women in general, would be good collaborators. This is not so, unless they themselves have had a reason to have a variety of cross-cultural experiences.

I was saddened by this. I called the two smartest people I could think of to talk about it. One was Gloria Steinem; the other was Barbara Johnson in women's studies at Harvard.

I talked with Barbara Johnson in January 1998, interestingly enough, just before the Monica Lewinsky story "broke."

We were on the phone, and she started off with: "I think that white women have benefited from the power of muteness."

In fact I had called her in part because I had read an article that she had written in which she gave many examples of the power of muteness for white women called "muteness envy." Perhaps the most riveting idea in the article was that every white woman who was nominated for an Academy Award for playing a mute woman had won. So that something about our cultures likes the "mute" white woman.

"Being *next* to power is more power than any of the other positions that they could envisage for themselves. The fear of being estranged or alienated, standing alone, standing up for themselves, standing out. So if the calculation of white women has been that not being alone maximizes your chances of being successful, not being exposed, not being out there, then it's almost second nature not to want someone to perform your identity."

This didn't entirely make sense to me because, after all, I had seen Cokie Roberts and many others on the David Letterman show. If they were afraid of being exposed, why on earth would they go on a show like that? She explained that on those shows they are speaking for themselves.

"Whiteness in women has always been fragile. That is, whiteness is something a woman can lose. In fact, femininity is something a woman can lose. In fact, femininity is something a white woman can lose."

I didn't understand that. "How can you lose whiteness? It's right there on your skin," I said. "How is talking to me a threat to that?"

She explained that the problem was they had no idea what I was going to do with their identity, with their material. "They wouldn't know what your story *is*," she continued.

"Oh, wow!" I said. "Wow!"

"Being a character in your play means being in a different position in the story than I'm in now. I'm trying to maximize my position, and you want me to be in a different position in a different story? No thanks."

I laughed from relief, not because any of this was funny.

It was quiet on the line for a moment. I thought for a moment before asking the dangerously obvious question. "How significant is my race in this?" I said, and then added, "If at all."

"We're in a weird political moment," she said. "In feminism, to the extent that it still exists, there's a huge prestige factor being in your play or in an anthology that's run by black women. The people who are maybe tied to the story of the presidency or the press may not be in the same moment," she said.

Then she added, "I think it's a moment where your race would play an unpredictable role."

CLAUDIA McCLAIN

CONVICTED FOR MURDER
MARYLAND CORRECTIONAL INSTITUTE FOR WOMEN

"Pretty Teeth"

The warden was basically telling us to watch what we say to you and
I said Well if you ask me I'm gonna tell it like it is.
He called me and Tyboria

um
he said
"It'll be a privilege for the segregation inmates
and I don't feel it's in their best interest."
You could look at 'em and just tell how they're livin'
and how they're bein' treated.
And people said
um you know
well
you know
and I told people
it was like
"Just go tell her the truth"
and it was like you know
whether it's gonna hurt me or don't hurt me
I just had to deal with it.
So yesterday I was telling a couple people I'm goin' up here [to talk
        to you]
because
you know they kept
trying to scare me
talking
"Are you gonna do it are you gonna do it?"
You know
kept axing and axing and axing,
and I said "If I said it once I mean yes"
and they kept
you know axing axing axing like they wanted to change our minds.
The officers
the warden called me back
and asked me that.
So
people said "Well Claudia
we know you're gonna go tell it all
everything you know"
and I said "You're right
because I said we're not dogs

we're still human beings regardless of what we might have done."
[She sits closer to the microphone and increases her volume.]
This is on the record!
We had one girl
her name is Zelda Mitchell [a pseudonym]
she has abscesses
an infection in her mouth.
And this other girl
she just caught hepatitis from the dentist using a dirty needle.
[She bares her teeth.]
But see I have pretty teeth
so I don't have to worry.

GRANDPOP'S NIGGER

THE PROBLEM OF GETTING TO "WE" WITH A DIVERSE CULTURE ON THE one hand and a profoundly patriarchal culture on the other has historical veins that are difficult to uproot. To find America in the presidency, I spent a lot of time getting to know Thomas Jefferson. I tripped over those historical veins. Those veins reach all of us. They are powerful veins. A friend of mine has a huge copper beech tree. It is gorgeous and shimmering and expansive. It changes color as the sun changes its position. Wild turkeys congregate under its expanse. I wonder, whenever I gaze at it, how it manages to pull the amount of water it needs from its roots. American history manages to weave its way into our daily lives in such a way. Sometimes the resulting tree shimmers like that copper beech. Sometimes the tree is not so pretty. In such a way American history has even marked my family.

1979
UPPER WEST SIDE RESTAURANT
NEW YORK CITY

My brother is eighteen months younger than I. He was born with platinum blond hair and blue eyes. People would stop my mother on the street and ask her where she got such a pretty little boy. I think they thought she had borrowed him. We have many colors in my family.

When I was a starving actress in New York, my brother would drive up from Baltimore after he got out of work on Fridays. He would spend the weekend and take me to restaurants to which I could otherwise not afford to go. One night at dinner, we started talking, as we often did, about our family. All of my grandfather's kids, that is, my aunts and uncles, left home as soon as they got through college. My father did not. He stayed in Baltimore and worked for my grandfather. Parenthetically, let me say that my father was the only dark-skinned member of his family. I asked my brother, who was very close to my grandfather, why it was that my father had stayed when everyone else had left. His explanation sent chills up my spine: "Don't you know that Daddy was Grandpop's nigger?"

SPRING 1996
MY WORK LOFT
SAN FRANCISCO

I was waiting for my research assistant, Nora, to drop off some Jefferson materials. I looked out the window, and Nora, who is a very petite white woman with a Louise Brooks type of hairstyle, was striding across the street with one of her classmates—a black woman wearing sunglasses. She had a very full head of hair that extended like a pyramid from her head. They had that "it's finally spring" sort of glee in their stride. Even San Francisco has to recover from cold, rainy winters. The confidence that they had, and the ease they had with each other, across cultures, was something that was nonexistent in my generation of women. They wore their intelligence with pride. Things have changed, I thought, as I leaned out the window to greet them.

As they entered, Nora's friend made herself comfortable without removing her sunglasses. She sat quietly as Nora and I went over a few things about Thomas Jefferson and some new material she had found. I said that I was fascinated by Jefferson.

Nora's friend suddenly broke in, with a kind of drone in her voice. "You've read the *Notes* of course?"

"The *Notes*?"

"*Notes on the State of Virginia.*"

I bristled just slightly at what seemed like the slightest bit of condescension, but quickly let it pass. She was a grad student, like Nora, at UC Berkeley. The conversation proceeded something like this.

"No. I haven't read them," I said.

"They're a must."

"What are they like?"

"I'm mixed about them," she said, as she lounged. "It's required, like reading Shakespeare."

"Oh."

"You can pick them up anywhere."

"But what are they like?" I asked again.

I think she may have said that it was very good prose.

I thanked Nora for her work, thanked her friend for her advice, and they left. For some reason I felt like I was Alice in Wonderland.

I was headed out of town to perform in New Haven. I picked up the *Notes* in a bookstore before I left. One night after a performance, I took them out. My heart sank. Thomas Jefferson was a racist, a *real* racist, and there was no way around that fact. I had known this, but now it was palpable. He wrote about blacks as if they were scientific specimens.

The first difference which strikes us, is that of color. Whether the black of the Negro resides in the reticular membrane between the skin and the scarf skin, or in the scarf skin itself, the difference is fixed in nature. Are not the fine mixtures of red and white, preferable to that eternal monotony, that immovable veil of black, which covers all the motions of the other race? They have less hair on their face and body. They secrete less by the kidneys and more by the glands of the skin, which gives them a very strong and disagreeable odor. They are more ardent after their female. But love for them is more an eager desire than a tender delicate mixture of sentiment and sensation.

Here I was, after a performance, in a dark, pinkish hotel room in New Haven, where the streets roll up at 10:30 at night, and I couldn't believe what I was reading. I was already down a path that had committed to Thomas Jefferson. We had done an enormous amount of research. I had known, of course, of his contradictions: that on the one hand he wrote the Declaration and on the other hand he had slaves. But this? He had not only a political dilemma with blacks but a "scientific" one. And he went further, to speak of "odor": "They secrete less by the kidneys and more by the glands of the skin, which gives them a very strong and disagreeable odor." All the ideas that we fought so hard from 1950 onward especially to dispel, were right there, deeply rooted.

He went on:

> In general, their existence appears to participate more of sensation than reflection. . . . Comparing them with their faculties of memory, they are equal to whites.

I tried to imagine how he did his testing. Did he do it himself, or did he have others do it? What kinds of tests did he use?

> . . . in reason much inferior. In imagination they are dull, tasteless and anomalous. They astonish you with strokes of the most sublime oratory; such as prove their reason and sentient strong, their imagination glowing and elevated. But never could I find that a black had uttered a thought above the level of plain narration.

Suddenly, the experimental elementary school I went to had another context. When our teachers and our parents fought to show that we could learn as well as any others, they were fighting a battle that Thomas Jefferson himself had helped create. When the white administrators sat in the back of our all-black classroom, they were watching the other side of a boxing ring that had been mounted as long ago as the mounting of the country. We may have been showing that we could do the New Math, but math was, of course, the very least of it. I had known all of this, but to see the *Notes* made it almost too palpable to bear. I was deluged with memories and feelings that I didn't even know I had.

He talked about the talent that blacks had for music but wouldn't concede that they could write compositions.

> In music they are more generally gifted than the whites with accurate ears for tune and time, and they have been found capable

of imagining a small catch. Whether they will be equal to the composition of a more extensive run of melody, or of complicated harmony, is yet to be proved.

The entire twentieth century, with the birth of jazz, would prove him wrong.

He even went further and into poetry—to take from us the possibility of making music of language!

Misery is often the parent of the most affecting touches of poetry. Among the blacks is misery enough, God knows, but no poetry. Love is the particular oestrum of the poet. Their love is ardent but it kindles the senses only, not the imagination.

Then, just as I really thought I could read no further, I read the lowest blow of all, which created for me a sudden suspicion about his motives.

Religion indeed has produced a Phillis Wheatley, but it could not produce a poet.

Why did he go after Phillis Wheatley? Why name names? And a woman who is the pride of so many blacks? I felt nauseated.

His imagination is wild and extravagant, [it] escapes incessantly from every restraint of reason and good taste, and in the course of its vagaries, leaves a track of thought as incoherent and eccentric as is the course of a meteor through the sky. Upon the whole, though we admit him to the first place among those of his own colour who have presented themselves to the public judgement, yet when we compare him with the writers of the race among whom he lived, and particularly with the epistolary class, in which he has taken his own stand, we are compelled to enroll him at the bottom of the column.

I felt nauseated because of that flood of memories. Memories that had been readjusted in a thirty-year public and personal therapy of blacks, whites, all of us, through study, culture, conversation, and some-times psychoanalysis. The public therapy, at least, was fairly successful. I was working on this very chapter in an office at Harvard University, the W.E.B. Du Bois Institute, where I convene the Institute on the Arts and Civic Dialogue. When W.E.B. Du Bois went to Harvard, he could not live with the other students. Now there is a plaque on the site where he lived. In the year 2000, the study of African-American culture is a solid study in the halls of the major universities in this country. It was a public therapy that was going on for most of this century but one that came full blast in the last thirty years: Martin Luther King to Colin Powell.

Jefferson's *Notes* were an unexpected shock. Not only were they a shock to my intellect, they were a shock to my entire physical system. I was just getting to know him, was intrigued by his vast array of interests. I had gone to the music store to buy a pile of CDs of violin compositions, because he had played the violin. I was planning my own trip to Monticello. I was treating him like any character I would play. Learning as much as I can, trying to fall in love with him. And all characters require that love, whether they are presidents, high priests, or child murderers, or racists.

But the *Notes*. It was like a fast-moving kaleidoscope that forced the return of terrible pictures, those "self-images" that many of us had before the term *self-image* emerged. I realized, in that dark, pinkish room in New Haven, a city with one of the best hospitals in the world on the one hand and one of the highest infant mortality rates in the country on the other, that there are so many people who still believe exactly what Jefferson pro-posed. Some in the human genome project even worry, politically, about what further discoveries could unleash in this area. Look at the affirma-tive action debate, be a fly on the wall in a tenure committee, a hiring committee, read criticism and even straight news carefully in our finest newspapers and journals, you will see the descendants of these attitudes.

White feelings of superiority are written in stone, as in our monu-ments. They are deeply encrusted in our presidency, and our Congress. They are deeply encrusted in our media. And if these attitudes in the presidency go back to Jefferson and his colleagues, these attitudes in our media go back to those times too. While Jefferson was writing his *Notes,* James Callender was concocting his images of Sally Hemings, singing them, publishing them in the newspapers of the day.

If down her neck no ringlets flow
A fleece adorns her head
If on her lips no rubies glow
Their thickness serves instead.

It's always hard to see what we're doing while we're doing it. I wonder if journalists today worry at all that a writer or student or scholar two hundred years from now will pull out an archive and read what they have written or what they have said on the air and hold it up as both shocking and rooted in the very problems that cripple us.

What though she by the glands secretes
Must I stand shilly shally
Tucked up between a pair of sheets
There's no perfume like Sally.

"We" is still a long way away. We could ignore history and say that things are better now, or even that mixed-race children are the promise of a better future. But that would be naïve. Sally Hemings was a mixed-race child, in fact she was only one-fourth black. An institution called slavery kept her in her place. We have institutions, subtle though they are, that keep many of us "in our place" and relatively silenced in public discourse.

I was dreading my work. It was going to be very hard to love this man. For actors the real test is the degree to which we can love the characters in spite of personal feelings, in spite of politics.

My disappointment almost immobilized me.

I thought back on the lounging graduate student. "You've read the *Notes* of course?"

Having read them, I decided to proceed. What choice do you have? As Anita Hill told me when I interviewed her, "To the extent that I am at peace here now, it's not because this place has fulfilled the promises that we thought it would. It's because I have fulfilled the promises and faced up to its limitations."

KEN BURNS

HISTORIAN

"Teacup: Regarding Sally Hemings"

It doesn't matter.
He owned her
get the story straight.
I mean he could have killed her if he wanted
he owned her
he could have done anything with her
he could have murdered her
they could have said, "Mr. President, where's Sally?"
and he could have said, "Oh I killed her last night, she displeased
    me," and there wasn't a law in the land that
could have touched him
the fact of whether he did or he didn't
this late-twentieth-century obsession with all things
sexual, titillating, and celebrity driven is an anathema to historical
    truth
he owned her and we forget the fact but the fact that
the man who authored the world's words which we consider our
    creed
held in chattel slavery more than two hundred human beings
one of whom
was a young and we are told attractive and potentially lover for
    him but it doesn't matter
the sexual politics are overwhelmed
by the fact that he owned her.
I like the frisson that comes from
both sides
"Yes of course he could have" "but no he absolutely didn't"
But he owned her goddamn it

that's the point he owned her.
And that's what we forget.
And we go "yes yes yes"
I say "Okay."
"So can I tell you about slavery?"
I said
"How would you like to live
in a one-room dirt-floored shack, fourteen by fourteen, in which you
    work fourteen hours a day?
Unless there is a full moon and then you work more,
you are not paid
you can be beaten
you can be separated from your family.
In fact they changed the wedding vows
for slaves
to read "Till death or distance do you part."
You are susceptible to every known disease of which there is no
    cure—
You are denied the possibility of an education, and in fact
in many instances you would be punished for learning a language
    or having a literature or having a culture.
Now tell me how long you would like to live under this.
I would say a generation's too long
a decade's too long, a year is too long,
a month is too long, a week's too long.
I submit if you were asked to do that
you might try it on for twenty minutes."
That's—
he owned her
you know if I own you
when I say he could have killed her
you say
"Hell yes but he wouldn't have."
His nephews murdered one of his slaves
and that slave's crime had been to break a teacup that had
    belonged to their mother
and there-was-no-recourse-in-the-United-States-of-America.

He's both the blessing and the curse
as John Hope Franklin said—
He ensured that we would inherit the poison of indecision on race
and yet he also wrote us the prescription for the antidote
for the serum that would cure us.
Jefferson said that slavery was "like holding a wolf by the ears—
      you didn't like it but you didn't dare let go."

SLAVES ON P STREET

ONE SUNDAY I WENT TO P STREET, AFTER HAVING BEEN IN TOWN for the Gridiron Dinner, to say hello to Priscilla and Amo Houghton. I brought along my mother, sister, and niece. We had a terrific time. My sister and Amo were chatting away, and Priscilla pulled me to the side. She had a slightly alarmed look in her eyes.

"Oh, Anna, I went to the library to look at the history of the house. . . ."

She took me by the arm.

"And, Anna . . ."

"I know, Priscilla," I said. "Slaves."

"Yes!"

I wasn't surprised at all. The house had been there since 1826; it made perfect sense. Priscilla had now versed herself completely in the facts.

"And the really shocking thing about it was in her will, she left slaves. She left one male slave, aged thirty-six to fifty-five. I mean, that's quite a range!"

I felt oddly more at home with this news.

"And she left one female slave, thirty-six to fifty-five, and three—young—boys. Michael, Henry, and James. She left two to one—"

"She split them up?"

"Well, it sounds as if she broke up this couple. She left this one servant woman, Mary, to her nephew, and then a servant man, Sam, to her niece."

I remembered when I first entered this house, and saw photographs of Amo and his family, and how I ultimately learned that Amo's great-grandfather had owned a big glass company, and they had made the light-bulbs for Thomas Edison. His history went way back—and so did Priscilla's. The documentation about Michael, Henry, and James—I felt like this connected me, in another way, to the house. We are all con-nected, in our ways, to a past.

"So this was really horrifying to me to find that out. Isn't it to you?" Priscilla asked.

My sister was putting her daughter into the car seat. Amo, the Repub-lican congressman, was concentrating on my mother, patiently helping her with her now stiff legs, into the car, telling jokes, filling P Street with his laugh. The slave Mary would never have thought she'd see such a sight, right outside the house. History takes a long time. But it gets there.

DENNIS GREEN, SR.

A DAD, A NONREADER

"Sweepin' the Hallways"

I had one over at 126
who said
"Oh he'll just be another statistic."
And I said What do you mean?
"Oh if he's not gonna read or write, Mr. Green,
you might as well look for him in the cemetery
or in jail."
That's it.
Bottom line
I been up in—
one they tell me at the end of the year

or during parent night
"Your son hasn't been doin nothin."
Yet instead
when I start comin to the school
I see my son
out of the classroom
walking the hallways,
and during lunchtime
he's eating pizza
with
the teachers,
having lunch with some of the teachers.
And this is how he's gotten by elementary school,
not being able to read.
They say, he's
the teachers are saying
Okay, since you can't stay in the classroom come um
come clean the book room.
He cleaned the book room
for three years
three whole years
he went inside of a book room
and just cleaned
and during that time
they said
when parent night
comes they say
Oh
I say "Well how come I wasn't contacted?"
"Oh Mr. Green you don't know what your child is doin?"
I said "No, not if I'm not here."
"Oh your child runs the hallway all the time" and
then some of them would tell me
"Oh you know the assistant principal said
your child is nothing but trouble
and if you watch, if you come up here during the day
you'll see your son cleaning up rooms

or sweeping the hallways.
And he eats pizza with the
dean
just to keep him
quiet
or keep things on the down low."
So I told her I don't believe that.
I did go inside the school
and I seen it with my own eyes—
That's the biggest shocking thing I seen in my whole life.

CREATING FICTIONS

A TWO-YEAR-OLD PROFESSOR

FALL 1998
STANFORD UNIVERSITY

My NIECE HAD COME TO VISIT ME. HER NAME IS ELIZABETH, AND at the time she was two and a half years old. She and her mother (my sister) were driving down to Stanford with me on a day when I was teaching. They wanted to see the campus. I thought of an exercise for my students, all young actors, that would involve Elizabeth.

"Do you have any Legos or crayons or things like that for Elizabeth?" I asked my sister.

Of course she did, she had a purse full.

"I'd like to use Elizabeth today in an experiment in class."

Her mother was all for it.

I entered the class—Freshman Acting. Their optimism and idealism was in stark contrast to the weary cynicism that hung over the more advanced students.

"Today we have a visitor. Her name is Elizabeth Allen. I would like you to observe her and take notes. Then I'll ask some of you to mimic her behavior. The great British director Peter Brook tells us in his book *The Empty Space* that the hardest thing for an actor to portray is a child."

They all eagerly got out their notebooks and pads and took places around the edges of the playing area. I walked Elizabeth to the center of the playing area and sat her down. Her mother carefully put down some crayons and some Legos.

Elizabeth began to draw, and she did so with an amazing amount of concentration. It will be much less relevant twenty years from now when she looks back on this, that she sat in a room alone at two years old being observed by nearly all white grown-ups, or people who in her eyes would have looked like grown-ups.

Was I repeating the scenario at James Mosher Elementary School, when the white throng of educators came to watch us learn?

No. With Elizabeth the situation was different. It was I who was watching, and I was actually watching my students as much as I was watching her.

Suddenly she dropped her crayons and covered her eyes.

My students looked up from their notebooks. Until that point, they had been steadfastly taking notes on every single breath she took. Everything was still, including Elizabeth. I looked to her mother for a clue. She merely shrugged.

Then Elizabeth began to move her hands away from her eyes and back, in peekaboo style. She repeated this several times. My students returned to their note-taking. No one laughed. They took it quite seriously.

Then Elizabeth stopped everything and looked at all of them carefully. Finally she did a very surprising thing. She roared at them. When she got no response, except one laugh, she roared again, longer and more ferociously, like a tiger.

I thanked Elizabeth for coming to our class, and she and her mother left to tour the campus.

I didn't ask my students to mimic Elizabeth. "Originally I wanted you to use this as a life study—but Elizabeth has been an even more valuable model for us than I thought. She has taught us something today about the position of any people who find themselves having to deal with the pressure of the gaze. It is totally abnormal for any of us to stand in front of many, alone, and to be observed. Yet performance and leadership require that. I think you figure out your relationship to being observed when you are very young. Elizabeth is only two, yet she already had a strategy to deal with the anxiety that your silent gaze could have caused. In your presence she became a tiger, which is her favorite animal, and to her it is a ferocious animal. In order to gain power over the moment, she roared at you, not as herself, but as a tiger. This allowed her to stay with you on her terms."

Elizabeth had created a fiction. Her fiction was not a lie. It was a persona. It was a tool that gave her power over us, and allowed her to speak to us, in fact it allowed her to roar, and thus to rule the room, for a moment. She caused the students to stop what they were doing. It was the single moment when they looked up from their pads, in a quandary. Was Elizabeth a tiger? No. Was she lying? No. She was presenting herself "as if " she were a tiger.

What we keep forgetting is that when a public person presents a persona, he or she is simply offering "It's as if I were." That "It's as if I were" is an invitation for us to begin to behave "as if we were" a group. That "as if " is very important for civic action. We are living with the death of metaphor. The media with their high-powered microscope and their incredible capacity to create metaphor behave as though they both love and hate metaphor. They build metaphor, but they insist on the literal, the mundane, the everyday. They take heroic events and try to make us feel as though these events can fit neatly in our living rooms.

Most humans adopt a persona in order to interface with the society around them, no matter how large or small. A person who is caused to move in a large and diverse society must develop a persona that is resilient, and perhaps more complex than, for example, that of a person who has developed a persona to operate in a small town where everyone is the same, and everyone knows everyone. These fictions, these personae are necessary for public life.

Perhaps these fictions are the clothing for greater truths, truths that such an individual accumulates by moving in and out of safe houses of identity in order to be effective in a larger, more complex society. That fiction is a kind of a bargain between the public figure and his or her public. The media seem to be particularly ambivalent about these fictions. On the one hand, they help create them. On the other hand, they are always trying to get under them to "find out exactly who this guy, or this woman, is." The danger of this was revealed most dramatically in the story of Mayor Rudolph Giuliani. Do we really want a society where personal confession goes that far in public? When we dig under a persona to find the "real person," we may not find the real person at all. There are also fictions that are useful to all of "us." These fictions should be allowed to blossom. The most effective fictions are those that allow many people to convene around them for good cause. The most destructive fictions are those that allow many people to convene around them for bad cause.

PLATO: A SUSPICION OF THOSE WHO CREATE FICTIONS IN THE NAME OF ART

FALL 1996
WASHINGTON, D.C.

NOW YOU'RE INVITED TO THE TABLE IN
WASHINGTON AND EVERYBODY LOVES . . .
AREN'T WE GLAD TO HAVE THEM AT THE TABLE
AND THEY SENT OUT A LIST AND EVERYBODY
KNEW AND THE NEXT DAY THEY SAY, CAN YOU
BELIEVE THAT STUPID FUCKING STREISAND?
WHO THE FUCK DOES SHE THINK SHE IS
TALKING TO COLIN POWELL ABOUT BOSNIA, YOU
KNOW? WHAT IS SHE, THE SECRETARY OF THE
FRICKIN DEFENSE, YOU KNOW. WHO IS SHE?

—*An Anonymous Man*

I wondered why there was such disrespect for actors in Washington and thought it might be a symptom of something else. The scholar Judith Butler told me that, in order to understand this, I had to go all the way back to Plato. So I called a woman named Shadi Bartsch, who, I was told, was an expert on this kind of thing.

Knowing in advance what my problem was, she had marked out the relevant passages in Plato's *Republic*, Book 10, Section 604: "Here he talks about theater and poetry as all being tainted by the fact that they're at this third remove from reality. Then where theater is concerned, he goes one step further and he says it corrupts people. It corrupts the human soul."

It *corrupts* the human soul. I had always thought that theater was *good* for the human soul.

"Why does it do that? Because it appeals to the baser instincts like pity and anger and grief and all these things, but it does so in a context where these emotions are not justified. We're weeping or we're rejoicing as we're watching something that's not truth."

This was giving me a horrible feeling, and I had that same feeling in Washington. It's that hopeless feeling you get when you know that people are really closed-minded. What a sweeping thing to say about art, but who in the world was I, who am not a philosopher, to question Plato.

"In other words we're warping our souls," she concluded. "In Plato's view."

We are *warping* our souls with theater and poetry?

LOGIC, ETHOS, PATHOS

FEBRUARY 1997
BELLAGIO, ITALY

I packed up everything I had gathered to date on the '96 campaign and in the two years leading up to it. I had a monthlong fellowship at a center that the Rockefeller Foundation runs to provide a workplace for artists and scholars. The setting is an extraordinary villa and grounds that sit on the shore of Lake Como. I was there working on the first stage version of this project.

I was told tales at breakfast of how John F. Kennedy had been to the villa. Apparently he had come to Italy to see the pope and for some reason was diverted and had to spend the night. The point of the story, however, was that (supposedly) an Italian movie star had spent the night with him.

One night at dinner, I found myself sitting next to a very warm woman named Ann Vasaly, from Boston. She was a scholar of antiquity. One of her specialties was the rhetoric of Cicero. Given my desire to understand what I had heard and not heard on the campaign trail, I pumped her for every bit of information I could get.

"There's a way of analyzing rhetoric that comes from Aristotle. He divides rhetoric into sources of persuasion: One is *logos*, which is $2 \times 2 = 4$, you know, the rational form of persuasion.

"And then there is *ethos,* which is extremely important. It's how you present yourself within the speech, what kind of person you become within the speech as it's given."

I asked her to watch some Clinton speeches I had on video and to define for me his rhetoric. I had videos of the two speeches that, by 1997, were considered to be among his best. One was the speech he gave after the bombing in Oklahoma City, and the other was the speech he gave at Ron Brown's funeral. She said she would.

"The third source of persuasion is *pathos,* which, of course, Plato said is the heart of the corruption of rhetoric, because when you move people emotionally, they cease to analyze and instead go along with all sorts of things simply because of that emotional involvement."

Later that week we watched the videos. Ann explained to me that Clinton is all *ethos* because his effectiveness is so dependent on how we feel about him at the moment. I was surprised that he was not *pathos.*

So it's not so much that Clinton made us "feel." It's that he made us feel *about him.*

I have come to the realization that the most powerful fictions are the ones that cause people to convene around them. The fiction then becomes more potent than the author. So it is with the president. We don't have a thoughtful, vital citizenry, and that's not only because the man may not be up to the task. The fiction is not up to the task. The president is only a man who inhabits the fiction. We as a nation can be a part, and we are a part, of creating a better fiction. We just need the space and tools to build it. The pundits, the governors, the media owners, the politicians, the lawyers need to give us the space. Or perhaps we have to show them how much we really want it.

Recently in performances, I was learning to be there *with* the audience rather than to be there *for* them.

1994 (JUST AFTER NELSON MANDELA WAS ELECTED
PRESIDENT IN NEIGHBORING SOUTH AFRICA)
ZIMBABWE
A PHOTOGRAPHIC SAFARI

The most gorgeous part of the safari was when we sat near the watering hole about midday, to see the many species that would gather. But during the rest of the day, we would sit in our Jeeps and watch all the animals, from many species, come to drink the water. The grace of the animals was unlike any piece of art I had ever seen. The giraffes bending, the birds, and finally the flock of elephants who seemed to glide from a long distance. There was room for all. The lion was not there. The lion eats at night, and, with very little work, maintains its place as king. Because nobody preys on the lion.

It would be wonderful if modern civilization could make a watering hole. If we could find some way to create even a fictive one that would allow us to convene and partake of the same thing, each one of us, regardless of our type. The president would ideally be that fiction. A man or woman would play the part of convener—and we could dress that man or woman any way we chose. The most important qualification would be that this fiction must have room for all.

As for going to watch the lions eat, well, it's a whole different feeling. Some of the people on the safari were most excited about that. The guides would tell us stories of kills they had seen just days before. The feeling was—how lucky we would be if we got to see one too.

During the day we sat quietly on a hilltop not far away. At night, while going to find the lions, we would ride slowly for a few moments with the headlights off. And stop. And wait. And move. It was furtive. Our observance. We were hushed, and the guide was hunched forward over the steering wheel. After all, we were in pursuit of the *king* of the jungle. We are waiting to catch him in the act, any act.

Many people assume that political life is theater. The theater is created to illuminate a truth. What truth is our political "theater" illuminating? True theater is not only text and subtext—it is a vast mélange of contradictions and paradoxes, associations and disassociations.

Is it indeed true that the press is the audience for our "political theater"? Is this informing what our theater is? Would the theater be different if it had a larger, more diverse audience? Would our theater look more like the watering hole and less like the guide crouched over the steering wheel of a Jeep furtively moving through the jungle at 2:00 A.M., stalking the lion, who stalks his prey?

MICHAEL DEAVER

Everyone talks about how Reagan was an actor. And they usually do not mean it as a compliment. They may be suggesting that he was a "fake," an "imitation," but an imitation of what? Would Plato have had a problem with Reagan, the actor president? Yet something about our culture embraces that which is "imitation." So much of how we run our lives in a society of mass production is in "imitation" of something. How far are we from truth as Plato would have thought truth to be?

Michael Deaver is the man who is credited with creating the image of Ronald Reagan, and with bringing "visuals" into the White House. He added a lot to "photo ops" as we know them. He now works in a consulting firm.

"I never worried about what Ronald Reagan said. Other people worried about that. And I really never had to worry about what he did, because he was a pro. And I really never changed any belief he ever had, because I couldn't."

What *did* Deaver worry about? He worried about how Ronald Reagan looked. Reagan had taught him that "the camera doesn't lie," so he believed that. It was all for the camera. He talked about the "tape" Reagan walked onto. By tape, he meant the mark on the floor upon which Reagan would stand while talking.

"And one of the things that I always strived to do with Reagan was that when he walked out to the tape, Ronald Reagan knew that that was going to be the best-dressed set he'd ever been on."

"How did you dress the set?"

"First of all, sound and lighting. I mean, lighting is the most important part of it. Ronald Reagan was a guy who was seventy-five years old, so you wanted to light him from the top of his head down, because what you'd do is you'd get the light to bounce off that wonderful head of chestnut hair, and you'd wash his face of wrinkles."

I was amazed at how open he was with all this information.

"If you lighted him either straight on or from down below, he'd have looked eighty-five or ninety years old. I used to kick the press photographers when they'd get down on their knees in front of Reagan and tell them to get up. If you want to take a picture of Ronald Reagan, you do it straight on; you don't do it from down below."

I was curious about how he knew to do this, and why he knew it would matter to the public.

Michael Deaver had grown up in a small town. His father, who worked for Shell Oil Company, had the nicest piano in town. He made a deal with the piano teacher—that the teacher could use their piano to give lessons if he gave lessons to the Deaver boys for free. It was a deal. Although Michael's brother was the one the lessons were meant for, it was clear to the teacher that the real student was "this little guy who stands around and watches during the lessons." Ultimately Deaver can play whatever you could hum. He knows what something needs to sound like. He said that his knack for knowing what something needed to look like came from the same source.

Deaver was onto something very important in our time. We live in a visual, not an oral rhetoric. He could compose ideas about the president by making a series of pictures of him.

1998

GRIDIRON DINNER

I was sitting in the midst of many journalists. Their motto is, "The Grid-iron singes but it never burns." The journalists do skits about the events of the year where they dress in drag and sing lyrics to the tunes of songs in Broadway hits. The president tells jokes too. When Clinton came to the podium, a hush fell over the room. Then I looked at the faces around me. There were three hundred and sixty degrees of intense gazes. These gazes were like laser beams. They were killer gazes.

All the examples that I have given are about watching. When the journalists were watching, it was as if they were trying to see *through* Clinton. The relationship of the eye to the subject is off balance. They were looking for something in his physical being, a tic perhaps, a slipup of some sort, perhaps he would drop something, do anything out of the or-dinary that would show him *up*.

They wanted a slip that would reveal more about Clinton and Monica Lewinsky. After having studied language and body language intensely for the last two decades, I have come to the conclusion that it doesn't always tell us as much as we think it does—particularly if the subject is used to being scrutinized.

The president is assumed to be in a planned physical state. That planned physical state is called, in the minds of those who observe it, an act. They think that the president is always acting, that he is in a constructed reality.

SUMMER 1996
RHETORIC LESSON
FAIRMONT HOTEL
SAN FRANCISCO

I am at breakfast with Hayden White, professor of rhetoric at the University of California at Santa Cruz.

"So, you see, association of images is the rhetoric to me, what image you put together with what other image."

"Okay."

"So, I think that's what rhetoric has to do with now, the association of a politician, not with a particular cause—but with another image."

"Yes, sure."

"Or several images."

So it's not about words, it's not about facts. It's about something else. It's about associations.

The age of the image as rhetoric would seem to follow right out of a time when commercials are more a part of our culture as artistic expression. And advertising is all about associations. But what happens when that technique of creating associations is used not only to get us to consume, to buy? What happens when that technique is the very lifeblood of how we learn to think about our process, how we learn to think about our American identity, our civic identity?

White said to me, "People identify democracy with the free market. This is what all the commentary on the elections in Russia has been—a triumph of democracy. It isn't; it's the triumph of capitalism."

"I see."

"The assumption is that the free market and democracy go hand in hand. If you buy into the free market, you have to take a certain amount of unemployment, a certain amount of exploitation, a certain amount of corruption, and so forth."

"Interesting."

"It has nothing to do with democracy."

"Oh?"

"I mean, that's been the greatest triumph of Western capitalism—it's been to identify democracy with the free market."

FALL 1995
MICHAEL DEAVER

There was one time when this idea of picture making backfired.

While he was president, Ronald Reagan made a trip to Germany for the fortieth anniversary of the end of World War II. Michael Deaver was responsible for organizing the logistics of the visit. The plan was that Reagan and West German Chancellor Helmut Kohl would have a photo op at a cemetery where soldiers were buried. This was to be on the theme of reconciliation.

Deaver went in advance, did some location scouting, and found what he thought was a wonderfully picturesque cemetery. He asked the chief of West German protocol and someone from the American embassy to check out the graves. As it turned out, there was no cemetery free of SS soldiers. They were buried all over Germany. Reagan was advised not to go to the cemetery for the reconciliation "scene." But he was adamant in spite of many vocal people, among them Elie Wiesel, expressing their dismay.

So, they went ahead with the plan. The plane ride itself seemed more somber than the graveyard.

"We were flying from Bonn to Bergen-Belsen that morning, and I mean to tell you it was somber on that airplane. Nancy was all dressed in black. She had said to me, 'You've ruined my husband.' So it was a terrible, terrible time." He concluded with, "Newsweek, of course, you know put Waffen-SS flags on the graves for their cover story."

Mixing images can be chemical. It's hardly that images are not strong. The adages all tell us that a picture says a thousand words. The only problem with reliance on the picture, particularly the photograph, is that there is no command really. There is not the opportunity to add breath into the mix. There's not the opportunity to stand in the moment and change the moment with the power of your own diaphragm, your own voice, your own power.

Michael Deaver, who brought movie lights into the White House, told me that at the end of the day, he would go into the East Room and play the piano because it allowed his soul to come forward.

MARLIN FITZWATER

PRESS SECRETARY TO RONALD REAGAN

"Ronald Reagan"

It sounds like that's description of a lack of intellect, or a lack of
    knowledge or whatever.
But having been there, I never saw it that way with Ronald Reagan.
If he got into an argument with Gorbachev, for example, and
    Gorbachev would talk about a 1925 chemical weapons treaty
President Reagan was a little chagrined with himself that he didn't
    know about that
and he knew
it didn't matter.
He didn't really want to know about that.
He didn't want to know about
how many bombs
we're going to allow on B-52s under this new treaty.
Is it ten bombs versus fifteen bombs?
Is it five nuclear warheads per bomb? Is it three nuclear warheads
    per bomb?
He says, You guys solve that problem.
My job is to see that it's done.

Reagan had this kind of instinct for knowing how to push big issues
    and big ideas.
And the mystery
that everyone is still wrestling with—
Did he know
that he knew how to do it?

METAPHOR'S FUNERAL

CIRCA 1959
1312 NORTH BENTALOU STREET
BALTIMORE

FOR MOST OF MY CHILDHOOD, I LOOKED OUT ON A GRAVEYARD. MY desk was by the window, and across the alley behind our backyard was a cemetery.

There was the sight of the graveyard, and the sound of the train. The train went under a bridge that was a half a block away. The graveyard looked like the end of the universe, but the train sounded like eternity.

I didn't find out until I was an adult that my parents were the first blacks to move in on our side of the street. I always remember it being an all-black neighborhood, so the whites must have moved out very fast. By the time I was able to understand such things, most blacks were trying to move out of the neighborhood I grew up in, and to find housing in a predominantly Jewish area in another part of town. We did eventually move from our first house on Bentalou Street to one of those predominantly Jewish areas, and my mother still lives in that house. That neighborhood is now an all-black neighborhood.

Behind Bentalou Street stood a graveyard. We would ride our sleds down its hill during the winter, but other than that we didn't really venture in. There was a No Trespassing sign. The lady who lived next door, Mrs. Johnson, was a friend of the caretaker, and once a year, we would walk with her into the graveyard and to the caretaker's house, which was in the middle. He and his wife were white. They had a grape arbor, and when it was time to pick the grapes, they would prepare several bags full for Mrs. Johnson. She would make grape jelly and pass it out up and down the block.

These trips with Mrs. Johnson into the graveyard were memorable. First of all, because as far as I could tell we were "trespassing," and nothing bad happened. They were also notable since Mrs. Johnson, weighing in at over four hundred pounds, never walked anywhere. Very occasionally she would be driven to church, but most of the time she stayed placed on her porch, or in her kitchen, and we would go to see her. On these occasions, we were quite a parade. The caretakers of the cemetery were likely the first white people I ever visited in their home.

One afternoon, something happened in the graveyard that brought all of us on the even-numbered side of the 1300 block of Bentalou Street to our back porches. It was stunning enough that we all stopped what we were doing.

Whenever there was a funeral, most of us, especially the kids among us, would take note. It was as if whites suddenly invaded the neighborhood. In addition to this being a white graveyard, it was a Catholic graveyard. This was before the sixties, so nothing about the pomp and circumstance of the Catholic Church was yet watered down—the priests wore elaborate hats, burned incense, and spoke Latin. True, there were surely black Catholics somewhere on our street, but most of us were Baptist, Methodist, or some other kind of Protestant.

So across the way, one would see an almost Felliniesque grouping of whites, some in robes, standing outside the dramatic entourage of cars, which had slowly pulled down Bentalou Street, turned the corner, and driven up the very slight hill of the cemetery. This particular funeral was nearly over, a lone car pulled up the hill, and the alley and our backyards burst open with the sound of a woman wailing. I can remember watching this and having chills go up my spine. Everyone from my family except my father, who was working, gathered, from whatever disparate parts of the house or surrounding play areas they had been in.

We watched a funeral of someone we knew nothing about, and yet we were saddened. We didn't know what exactly was going on. But somehow, through the grapevine, we were told that the wailing woman had come from out of town, and had missed the funeral of her father. She had to be held back from the grave. We watched as she was taken, by each arm, back to her car.

It was also an important moment because, in spite of what I was learning about "white people" and how different we were, I could imagine the circumstances, and I felt for that woman.

I came back to that sixties expectation that education is the answer to racial strife and inequality. The idea was that, if we were all educated, if we all learned our ABCs, we could all have the advantages of the American dream. My education was a product of that idea. *Along with that,* as a bonus, an important bonus, was the notion that, having gotten *to know* one another, we would make a better, more equalized society. But as we watch affirmative action burn at the stake, as we watch the numbers of incarcerated people of color climb, we have to ask, what happened?

Education gives us more facts, more evidence, but it does not give us empathy. The proof is staring us right in the face. What profession of people are thought of as the *least* empathetic of all? The media. And they have the resources to *know* everything. In fact, perhaps they know too much to be empathetic.

I suggest here that knowledge will *not* save the world. We have shrunken hearts.

In those days when I stood on the porch, I had perhaps more empathy than I have on this day, with a terrific education. In those days, when I was standing on the back porch, and watching those few white people who came to the graves of their loved ones, my curiosity was enormous. My *desire* to know them, to be among them, was enormous. And when I stood on the front porch, and looked up and down the even side of the street, at all those black folks—or looked across to the odd side of the street at all those white folks, my heart was an open heart. Education did not make me a more empathetic person. It made me a tougher person. It helped me develop a persona, it taught me how to fight, but it did not "open" me to the world. I was born with a certain openness. Life has caused me to resist those things that through the process of education would shut me down.

And, from the looks of it, many of my colleagues, educated as they are, do not have healthy hearts. They may have healthy hearts for those closest to them, but it is difficult for them to imagine the pain of the other.

These very people, who can pay big bucks to go to the theater, or to see other works of art, talk in a vocabulary of "what they identified with," what they "personally connected with." It's rare that they can reach beyond what they can identify with to *feel* for the other side. America needs heart surgery.

1996

LOBBY OF THE ESSEX HOUSE HOTEL

NEW YORK CITY

I have just returned from a magnificent dinner with Studs Terkel, at a "joint," as he called it, named The Crocodile. We have been out all night. Studs has had much more to drink than I could ever handle, and yet, in his eighties, he is wide awake and telling me stories as we sit on a huge sofa in the lobby. And this particular story, of all the stories Studs has told me, stands out as one of the most important. If there is ever a genuine, real funeral for metaphor, Studs should give the eulogy.

He told me the story of his friend Bill, a blues singer, a black man who sang the blues and who laughed when he was angry. And one time Studs was the emcee when Bill was singing the blues.

It was a story about a mule that had died, it was a song called "Plow-hand Blues," and Studs said that it was "a long wail of a blues, like a Spanish flamenco, a *canto hondo,* a deep song," and "Bill's guitar cries out like a human voice"—"this incredible moment" and "just at that moment, these two kids, one black and one white, in the audience, got up and scraped their chairs and walked out, disdainfully." And Studs was furious— he was furious that they ruined Bill's song.

And Studs says that he said to Bill, "They ruined your song those bas—— they ruined your song." And Bill of course laughed at Studs's anger, and Bill said, "What do they know about the blues? What do they know about a mule? It's a horse-and-buggy song to them. What the hell do they know about a mule dying on 'em? This mule died and it was a tragedy for me or my father, but they don't know anything about mules."

Bill said, "It's like me and the bomb." He said, "What do I know about a bomb? They had it in Europe, Italy, Germany, and I saw the rubble, and I saw people crying when their houses fell down, but what do I know?"

And then Studs said to me, "Bill raises the big question, that may answer everything you're searching for!" And he said, "And Bill said, In order to *sing* the blues you have to *experience* it." And so Studs says, "If that's the case, if you have to *experience* the bomb, if you have to *experience* it to understand it, then we're in for it! Do we have to have a bomb fall on us?" he said. "Must our mule die on us in order for us to experience the horror of it?"

Knowing, experiencing, witnessing, is limited in its reach. Just because you "know" doesn't mean you are "of." In fact, there are ways to be "a part of" without direct experience. With all our potential to be brought "up to the minute," many of us are not "a part of."

RICK BERKE

THE NEW YORK TIMES

"Fondling Breasts"

I think, we've always hated sex, these kinds of stories. We've
    always been last. From the beginning, there's a host . . .
It was like a hundred years ago, we just had to . . .
We've always stayed away, the Gennifer Flowers stuff,
the Gary Hart, we've always been the last,
and we've always been very uncomfortable about it, in not
    knowing how to deal with these stories or what to do with
    them.
Sometimes we've been, waited too long, when they've become
    stories that were unavoidable.
But I'd rather be last than stoking the whole thing.
So we've seen a lot of changes in what the *Times*,
because of this scandal,
of what the *Times* would write about, would cover.
I remember covering, I covered, the Thomas-Hill hearings.
And I remember thinking,
Do they put pubic hair on Page One? and, you know, penis, and
    all this?

Because we'd never, like, gone there before.
And I thought that was, like, new ground,
you know, however many years ago that was.
And then I find myself last year writing about oral sex in the *Times*,
on the front page, fondling breasts, and things that I never thought,
you know, my God,
the *Times* would never have touched. So we're very uncomfortable
     with these kinds of stories.

POLICING

We have both visible and invisible violence now. The invisible violence is the mean-spiritedness, the lack of forgiveness, the lack of interest in rehabilitation, the numbers of black men and now women incarcerated all across the country. At the *Vanity Fair* Oscar party in 1999, Tom Hayden told me that the biggest supporter of political campaigns in the state of California is the union of prison guards. He told me this just as they were announcing best picture. I was so shocked I missed the announcement.

Cynicism, wit over wisdom, and the prevailing mean spirit entertain us, but at what price?

FALL 1998
SAN FRANCISCO

I began to think that there were reasons for us to fear the media. I was having coffee in a Noe Valley café with Jim Risser one morning. Jim is a Pulitzer Prize winner who runs a journalism program at Stanford called the Knight Fellows. I asked him what he thought about our fear of the media.

"It used to be said that you have no reason to fear the media unless you've done something wrong," he said calmly.

I said, "Well gee, that reminds me of when I was a girl, growing up in segregated Baltimore. When I told my mother I was afraid of the police, she said, The police are here to protect you, you shouldn't be afraid of the police unless you've done something wrong."

He suggested that I ask the Knight Fellows myself.

I met with the group. The Knight Fellows are professional journalists, representing news organizations from all over the world, who take a year off to study whatever they like at Stanford. I asked them, "Should we be afraid of the media?"

The general consensus was "You should be afraid of the media. And if you're not afraid of the reporter him- or herself, you should be afraid of the conglomerates who run the media."

Where are we if the media themselves think we should be afraid of them?

Sometimes when I see how the press treat people, I find myself thinking about the police and the press in a similar light. Neither is a uniformly bad institution. But they do not always use their power responsibly, and there's not a lot we can do about it. Nobody monitors the media. When asked about that, some of them bristle and say, "We monitor each other." People have been fighting police brutality vigorously for forty years. How many citizens' review boards are there, and how effective are they? What can we do to get better media? Just don't buy the papers, people say. Just don't turn on the news. I think that's not a good enough answer.

Both the police and the media represent fairness and unfairness, justice and injustice, and both have the power to practice brutality should they choose to.

SATURDAY NIGHT, NOVEMBER 1995
THERESA FENWICK HOUSE
WASHINGTON, D.C.

I came back to the Houghtons' house on P Street in Georgetown one Saturday after having been out at the Maryland Correctional Institute for Women. I'd stopped off to have a swim on the way. It was fall, and at 6:30 or 7:00 it was dark out. I tried to open the front door. The inside chain was on. This was strange for a Saturday. I thought that perhaps my assistant, Marcos, was upstairs in the office working, but I couldn't remember having asked him to do anything that would keep him working this late on a Saturday. I took a few steps backward to see if lights were on. There were no lights on on the third floor. On the other hand, there *were* lights on in a section of the house across the garden. I knew for certain that the Houghtons were away for the weekend, so this bothered me. I took out my cell phone and called Marcos to see if he was, in fact, upstairs in some way that I could not see from the street. He was not.

I went in through the garden gate, entered the house from the ground level, into the kitchen, and called the police. I explained that I was a guest in the house, that I had returned home and found doors locked in an unusual way, and lights on that shouldn't be on. I worked through the monotoned responses of the 911 operator, who did not seem to be listening at all.

"No, I'm saying that this is *not* my house, that the people who live here are *away,* and there are *lights* on in their house. . . . I'm a *guest.* . . . Well, I'm afraid to go upstairs. . . . Look, this is a congressman's house, it would seem that you would at least . . ."

Finally she droned that she'd send someone by to take a look.

"How long do you think this will take?" I asked.

"There's a lot going on tonight. They'll be there as soon as they can, ma'am." She sighed.

I had visions of sitting in the garden till dawn. I was very tired, and contemplated going to a hotel. But if I did that, and they were destroying the Houghtons' property—or stealing something . . . No, it was clear. I couldn't leave.

It seemed like I had barely hung up the phone and the police were there. Relieved, I went to the garden gate and opened it. Much to my shock, I found myself looking into a semicircle of about a dozen police officers with guns extended toward my face. I had never looked into the barrel of a gun before. The barrel was bigger than I would have thought.

But no sooner did the guns register than they started a very loud chorus: GET BACK!!!! GET BACK!!!! GET BACK!!!!!

My heart started racing. But this was a misunderstanding.

Somewhere, I found the wherewithal to strive for clarity. I thought if I was reasonable, they would be reasonable.

"Actually, I'm the person who called you."

They didn't seem to hear me, or listen.

The officers were all of different races, women and men. As I stepped forward, they shouted again: GET BACK! GET BACK! GET BACK! GET BACK!

I tried to explain: "I'm a guest in this house. This is Congressman Houghton's house. He's away and there are lights on that . . ."

I looked around for a neighbor. The streets were vacant. Not that I knew anyone on the block anyway.

They lunged closer, bringing their guns even closer to me. GET BACK! GET BACK!! GET BACK!! GET BACK!!!

I moved forward a little and tried to talk to them, one human being to another: "I'm just trying to protect their property I'm afraid there's someone in the—"

GET BACK! GET BACK! GET BACK! GET BACK!

I decided to give them all I had—I put my hands up, began to back up, and said in the vocal intonations of a confession, "Okay. Okay. Look, I'm afraid of you. I'm afraid of you! No really. I wrote a play about the police. You remember Rodney King? I'm afraid of you. I'm afraid. Okay? So I'm terrified. You've really frightened me."

This time they didn't shout. They were still for a moment. There was a Latino woman who kind of glanced at the black man in the middle. He glanced at her but looked quickly back at me. I continued: "You know, Congressman and Mrs. Houghton are humanitarians. I'm their guest. I can only *imagine* how they will feel about this."

One of them, the tallest one, who was in the middle, a black man, stepped forward. They put their guns down. He said, "All right, miss, just calm—down."

I continued, with more things that I had on my mind, now that I had their attention: "Here I am trying to be responsible to this property, and you pull out your guns before finding out a *thing* . . ."

The tall black man was about to lead me into the house as the Latino woman and an Asian man went to the front door.

"Hey!" I shouted. *"Don't break the door down!"*

They ignored me.

"Look, miss, just—relax," the tall black cop continued. He reminded me of a physical trainer I had had years ago in San Francisco.

"They can't break the door down! This house is a historic *landmark*." I moved about, up and down the street, frantically looking for the plaque that said THERESA FENWICK HOUSE.

"They have to get into the house if they're going to help you, miss," he said, as if he were talking to a child.

"Well, why can't they go in through this way?" I pointed to the kitchen door.

They immediately scurried down the path and into the kitchen. Another crew of them scurried over to the side that the Houghtons lived in. They all seemed like animals, or let's say the animal side of their nature was what I saw. I stood in the street and looked up at the house as their flashlights reflected through the windows. More police cars pulled up.

"My God," I said, "did they send out the entire precinct?"

Then it dawned on me. Well it *is* a congressman's house.

The Asian man officer and the Latino woman officer came out through the front door. "It's all clear."

"How did the inside get locked?"

"I couldn't tell you," the tall black policeman said.

We went into the kitchen, because he wanted to ask me a few questions. As he finished he said, "Now, miss, I want you to understand why we did what we did."

"I know why you did what you did. I was moving forward, and when you screamed, 'Get back,' you wanted me to get back. I wasn't hearing that. All I heard was that you were treating me like a criminal, and I wanted you to know that I was the one who had called you."

"Look, miss . . ."

"So once I stepped back, you put your guns down, but if I hadn't stepped back you probably would have shot me."

"Now, miss."

"That's how people get killed innocently by the police," I continued. "You know we don't know what you know. We didn't go to your school. The only reason I knew to step back was that I had done some research with the Oakland cops, and I know that first you make noise, and then you shoot."

"I just wanted you to understand . . ." and he continued to do "public relations," I suppose because it was, after all, a congressman's house.

The fact is, they did tell me to "get back" and I didn't understand it. They were very literal. I was on the metalevel of right and wrong. And I didn't trust them enough to do anything they were telling me to do. I was so shocked by the guns. I immediately went into a mode of trying to convince them of my innocence. I had an increased understanding of what black men had been telling me all my life.

It took me weeks to get the feel of those gun barrels out of my system. And I thought, If they had shot me, the real story would never be out. All kinds of people would have been brought forward to paint a picture of me as someone who deserved being shot, and another side would have painted a picture of a tragic loss.

Having observed people dealing with the media, and using "confessional" behavior to get them around to their side, I used the vocal tones of a "confession" to bring the police to put their guns down. "Okay. Okay. Look, I'm *afraid* of you," I had conceded. "I'm *afraid*." It had worked, but for days, weeks, I would still see those guns, smell those guns, and feel as I did then, that I was close, very close to something that could have gone another way. Thinking about fair and unfair, right and wrong when they're standing there with all their might and power won't help.

Although we live in a society permeated by media, most people do not, actually, know how to deal with it. And when it happens to them, it's very surprising. I suppose it's like sex. You see it in movies, you see it on television, it's in music and in magazines, but until your first time, you really do not know. And when it's your first time, you're on your own to put the pieces together. It helps to have a decent partner.

I went inside after the police left. The phone rang. It was Priscilla. "I got your message. *Anna*, what's going on?"

I decided not to tell her about the cops and their guns. I knew she would worry.

I told her about the door being mysteriously locked. I had been so caught up with the cops, I had almost forgotten that the door being mysteriously locked was what had started the escapade.

"Oh!" She laughed. She explained that the handyman always chainlocks that door no matter how many times they tell him not to.

Thanks, Mr. Handyman, I said to myself, for causing me a traumatic experience.

There are a variety of ways to keep us back. For folks who are really stuck, in the bottom of the system, those means permeate their lives. We like to believe that America is about fighting your way up and that you can make it with tenacity and brains and guts. That is not true. There are actually many, many ways to keep people back. Not all of us will have to deal with policemen, drugs, abusive mates, and much more. But in the finer and more refined circles of our society, infrastructures do keep many people locked in. Some people don't even know they are locked in until they try to move. Often we are happy to stay exactly where we are. But when you move, you are vulnerable.

GET BACK!!!! GET BACK!!!!! GET BACK!!!!!!

I was also chilled by the realization of how dangerous it is that we actually learn very little about what citizenship requires. If the police have certain techniques, and we don't know what they are, we could literally be dead. The police, like many professions, exist in their small circle. For those of us who have little reason to interact with the police, we end up as strangers in their land; that is, when they make our land their land.

The media are one of those instruments that can, from time to time, keep people back, inasmuch as they perpetuate some aspects of American identity and obliterate others. It's like we are in a state of house arrest. Stay exactly where you are.

SUMMER 1997
NEW YORK UNIVERSITY LAW SCHOOL

I am talking about freedom of the press to a legal scholar at NYU, Bill Nelson. The conversation drifts to policing. I had asked him what the first police force was in America.

"I think the New York City police force is the first police force in the United States, and it's the early eighteen thirties. The London police force is a couple of years earlier than that," he answered.

Nelson had several books out to help me understand a very peculiar time in the earliest days, during Thomas Jefferson's time, when James Callender, a journalist, had gone to jail for things he had written about then President Adams.

"Now, is it true that the London police force was created . . . Apparently they weren't there to fight crime," I offered.

He finished my sentence: "But to keep the lower classes in their place."

"Right," I said.

"That's a big, that's a big job of police at all times. I mean, I think to be realistic about what police do, that's a big job of police forces at all times. That's what the New York City police force mostly does now, right."

"Are you speaking as a lawyer or a historian?"

"As a historian. Friday night. We had dinner with some friends. And, uh, I had in fact gotten a parking space right here, and we walked to the car, we got in and we drove, and shortly before we got there, the police decided to set up a barricade to check out drunk drivers. This was about ten-thirty Friday night. Uh—so I finally got up to the front and he asks me, had I been drinking? I said, Yes, I had two glasses of wine with dinner over the last couple of hours. Uh, and, uh he asked to see my li—— do you have a license? Yes. He asked to see it, and I, by mistake, uh, pull out an NYU ID card, and he says to me, Oh that's not a license, it's an NY—— an NYU ID card. Go ahead. I can't help but think that the police, you know, it was a very polite, nice policeman, but he's dealing with an older white guy who clearly is on the NYU faculty, fine, we'll let him go. He's certainly not gonna treat a nonwhite person that way."

There are current brutalities of the police force against brown and black men. They don't seem to go away. Even when we see the images of them. Even when they are obvious.

Billy clubs and guns are not the only instruments we have in our society to keep people in their places. There are more subtle ways that this is done. The neglect of the educational system, of public schools, in a culture that professes to believe in knowledge as a cure, is the most obvious way.

In Washington people are kept in place in a subtle way. But seemingly small things could have been warnings for what was going to happen to the president.

Washington is a place of organized seating. It is very important to keep your place. If you are not in the club, then you must accept your fate. If you are in the club, you must behave a certain way. In the course of my time there, I saw people misbehave and get their hands slapped. Small slappings in a generation that was hungry for another Watergate.

I didn't know enough to take sides in Washington. I couldn't read the "text" of the place well enough. I only knew broad strokes. My intuition, however, did cause me to pause when something seemed out of balance.

JOE KLEIN

I questioned what happened to Joe Klein when it was discovered that he was the "Anonymous" who wrote *Primary Colors*. Why—is—this—such—a—big—deal? How does it really affect the quality of our lives?

It was before daylight, and I was down in the Theresa Fenwick kitchen making coffee when I opened the papers and saw that Klein's confession was on the front page. It happened just as the '96 campaigns were taking off, and people were in full sweat about the matter. I heard very passionate explanations: "He *lied*. I mean, my *God*, if you're in the press you're not supposed to lie, it gets to the very base of what we *are*."

The fact is, most of us don't believe the press tell the truth. Nevertheless, we believe, and quote what we read as truth. It's nonsensical. It can only mean that we have given up on truth, and only pass information. We're in the "know," but we know that we are not in the "truth."

I called Judith Butler, scholar of rhetoric, to get her take. "Well, I think it has got to be the media's infatuation with itself, in part. You know, they do think they are the center of the world, I think it is maybe the media feels that it was—that it had a hoax played on it, so what it can do now is turn on this guy who clearly has broken ranks with them."

I thought the Joe Klein event was a warning, a warning of what was going to come like the day of the locusts with Clinton and Monica. And for those readers who don't care about Clinton and Monica, it's possible that Clinton and Monica warn us of things to come that we will care about. We will need the media, and they will be off in a language of their own, making their own sets of small slaps, unable to understand us.

ELLEN DeGENERES

Then there was the story of Ellen DeGeneres.

Every year there is a big dinner, called the White House Correspondents' Dinner. It is black tie. News organizations invite celebrities to be among them. The president attends. It's in a huge ballroom at the Hilton. There are small cocktail parties before, and parties after. There is a parade of celebrities with the usual suspects, Annette Bening, and Warren

Beatty. Sharon Stone, George Clooney. *Vanity Fair* usually gives a party. The party that *Vanity Fair* gives after the White House Correspondents' Dinner is a lot like the party they give in Beverly Hills, at Mortons, after the Academy Awards. Sometimes it gets very confusing. For example, just after Clinton brushed by conviction by the skin of his teeth, I went to the *Vanity Fair* Oscar party. Monica Lewinsky was the star guest. She seemed to get at least as much attention as, if not more attention than, that year's best actress, Gwyneth Paltrow. She was surrounded by people I had met in Washington—correspondents from major news organizations and former White House staffers.

Graydon Carter invited Ellen DeGeneres to the White House Correspondents' Dinner in 1997. She came to the dinner with her girlfriend, Anne Heche. This was just before she was to "come out" on her sitcom. Her attendance at the White House Correspondents' Dinner was regarded by many as a publicity ploy.

In the course of the dinner a comic performs, and Clinton makes a speech. It is expected that the president will be funnier than the entertainment, and sometimes he pulls it off.

At a certain point in the evening I noticed that the people in front of me were not looking at the stage—they were looking at something else, and their mouths were hanging open. I turned to see what they were looking at, and I saw two women with their arms around each other. Apparently they displayed more affection than many thought was appropriate. Before the dinner, Graydon Carter was looking straight ahead at the stage, while his guests, Anne Heche and Ellen DeGeneres, were causing quite a stir.

This went further when Graydon Carter took them upstairs to a room in the Hilton to meet the president, and they approached the president with their arms around each other. People from both camps—those who want the sexual status quo to remain soundly heterosexual, and those who fight for gay rights—expressed displeasure. After all, it was a "photo op."

Their behavior, and the general response, did not surprise me. What did surprise me was the following editorial in *The New York Times*:

After all the hype and exploitation surrounding the actress Ellen DeGeneres and Ellen Morgan, the woman she plays on television, it was easy to lose sight of what actually was taking place on ABC last night. The "coming out" of the title character on *Ellen* was accomplished with wit and poignancy, which should help defuse the antagonism toward homosexuals still prevalent in society. . . . Unfortunately, Ms. DeGeneres was not immune to exploiting the situation, most notably by her ostentatious display of affection with her lover in front of President Clinton at the White House Correspondents Dinner last weekend.

I understood the text of the editorial, I just didn't understand why an editorial in *The New York Times* would take a moment to refer to her behavior at a dinner that most Americans know very little about.

I did the rounds of asking people to explain to me why this was such a "big deal." One of the people was Paul Costello, who had worked in press relations for quite some time in Washington. He put it this way: "Talking about something Washington can't handle at all. Sex. Any kind of sex. But gay sex? It's just not part of the game, it's just not part of what you do. Washington is a town where you don't talk about foibles, you don't talk about depression. . . . You only talk about strength and manipulation and Machiavellian points of view, you don't let on weakness. It's the most unsexy place, it's the most sexless place in the world."

Okay, so the trespass was a trespass into sex, and sexuality. Still, this is the nineties, we're liberated. I called Judith Butler. She put it this way:

"I mean, it doesn't strike me as gay pride in its finest hour if that's what you're asking me. I mean, I think it's a scream! And the fact that people got so worked up about it is the most interesting part of this. I suppose that people who consider themselves liberal and tolerant in their everyday lives, who nonetheless, people who think [laughing] that you're not supposed to do it in front of the president, think you shouldn't be doing it in public.

"It's okay if that's what you do if you do it in private and they love feeling liberal and tolerant about that. But to do it in that public a setting and in front of the, the symbolic authority of the nation—is really to not have any shame at all."

Counting on a sense of shame is a kind of policing too. But this gets tougher in a diverse society, where that sense of shame begins to disappear in some lifestyles. It may be that the "freer" we get culturally, the more other kinds of restraints begin to appear.

I then went to the Condé Nast building on Madison Avenue, and went into the offices of *Vanity Fair* to talk to the host himself, the editor, who had invited Ellen and Anne to the party. For him it was all fun. When I asked him about the *New York Times* editorial, I felt like some kind of a fuddy-duddy.

"Oh fuck them," he said dismissively as he took a drag of his imported cigarette.

Although he gave the best party in Washington, he himself had never been invited to the White House.

"I've never been invited to the White House, and if I was I wouldn't wanna insult them but I probably wouldn't go."

"Really."

"Well, you know, it's the most uptight place in the world. I'm sure it's a perfectly nice place to live, but I'd be too terrified, it's too built on power."

As I left his very elegant office at Condé Nast, I questioned why he dismissed power, as if he was not himself a prince on a mountain of power, power in the fashion world—a world that affects many more people than Washington affects them. Psychologically, at least, the world of fashion has a greater presence in our everyday lives. Yet in reality, decisions made in Washington have a tremendous effect on how we live our lives. Many of us know more about hemlines and hair color than we do about candidates for office. Graydon Carter is powerful, and his power looked like a heck of a lot more fun than the power I saw in Washington.

There was also the issue of simply how artists are regarded in Washington—which of course has ramifications with regard to how the arts are thought of in this country. We are the only superpower in the world, and we do not support the arts. We do not have financial support and we do not have intellectual support. There is a lot of media about controversy, and there is media about art with celebrity participation. That media goes hand in hand with advertising. There is little or no attention paid to the people who work very hard in the arts because of a series of beliefs, either in the health of their art form or in the health of a community that benefits from the arts. There is ambivalence about artists in Washington. We are still seen, as Rousseau and others saw us, as derelict.

The media are a part of bringing us into the public eye. And when they bring us in they put us in a "place." To move from one place, that is, to move from what is assumed about you, to another place is very hard to do. People who don't seem to be in any one place are very hard to police. Clinton was said to have had a hard time because it wasn't clear "where he stood." Our culture is in transition, even as we know change is inevitable, those who communicate and define culture put up a series of dams. But Congress and the media lately, and in the Lewinsky-Clinton scandal, showed how ineffectual their dams are.

Policing is the protection of property. The status quo is a kind of nonphysical property, which is policed by nonphysical means.

JAMES CARVILLE

"Herd Mentality"

So what!
I mean sure.
But, but see
again
I wasn't put here
to
agree with these people.
I'm not put here to dislike 'em.
I like 'em.
I love
they wonderful
they nice parents
they're very bright people
terrific table manners
they're charming
they witty
they just wrong
that's all!

See the problem is if you think differently than they think they attack
    you
it's only one way to think
and that is the way that they think
and I think it's a shame.
This is my question.
As I understand
that, that
in, on rough terms is that the national media, the media here in
    Washington
they are people who are supposed to be more knowledgeable
in
and closer to the situation than the rest of the people in America
and as such it's their job to inform people what's going on.
I mean
I think that's a reasonable hypothesis
we have a free press in this country.
If so many of them were so wrong
it's my job to tell the American people about that.
It's part of their mission
here is to be right about these things.
They all
make
and they should, they make
make nice salaries
they got nice offices
they have access they go to the right parties
they talk to the right people
they have access and everything
and if they're consistently wrong
then
somebody gotta sort of say
it.
See.
In any other endeavor in life
you will suffer
public humiliation

for you being wrong
any other endeavor
you make the stock market
you make the right investment
you get to add a room to your house
take a trip to Hawaii.
I'm going to Bob Woodward's house tonight
who is a lovely man
as is his wife
Elsa
and they have a
wonderful home in Georgetown
and I'm sure that he sells
millions of books
and you know what?
He should
He was right about a big thing
he has reaped the rewards of that
what about all of these reporters
who were all dead wrong about Whitewater?
The media is the only business that I know,
okay?
That suffers
no penalty for being wrong.
It's, the herd judges itself,
and the herd exonerates itself all the time.
And anybody who criticizes the herd
the herd turns on.
Ask me I know.
They called me a buffoon and this and that.
I criticize the sort of mentality.
I think that what Washington needs more than anything is people
that think different than they think.
I guarantee you
that there are fraternities that have more diversity of thought.

SWINGING

I. THE PRESS AND PRESIDENCY
PROJECT HEADQUARTERS

EARLY SUMMER 1996

WE WERE IN FULL GEAR. THE ARENA STAGE THEATER, WHERE I WAS in residence, didn't have enough space for our headquarters. We'd outgrown our office there. They rented us a two-bedroom apartment across the street, and we turned it into command central. The empty apartment I walked into in June, with its smell of freshly laid carpeting, eventually housed an enormous amount of activity. These headquarters would end up housing all of the activities that put me on the campaign trail, and all of the activities that would lead to the productions of the play *House Arrest*. Production would follow my journey on the campaigns. It would start as a place that was centered on phones and faxes, and end as a place that was centered on turning four hundred audiotapes into what actors needed to "become" the people I had interviewed. By the end we would create, out of those four hundred audiotapes, ten thousand audio tapes as part of our editing process.

The first team was diverse. Nora, a graduate student in history at Berkeley, was already onboard, and by now had read a library's worth of books. Marcos had been with me in Washington since the first day; Andrew came to us with an interest in history and theater from Amherst; Erin was from Yale. Matthew, a former student of mine at Stanford, who I'd talked into coming to work for me on this project, was born again. He did advance work. Cori was a sensitive poet, who had been a student of mine. She did research. The office was run by Kitty, who was the daughter of Washington politicos. With a background in radio research for Ken Burns's films, her job was to organize and think up the vast range of activities that would entrench me in the campaign of '96. Lynette ran my life from D.C. Others came in and out during the summer and fall. Shawn, a law student at Yale, created dossiers on people alive and dead.

They managed together to make for me an impressive but grueling schedule. It involved going on the Clinton and Bush campaigns, preparing for and attending both conventions, writing for *Newsweek* at the conventions (I had never done political journalism before), going to the presidential and vice presidential debates on both coasts, traveling with Jesse Jackson, going to the "border" in El Paso, Texas, continuing to do interviews of Washington media and White House figures, going to the South to visit churches that had burned that summer, helping with fund-raising for the project, and doing other, tangential things—like visiting Willie Horton in prison.

There were no "down" days between June and election day in November. They had to cut through an enormous amount of red tape to pull this off. They also had to prepare me intellectually for everything that was about to happen. They read books, dug into the Internet, and created a mountain of dossiers. They also chased potential interviewees with the vigor of terriers. They got me "in." None of them was an "insider." Powell-Tate, a consulting agency, generously helped us knock on doors in the fall of '95. We couldn't have done it without them. But basically this motley crew of people freshly out of college in theater, and in history, with no campaign experience, created a schedule for me that was as if I myself was campaigning. It was the hardest work I had ever done, going on that trail and writing about it.

Watching without being soundly in an organization whose business it is to "watch" is hard work. Theaters are not in the business of "watching." They are in the business of "presenting," and usually that presenting is done inside a fairly safe place. It is safe because the risks that theater artists take are usually aesthetic ones. We don't normally face the public until we are "ready." The Arena had to turn itself around in order to do this, and it did. I did too. I was basically doing my work in a setting that was not safe at all.

My schedule—some of it being with the press corps, some of it on my own—looked something like this:

July 19 Atlanta—opening ceremonies of the Olympics
July 21–23 West Coast trip with president—flew with press corps
Denver,
Los Angeles,
Sacramento
San Francisco
July 25 Greensboro and Tuscaloosa, Alabama, attended revival meeting
  for a church that burned in June; Birmingham, Alabama
July 26 Atlanta—Return Olympics
July 27 Columbia, South Carolina, St. John Baptist Church, visited small,
  two-hundred-year-old black church that had burned
July 28 Greeleyville, South Carolina, visited Mt. Zion AME, which had
  burned
July 29 Library of Congress, Washington, D.C., research on past
  conventions
July 30 Fund-raising, Washington; Preparation, Schlesinger interview,
  Library of Congress
July 31 Meeting with Michael Deaver; Preparation, Schlesinger interview
Aug. 1–3 Research, listening to recordings of radio coverage of past
  conventions, Library of Congress
Aug. 4 Interviewed Osborn Elliott, former editor, *Newsweek*, Century
  Club, New York City
Aug. 5 Interviewed Arthur Schlesinger, Cote Basque, New York City
Aug. 5–9 Screened television coverage of past conventions, NBC. Other
  convention prep
Aug. 9 Joined Young Republicans train to San Diego in L.A.
Aug. 9–16 Republican convention, San Diego

It was an adventure. When you're on your own, you have to create
your own advance team.

II. SWINGING WITH CLINTON

I went to visit Ann Lewis, the deputy campaign manager for Clinton in
the '96 campaign. In the midst of the flurry that accompanies a campaign, I was surprised to find her with pearls around her neck, seated
calmly at her desk, with an elegant porcelain dish of fruit on the guest

side of the desk. There was a knife on the plate, and one piece of fruit had been cut. It looked like a still life. I imagined that the pearls, the containment, the fruit were all a kind of centering device. She told me that her strategy for press conferences was to be like a fifth-grade teacher.

"I concluded what I wanted to remind people of was sort of the best fifth-grade teacher in school, the one that all the parents wanted their kids to go to, because that was somebody that—because that was somebody whose word you could depend on or you could believe. She had authority, but she wasn't threatening, and that's who I try to be."

Lewis told me about a trip to California in late July that the president was making and suggested that I try to get on it. I had *Newsweek* credentials, because I was going to be writing for the conventions.

So Kitty went about getting permission—sending letters and making phone calls, until we finally secured authorization, from another very pleasant woman, named Ann Edwards. Kitty took care of the security clearances, and of course billing. The trip would cost us $3,300 for airfare and about $400 for hotels. Kind of an expensive trip to California, considering the fact that the press plane is coach class (except for the bigwigs— *The New York Times, The Washington Post,* et cetera, who fly first class). There's a lot of hierarchy in press travel, and in the briefing room, with the major networks and the *Times* and *Post* getting first dibs.

I went over to *Newsweek* to get briefed by their White House correspondent Bill Turque and by Tom Rosenteil. We also spoke to David Broder, a friend at *The Washington Post,* to find out who was flying for the *Post.* He told us about Kevin Merida, who was "a great guy."

So the day that I was headed out on this "swing," Nora and Kitty came over to the Theresa Fenwick House on P Street to give me my final marching orders before I set off for Andrews Air Force Base. They were very excited. I was very nervous. We sat down at the kitchen table. Nora had in hand a couple of huge dossiers, just in case I was able to do an interview or two. "Like the president," for example? she suggested.

"There's no way that's going to happen," I said.

The idea was that I could use all that time I had on the plane to bone up, just in case an interview with the president came up. We knew that whenever that interview happened I'd have to grab it, and be ready.

Kitty planted an itinerary on the table, right next to Priscilla's bowl of angel cards.

12:30 P.M. Depart P Street for Andrews AFB
1:30–2:30 Check-in, Andrews AFB
3:15 Wheels Up, Press Plane Departs for Denver
4:45 Press Plane Arrives, Denver AFB
Remain Overnight, Brown Palace Hotel

The idea was, I would travel with the press and the president from Denver to Los Angeles to Sacramento and San Francisco. I would leave the press and the president in San Francisco, and have one day at home to prepare for my trip to the South. I would then leave early in the morning (like 4:00 A.M.) to go to Birmingham, where I would visit one of the churches that had burned, and head from there to the Olympics, and onward to South Carolina, where two other churches had burned.

Kitty had lists of people's names, and all sorts of backup plans.

I felt like I used to feel on the morning of an exam, without the adrenaline. Midsentence Kitty looked down at her pager. "It's the White House!"

Nora seemed thrilled by the news. "The *White* House!"

I was starting to have a feeling I knew all too well. It wasn't a good feeling. It was a feeling I associated with a kind of pressure to perform. Even though I was going on the press plane as a "mere" observer, there was something about it that was not just like your normal plane ride. Your normal plane ride, by the way, is not without stress—you have to make sure that you have your ticket, your driver's license, and that you are ready and alert at every turn: at security, that you check all signs to make sure everyone's given you the correct information, et cetera.

But this, with all its details, was more complicated. It wasn't the pressure to perform, say, on opening night on Broadway. Perhaps because it was about being with a group of strangers for several days. Also, opening night on Broadway, or performance at any time, gives you the anticipated release of "it's over." This would be three days of hoping nothing went wrong, and moving in a territory I did not know. I had signs already, from my previous months in Washington, that this was not a summer camp atmosphere, to say the least. I was having a flashback, for some reason, to those days at Elementary School No. 144 when the white people came to watch us learn. But *I* was doing the watching this time, so what was the problem? Well! Maybe the problem was that I was with a planeful of journalists. I was reminded of being on the safari in Zimbabwe. Sleeping in a tent, with the danger of lions lurking.

Kitty was jotting down notes as she talked, presumably to a Clinton staffer. She wrote on a piece of paper, so that Nora and I would know what was happening:

"Ann Matthews"

She moved the paper toward us.

Maybe the trip was being called off. No. It didn't sound like that.

The Sunday papers were on the table. I glanced at them. The previous week a TWA jet had crashed. They still didn't have very much information.

Kitty was getting more and more specific. Her conversation went something like this. "And what will she be able to observe?" She was writing notes. "Uh-huh, uh-huh."

Kitty put down the phone and gave us a long, intense look. There was a pause. "You can get on Air Force One."

I seem to recall that Nora screamed out, or gasped, in a way that you would think of as an eighteenth-century way. She was in her early twenties, but she used expressions like "Heavens," always with the slightest sense of irony. Nora was laughing.

I did not laugh.

"Woah, woah, woah," I said. "Air Force One?"

Kitty nodded.

"I am not prepared to go on Air Force One," I said.

Prepared or not, it seemed to be in the works. "How did that happen?"

"Ann Edwards volunteered it."

"Just like that?"

"Our office did not broach this at all at this point."

"Because I thought the idea was we were going to wait to get some 'big donor' that we might know through the grapevine to get me on Air Force One. That's what George Stephanopoulos said I should do."

It seemed to me that both Nora and Kitty had kind of now-or-never looks on their faces. This was more than I'd bargained for. I was having enough trouble with the press plane part of it, and now Air Force One. I felt very in the dark.

It's interesting, when you work with people you begin to absorb their desires too. Since the day I arrived in Washington, press people had been saying to me, "Oh, you have to go on Air Force One." I didn't know how I felt about it. It was beginning to feel "mandatory."

Kitty simply continued giving me instructions. The official pool reporter on this trip for the newsweeklies is from *Time*. Pool reporters travel in the press "pool" to events that are not open for the entire press. They then report to the rest of the press through something called a pool report about what happened.

"The *Time* reporter is named Jeff McAllister. All you have to do is check with him and see if he'll let you take his seat on Air Force One for a short leg of the trip."

"But why would he do that?"

The doorbell rang. "I'll get it," Nora said.

"It's no big deal. They do it all the time." Kitty was speaking quickly.

It's in moments like these that I tend to speak very slowly. "I don't get it."

"That's what Ann Edwards said. Just let her know if you decide to switch with Jeff. For security reasons, she will need to know if you are going to switch with Jeff."

Nora came back downstairs. "The car is here."

"What else did she say?"

"Most of the events are private fund-raisers, which won't even be open for the pool to observe."

I didn't like the way I was being given this information at the last minute. The call had come from the White House literally as I was leaving. To be perfectly frank, at that point I would much rather have spent the night at the Maryland Correctional Institute for Women, in the cell of a child murderer, than sit on Air Force One. I knew a woman who had allowed her boyfriend to murder her daughter, actually, and from time to time I would talk to her, either in her prison or on the phone. Given what she'd been through, she had a very philosophical view of life that I rather appreciated.

That's a bit of an exaggeration, but I think it is accurate to say that if I had been able to get clearance to spend the night in jail with a child murderer, I would have felt a lot like I did before leaving for the press plane. It's a feeling of dread and fear that one might have before crossing boundaries. I say all of this to admit that, for all my talk about coming out of safe houses of identity, it is not easy. It is not comfortable. How much nicer it would have been to spend the afternoon in the garden, and go out to dinner that night, or even take the shuttle to New York, than to go on this campaign "swing."

"So, that's what the White House said I should do? Ask this guy Jeff McAllister?"

"Yes."

Apparently this was something that was done all the time. Even news organization interns did it, I was told.

Kitty and Nora walked me upstairs. I went over all my gear. Cameras, computer, clothes, itineraries, dossiers, David Maraniss's book. I locked up the house, got in the car that was going to drive me to Andrews Air Force Base, and waved good-bye to them. They looked awfully cheery as I pulled off down P Street.

I was the first to arrive at Andrews. Very military. I was about an hour and a half early. Kitty had given me enough time to get lost twice. The room that I waited in was rather nondescript—large tables, chairs. From being in the briefing room, I had developed a caution about sitting down. Even though I was the first one there, and all the seats were empty, I was worried that I might sit down, unknowingly, in somebody else's seat.

One by one the photographers, cameramen, and writers began to show up in the waiting room. I noticed that all of the photographers and cameramen were carrying or wearing rainproof outerwear. As people arrived, they sat alone, usually, read the paper. It was a fairly quiet place. I noticed here and elsewhere that no one read the paper "idly." They all seemed to read it with a sense of purpose, as though they were looking for something specific, the way we in the theater read reviews.

Air Force One was on the ground, as was the press plane. I tried to get a photograph of Air Force One, but I couldn't fit it in my frame. I noticed a very outgoing, rather upper-class-looking woman with short hair and a red jacket and a baseball cap that said TIME. I had noticed her before in the briefing room. She was a photographer.

III. THE PRESS PLANE

I boarded the press plane. All of the seats have white pieces of paper on them, with the names of publications. Nothing is random. I looked for the seats marked *"Newsweek."*

"But which *Newsweek* seat shall I take?" I asked someone who was in charge. "Any one." This made me nervous. I knew from a ballet I worked on with the Alvin Ailey Dance Company that seating—where a dancer sat on a bus, for example, or where she stood in class—was not to be tampered with. I figured the press would be the same.

I sat in a *Newsweek* seat. A very tall, rather good-looking man got on the plane. He was one of the *Newsweek* photographers. He was looking around for where to sit.

"Is this your seat?" I shouted out, already rising.

"You're fine. You're fine," he said.

After a while Joe Klein got on. I wondered how it must feel for him to be among these folks, many of whom were hostile to him. After the plane took off, I saw that there were more seats in the back, and I left my seat to find a place to stretch out.

This was just like any other plane, except they brought us more food. I had already decided that the safest strategy was the Audrey Hepburn Seafood Diet: "See food. Don't eat it." I wasn't going to eat anything on the plane, except coffee and whatever wilted lettuce and shredded carrots they brought by from time to time. But as for the Chicken McNuggets, the sirloin tips, I was glad to be a vegetarian.

I was sort of napping, and the woman photographer I had noticed before came over. She introduced herself. She was literally the only person on the plane who seemed outgoing in that way. "Diana Walker," she said, extending her hand. She began to talk to me while standing by my seat. She had apparently covered presidents since Carter for *Time*. I wondered if she were the sort of unofficial welcome wagon. She was very elegant, and very nice. And very funny. In the course of the trip, a moment on the bus here, another moment standing at security there, I would get a picture of a very interesting person. I gathered that she lived in Washington, grew up there, was married to someone named Mallory. She seemed "established." Had gone to Foxcroft. Fancy boarding school. For the greater part of the first conversation, she stood in the seat behind me and talked to me over the back of my seat.

I mentioned to her that I was to talk with the reporter from *Time* about taking his place on Air Force One. In a way I was floating the idea.

"Oh, Jeff! He's a great guy," she said. "He'll let you do it."

"But why would he give up his place on Air Force One?"

"It's no big deal."

The plane landed in Denver. We got off the plane and had to get on a bus on the tarmac that would take us to our hotel.

I spotted Todd Purdum, with whom I had dined and spoken several times. He was very well educated, was given to quoting Yeats in the middle of, say, an otherwise uneventful explanation of the day-to-day work of a journalist. I congratulated him on a huge piece he had done on Clinton in *The New York Times Magazine*.

"A group of us are having dinner tonight, want to join us?"

"Sure," I said.

There was a very friendly looking aide—named Kris Engskov. He sounded like he was from the South, or the Midwest. Our conversation went something like this. "Miss Smith?"

"Yes?"

"I was told you wanted to go on Air Force One?"

I wondered who told him. I reiterated what I already knew.

"Jeff's a good guy. He'll let you do it."

Everybody kept saying that Jeff's "a good guy."

We got to the hotel and went to our rooms. Our luggage was delivered. On the one hand, this is simpler than other kinds of travel because they do everything for you; on the other hand, it's odd because you have no control. I imagine the army would be like this.

I met Todd and his friends for dinner. The anxieties, the ennui, the general air of the work to do, the work to be done, permeated things. These were people who wanted to get it "right." This felt nothing like "Boys on the Bus." It seemed uptight.

IV.

The next morning we all went to a speech about "deadbeat dads" and then traveled on to Los Angeles for a speech on juvenile crime.

We were given rooms at the Loews Hotel by the beach in Santa Monica. That night I had dinner with Kevin Merida, a black journalist I had met the day before, and his brother-in-law.

I was, at this point, scheduled to go on Air Force One in the morning, for the ride from Los Angeles to Sacramento. It seemed that I was on for about thirty-five minutes, at the most. Kevin was giving me the lowdown. He kept referring to something called the pool report. "What's a pool report?" I said.

"You'll have to help write it."

I thought he was kidding. But I wasn't sure. I got my hands on a pool report, took it back to my room, and read it.

It was lighthearted in manner—"The president was not feeling our pain tonight." It started with a complaint about how long they had had to wait for the event to begin. At any rate, I concluded that Kevin was joking about the fact that I would have to help write it. He had a laid-back, warm manner.

The next morning we all arose and went downstairs, where we had to wait in a holding area before taking off. Each time we left a hotel, we would have to go through security. We'd bring our bags down early in the morning. Dogs would sniff them, et cetera. The fear, or expectation, that something could endanger the president is palpable always.

We were then whisked away in the entourage of the president. This was much different than traveling on the press plane. The first thing that is unusual is that, when you travel in the entourage of the president, there is no traffic. They shut down the Los Angeles freeways. I had never in my life traveled the 10, the 405, or any Los Angeles freeway without traffic. It is an amazing experience. I can only imagine that this would be very empowering for the boy next door who becomes president. And this would be the least of it.

Then we took a helicopter—a military helicopter. Very dramatic. And then the flight on Air Force One. Air Force One in and of itself is not remarkable, so I don't know what the people who told me I must get on

Air Force One meant. Did they mean I should try to get access to the president on Air Force One? I was not with the president. I was with the press.

The press area on Air Force One is more comfortable than the press area on the press plane, but it feels more like business class than first class on a normal flight. The flight attendants give out souvenirs—Air Force One M&M's, napkins, and so forth. The food's better than it is on the press plane, and it's served on Air Force One china. I was seated next to Kevin Merida. We spent the thirty-five minutes as black folks often do, talking about a black folk. In this case, Jesse Jackson.

Leon Panetta came to the back of the plane, which is where the press were. He spoke very quietly. It was nearly impossible to hear him, and, although he had a huge smile on his face, he did not seem to be making any kind of great effort to be heard. His ease, his smile, was in direct conflict with the urgency of the press. They wanted information on TWA. As he walked off, and some of them tried to get further access, one reporter asked me exactly what he said. I told her what I heard. "That's all I could hear," I said. "You should probably talk to someone else."

I had a sudden pang of fear. I'm not official. She was asking me a question as if I would know the answer. Suddenly I felt as though I were watching surgery and a nurse turned and asked me to pass an instrument. Here is the danger of being an observer. Yet the press observe all the time, and their work requires that they get as close to the subject as possible. How do they do that without getting confused *as* the subject?

The ride on Air Force One was over. I was still in the "pool" and was shuttled to a series of events. Everything the president did was staged within an inch of its life.

When we got to Sacramento, we were taken to the home of a wealthy person where the president was having lunch. We were "held" in the backyard of a neighbor. Lunch was served. The food, the folding tables, the sitting and waiting reminded me of the days when I had done work as an extra in movies. Kevin, and a few others of the pool, were writing the "pool report." In this case, the "pool" was not even inside the house where the fund-raiser was taking place. All they had to go on was what they'd seen of the president as he went into the house.

At one point Kevin asked me a question. It was something like (although I can't remember exactly what it was), "What color were the umbrellas outside the house?" or, "Was that a canopy or an awning?" He wrote down what I said. I had an eerie feeling, and soon moved away from his table.

There is a combination of idleness and sense of importance to the behavior of the press. They are literally trapped or, as Ed Bradley said, held "captive" by the president—hanging on his every word, in spite of their suspicion that his words are not truthful or meaningful. The more cynical ones among them say that they are held captive by the deathwatch—the possibility that he might get killed on their watch, and how important it would be not to miss that. But how they move from idleness to seriousness is what perplexed me. It's a little like veteran movie stars, who can tell jokes before a scene is shot. I have to hide in my trailer and meditate, even before the simplest of scenes.

Diana Walker distracted me—she was taking pictures of me. I saw her out of the corner of my eye. I asked her to stop. She thought it was amusing and kept snapping away. What was worth her film, it seemed, was that I had been in the movie *The American President,* and now I was actually traveling with the real president. I wasn't amused by that, but I was amused by her, and her mock gotcha-ness.

We soon gathered up our gear and took off for the next stop.

Each stop had on the dais, with the president, civic leaders dressed in their finest. There were very long introductions in each case. These people would often give speeches. It seemed that their presence had less to do with what they were saying, and more to do with the fact that they were in proximity to the president, at least for those few moments. This, I suppose, legitimized them—they had been with the president of the United States.

There was one event outside under a cluster of trees. The president was talking again, about "deadbeat dads" and how these deadbeat dads would not be able to get away with deserting their families. I noticed, for the first time, the men in black.

They were dressed in black jumpsuits and carried automatic weapons. They traveled in black vans, whose windows you could not see through. They traveled with black dogs. They lined the roofs of buildings around the event. It's as if the president were the nation's most precious possession.

Again Leon Panetta emerged, and a group of press huddled around him trying to get the latest on TWA. Again, he spoke so softly that he was nearly impossible to hear. Again, he had a huge smile on his face, in direct contrast to their furrowed brows. Again, he walked off before they had seemed to get enough of him. Again he deflected their questions. The onstage presentation continued. What was clear was a subplot, always to the president's staged performances. Life went on behind the scenes.

Someone came out with the "pool report." I read it, and suddenly my heart began to race. The authors had signed my name to the report. Were they joking?

My beeper went off. I called in. Richard Ben Cramer had called. He was in San Francisco working on his book about Joe DiMaggio. He congratulated me on winning the MacArthur award, would I like to meet for dinner? I determined that I would actually be in San Francisco for one night, and that it would be great to have dinner with him.

I went outside and stood on a stairway, watching Clinton work the rope. A sight to behold. He throws himself right into the crowd. Why does it mean so much to the crowd to shake the hand of the president? And while the crowd is grabbing at his hands, the men in black, the Secret Service, the dogs, patrol the crowd. We are all suspects. Any one of us might plunder the crown jewels.

V.

This trip was winding down. Clinton had one more event, inside an airport, in a rather plain-looking room, almost like a classroom. I was standing in the back. I thought I caught his eye. It was as if he was standing right next to me. Clinton has presence. That "deep surrender."

I picked up my gear and took off. I was approached by J. F. O. McAllister, the reporter from *Time*. "I'll take over now," he said. He was going to come back to the pool. It reminded me of getting off a ride at the amusement park. Not quite a roller coaster, but more at stake than a merry-go-round. "Thanks," I said, heading off for the last leg of the trip. A woman journalist from *USA Today* approached me. "Are you okay?" I didn't know what she was referring to. "Was there a problem about your name on the manifest?" I didn't know what she meant. "Not as far as I know." She looked concerned. I looked over my shoulder as I headed to the regular press plane.

The press plane landed in San Francisco, and I headed to our new holding pen, the Hilton, downtown, across from Glide Memorial Church. I waited to have my bags released and took off, with an amazing sense of freedom. What was I free from? I got a cab and went home. That night I had a terrific dinner with Richard Ben Cramer. Newly awarded the MacArthur, I picked up the tab. In a day or two I'd get a call of congratulations from Susan Sontag, who would say, "And don't take your friends out for dinner, it's not a lot of money. It's no more than a modest academic salary." Well, modest or not, it's the only money I've ever gotten in my life that I didn't have to work for or, better said, the only money I ever got that I got by surprise, out of the blue. I ultimately took her advice, but at least that night, I still thought I was rich, and so Richard and I ate well, and drank well. He and I had something in common. As far as presidents are concerned, Richard commented, "We both know these guys are special."

VI.

The next day I went to my loft to do some work. I had just gotten in from the gym, and purposely didn't check the answering machine, because I had a lot of reading to get through. Dossiers of potential interviewees. At this point, I was still learning the language of the culture, and the conventions were in front of me.

I began poring over what my team had gathered about the church burnings. Nora had gone to a gathering of preachers in Washington to take notes while I was on the road, and Kitty had been on the phone all week trying to put together an itinerary. People had been hard to get ahold of. Even as I was reading the material, Matthew was on country roads outside Tuscaloosa predriving all the routes I'd be taking, so that we wouldn't get lost on the way to the interviews we'd scheduled.

Churches had been burned throughout the South since December of the previous year. It was unclear if they were random or connected in some way. My first destination was Greensboro, Alabama, the location of

Rising Star Baptist Church. It was a church that had literally been built by its members. One of them had put up his milk cow as collateral for the land. It was sixty-five years old when it burned, at 3:00 A.M. I would also go to the site of an old slave church, called St. John, which had burned near Columbia, South Carolina, and finally to the church Clinton had chosen to visit during the rash of burnings, Mt. Zion AME in Greeley-ville, South Carolina.

I was anxious about going to Birmingham. All that footage of the South in the sixties, the dogs, the fire hoses, the men, the women, being kept away from lunch counters, and schools, those big fat white men with crew cuts.

From the press plane to the country roads of Alabama—what a mix. The press plane is remarkably clear of "race." Kevin Merida and one other woman were the only blacks I saw on the trip with the president. I had thought it was so odd that, in 1996, the U.S. media was not more diverse. I wondered how hospitable or inhospitable it was for reporters of color. The nineties were an odd time. At the very moment when you were inclined to agree that things *are* better, black churches would be burned, and at that same moment as your gaze peruses newsrooms and press planes, the place where "news is made," where the "rough draft of history" is written, you marvel at the lack of writers of color. White women, yes—colored people, no. Left in the dust. Still not a part of making the story.

The phone rang. My assistant was frantic. "*The New York Times* is trying to get ahold of you."

One of the first things an assistant of mine learns is to refer all calls from the press to my press representative. I don't talk directly to the press until it's organized by my rep. (That's odd in and of itself—except that talking to the press requires a specific language, a guarded language. You can even get a "media education." I haven't gone that far yet.)

"Didn't you tell them to call Stephen [my press rep]?"

"I did, but she was very aggressive."

"They have to talk to Stephen."

"He called too. You need to call him back right away. It's urgent."

I called him.

He had just gotten a call from the *Times*. They had assigned someone to find out why I was on Air Force One.

I gave Stephen the whole story. About how Kitty and Nora and I were sitting in the kitchen, and we got this call from the White House, et cetera. He's been around the block several times, is very versed in the worlds of Hollywood, Washington, and *The New York Times*. Normally he allows me to finish my sentences. Suddenly he cut me off.

"It's Maureen," he said emphatically, as though he had the winning answer on a game show. He meant Maureen Dowd. He sensed that she was somehow involved with this, although she herself had not called. When I had arrived in Washington in 1995, I had been told that Dowd had advised her colleagues at *The New York Times* not to talk to me.

I flashed on a moment that had seemed odd to me during the trip. I was walking down a hallway of a high school, just after Clinton had saluted a number of policemen, and I saw Todd Purdum talking to Maureen Dowd. She grabbed Todd and pulled him into a classroom. The door slammed. They had the look of two junior high school kids up to mischief. I had not liked the feeling I had when I saw that, but it felt too much like junior high for me to think this was really serious. Besides, Todd had always been such a gentleman.

Whatever Maureen Dowd was doing, the *Times* was writing a *second* story to back her up.

Stephen interrupted whatever I was saying. "Let's get Kevin Merida on the line."

The *Times* had called Kevin Merida too. My trip on Air Force One was being made to look nearly criminal. They had also called J. F. O. McAllister of *Time* and Ann McDaniel of *Newsweek*, since I had *Newsweek* credentials. The issue seemed to be that I had written the pool report.

I was shocked. "Well, I didn't write it!"

Kevin consented that that was true.

"Well, what's the problem?"

Stephen chimed in that interns write pool reports—they're very informal documents.

Kevin then cautiously added, "Well, remember you did help describe . . ." He was referring to the umbrella, or canopy. I believe I had said no more than "It's yellow," or "it was an umbrella."

"Yeah, but, I didn't *write* it."

He agreed.

I never know if people mean it when they say you're right, or if they just want to get you to stop talking. "Kevin," I said. "Why *did* you put my name on the pool report?"

"It was a kind of salute to you," he said after a pause.

A salute? He had thought it was interesting that I had been in *The American President,* playing a press secretary, and here I was on a press plane. It may have been well-intentioned on his part, but *The New York Times* was certainly not looking at it as a "salute," they were looking at it as serious trespassing. I couldn't help feeling a bit of an edge—a bit of racial edge—about it all. I wondered what would have happened if a white colleague of mine had traveled on Air Force One. I doubt that it would have provoked the same type of response.

"Why don't we tell them that the White House put me on, or told me how to get on? That's really what happened."

"I don't think you need to do that," Stephen said.

"I'm really sorry about this," Kevin said.

This was sounding worse and worse. The guess was that Maureen Dowd was going to write something about it. She had, I was told, "hit the roof" about me being on Air Force One, and perhaps Andy Rosenthal had too.

"Andy Rosenthal?" I said. Andy had been at the first party given for me in D.C. It was at that party that I had heard so much about Air Force One, and about how important it would be to go on Air Force One.

We finally got off the phone. I had plans to go out to dinner. The Slanted Door, a wonderful Vietnamese restaurant. All night I felt lousy. Stephen told me to expect something in the paper the next day. I was going to be leaving for the airport at 4:00 A.M., headed to the sites of the church burnings.

"I GOT THE *NEW YORK TIMES,* IT AIN'T NOTHIN' NEW NEWS BLUES"

UNITED AIRLINES RED CARPET LOUNGE

The New York Times wasn't being delivered because I had been out of town so much. The next morning, after I got to the airport and checked in, I bought a copy of *The New York Times*. I didn't want to read it to my-self. I knew already the likelihood was whatever was written was going to be disturbing, I had that same feeling you have when you read a review. On the occasions when I had to read reviews because they would dra-matically affect my immediate future, I had them read to me—I didn't read them alone. So—I called a friend, at 5:00 A.M., and read the articles aloud over the phone in the United Red Carpet Lounge. It was a one-time performance.

The big story on President Clinton's Western swing this week was that *Newsweek* sent Anna Deavere Smith as its White House correspondent. Let's put aside the absurdity of *Newsweek* assign-ing the writer and actress, who played a White House press secre-tary in the movie *The American President* and is now working on a book and a play about political reporters, to cover a news story.

The White House was philosophical. "She writes plays and Joe Klein writes novels," said a top Clinton aide, slyly. *Newsweek* has a precedent.

And certainly if Ms. Smith is looking to document the feck-lessness of the press, what better evidence than her own instant and bizarre accreditation? The real issue in sending the talented Ms. Smith on the campaign trip is whether it was unfair to give the President such tough competition in performance art.

Robin Pogrebin's article, printed on page 20 of Section A in the *Times,* started, "*Newsweek* yesterday found itself explaining how it was that a performance artist, Anna Deavere Smith, wound up representing the news weekly on Air Force One."

Several things seemed odd in this new land I was visiting. I was iden-tified in each case as a "performance artist." I could be called actress, play-wright. I could also have been called professor, or Stanford professor, or even Ann O'Day Maples Professor of the Arts. In actuality I have been an academic much longer than I have been called a "performance artist." I have been teaching since 1976, have held academic rank in a variety of universities since 1978, and have tenure.

Stranger still is the ease with which these two journalists refer to "performance art." And perhaps what troubled me most about the articles was the use of that term. I'm more worried about the way the identity of that term was misused than about how my identity was being handled. I don't know what a performance artist is. Do the journalists know? From what I can decipher, *performance art* is a catchall phrase meant to serve a variety of people in a variety of art forms, not just theater, who cannot be easily categorized. When my work hit the scene, many people said they had never seen anything like it before. I was soon placed in the category of "performance artist" by the media. There have been some debates about whether or not I am a playwright. I like to think of a playwright in the old way. The word, as you see, is spelled play-w-r-i-g-h-t. It's not w-r-i-t-e. That's not a typo. *Playwright* is like *wheelwright*. A wheelwright makes wheels. A playwright makes plays.

Around about the time that the theater made some efforts to get to a bigger "we," that is, around about the time it was clear that it could no longer mirror society if it made room for only Williams, Simon, O'Neill, Miller, and Shakespeare, a variety of people emerged. They worked outside the limited box of art as mirroring only the lives, dilemmas, and stories of white families, white people, and particularly white heterosexual men. They were of color, they were women, they came to art with questions about society and about art that were not answered by the status quo. This group of people, adventuring to make a bigger expression of who "we" are, often worked in unusual ways, mixing forms, working outside forms. Many of them were called performance artists.

Because of controversies around the National Endowment for the Arts, the term *performance artist* connotes controversy, and even that which is outlandish. I believe that performance art may contribute to a significant change in culture. A change that allows a bigger "we." Here *performance artist* sounds a little sleazy: "whether it was unfair to give the President such tough competition in performance art."

Clinton was being called a performance artist too. Dowd had continued, "Bill Clinton, after all, is a metamorphosis artist, performing roles of New Democrat, Old Democrat, radical liberal and conservative all in his first term." Under this light, the idea of metamorphosis, or art, or performance art did not sound very positive. Moving, changing, evolving is not respected in politics; it is honored in art. I wonder if some scholars of performance would see Maureen Dowd as a performance artist. Would that be an honor or an insult?

Far from the facts is the notion that I was traveling only for *Newsweek*. In fact the Arena Stage paid for my trip, and we had gone to great lengths to get access—a staff of six working day and night.

And then the question of whether I was worthy of credentials in general. Who can be credentialed? "Who is credible?" has been a part of the blood on the floor in the battle to make a bigger "we." The easiest way to silence a voice is to question its credibility. All sorts of people have gotten credentialed in the past. I see colleagues of mine, from the arts, with by-lines in *Newsweek* and *Time* and other magazines. No one lifts an eyebrow. Jean Genet, the French writer (and a thief), covered the Democratic convention in '68.

Who is credible? The person who has the most ink, the most airtime? The idea of who is credible and who is not changes with time. Slave narratives were not credible. The story of Sally Hemings was not a credible story for years, although there were slave narratives to support it. Finally there was a debate, and finally there was DNA. Neither history nor science could have stood on its own. Supposedly we have expanded our idea of credibility, we have gained enough evidence that we shouldn't be so quick to judge who is credible and who is not. In Washington they have not expanded that idea.

"Oh they love when Streisand comes to town, yet these same people are the ones who at a dinner party would say, 'What the fuck does she know about Bosnia? Who is she?' " an anonymous insider explained to me.

Misinterpretation is a way of life in Washington and in the press generally. My brush with it was extremely mild, compared with how it works in a real way in the everyday lives of the people whose careers are politics and image building. I have a lot of tape to attest to this. Perhaps one of the clearer statements came from Alexis Herman, secretary of labor: "They want to misinterpret, you know, the feeding frenzy. And unfortunately there is an element today that can paint you to be a very different person, that you may not even recognize. . . . And then the funniest thing to me was that somehow I was labeled a 'Washington insider.' That was really, you know, you're on the outside looking in, trying to bring down the walls, bring down the barriers, to be in the room, to get to the table, you know? And somehow to wear the mantle of a Washington political insider was just funny to me, you know. It was just funny to me."

Probably the biggest fiction being created here was the idea that my being on Air Force One was in the lead of Dowd's column. The idea that I was the "big story" on the president's western swing. Actually, the big story on the swing was the TWA crash. The reporters seemed eager to get details of what had happened, and those details were hard to come by.

So those were some of the subtle fictions and not so subtle fictions being created around my name, around the term *performance artist,* around my trip to follow the president, around my desire to know more about the circle of people who create America and those who tell us about their work. This was a subtle and not so subtle fiction that put a public frame around my search for American character on the campaign trail. What truth was that fiction trying to tell?

Even as Dowd's writing could be enjoyed by some as a kind of performance art itself, a kind of dark insightful clowning, Robin Pogrebin, who had written the second article, seemed to have the task of making this very serious. Why had the *Times* printed *two* stories in section one about thirty-five minutes on Air Force One by a little-known (in the big scheme of things) African American playwright-actress?

Sitting in the little phone cubicle of United Airlines, with my morning coffee, I waited for my flight to Birmingham to board. I thought about how afraid I had always been to go to Birmingham. When I was a girl in Baltimore, we were afraid to go any farther south than Washington, D.C. It was the first place I was called "nigger." My father had a saying, which was that he hadn't been to Mississippi in so many years she could be married by now for all he knew. And then there was the awful news of the four little girls who were killed in the bombing of the Sixteenth Street Baptist Church. I can still remember learning that news from my mother, in our kitchen on Bentalou Street, before we were in integration. That morning I was more afraid of what would be written about me in *The New York Times* than I was of going to Birmingham. I realized how out of balance my reaction was.

VII. O'HARE AIRPORT, CHICAGO, ILLINOIS

I had to change planes in Chicago, and when my plane landed at O'Hare, I called my office to check in. My assistant said that I should call my press representative.

I started looking for a pay phone that wouldn't be too noisy. I decided I better first get to the gate, so that I would be ready to board even if the phone conversations got complicated. I had several calls I knew I had to make. I called my press representative. He was already getting calls, and he needed a response.

"A response? What for?"

"We have to come up with a response right away."

"You mean a response that will be printed?"

"Yes."

I was suddenly worried that we should bring my agent in on this, since she had been a part of the *Newsweek* deal, and a book deal. We decided to conference her in.

"Hello. Hello. Are you there?" They were both on the line.

"Okay, everybody's here."

My agent was curious about what Maynard Parker, the editor of *Newsweek,* would be thinking, since I had been flying with *Newsweek* credentials. Some people thought that when *The New York Times* asked *Newsweek* to comment, their response had sort of left me hung out to dry.

"I haven't talked to him."

To tell the truth, I have never understood this part of the "game." Something goes out, it's not entirely true, and we have to find a way of responding. The whole thing was a disruption in my already overly ambitious schedule, but it was coming clear to me that it was not to be ignored.

"I think we should just tell the truth," I said. "Tell them what really happened. Tell them the White House put me on the plane."

For some reason, neither one of them thought I should say that.

"Why shouldn't we just tell the truth, just say what happened—"

My press rep cut me off. "That's too Talmudic," he said.

"Excuse me?" I said.

Too *Talmudic,* I thought to myself. What did that mean? Did that mean the truth is too studied? It did have a ring to it—"too *Talmudic.*"

My agent agreed with my press rep that I ought to come up with something short and to the point. They waited—I was under the gun. It was a little like a game show, with a loud clock ticking.

"Say that I came to Washington to learn how things work and now I know."

They both laughed. I wasn't laughing at *all*.

"That's good!" one of them said, very animated and relieved.

"See, that's the kind of thing that will work!"

"It's quick, to the point, and it's light," my agent said.

"I like it because it has a couple of layers of meaning. And it has a little bit of an edge," my press rep said.

"What do you mean?" I asked.

"It's sort of like, this is how you play the game. Now I know you guys don't play fair," he said.

"Hmm . . ." I said.

My agent still wanted me to make sure to call Maynard. "Just to check in."

"Okay," I said and hung up.

Just to check in. I looked down at my beeper, the first beeper I ever had; I had gotten it for this project. I was surprised that I hadn't heard anything from the office in Washington, or the theater for that matter. I couldn't imagine that they hadn't read *The New York Times*. They were probably scared to death. All they had done was follow procedures given to them from others.

I quickly dialed the office in Washington. One of the interns brought Kitty to the phone.

"Did you see *The New York Times* this morning?" I asked.

The phone was silent on her end for a few moments. "I was just *sick* when I read it," she responded. She let out a long sigh.

"Maybe you should write a narrative about what exactly happened, I mean with the White House and all, you know, for our own record."

She said she would, and she did.

I hung up.

I still had a few moments left before boarding. I called Richard Ben Cramer. "What do you make of this?" I asked him.

"Don't worry about it, Anna," he droned, in a kind of weary, Jack Nicholson–esque, high pitch. He then said something like "These things last two minutes."

They last two minutes. And Andy Warhol said we have only fifteen. There were a million things I had planned to do with my fifteen—and they didn't include this. My trip to Birmingham was a part of what I would like to do with my fifteen minutes. And somehow it was being sidetracked.

What if I had gotten as many calls about the church burnings as I did about the *New York Times* articles? In retrospect, I decided it would have been nice if just as many people had called when the church burnings started to say, "Anna, why don't you go South and check that out?" I even got a call from one of my funders when the Dowd article appeared. Even my *accountant* wanted to know what was up. Shortly before this happened, perhaps no more than two weeks before, when I had been awarded the prestigious MacArthur award, my mother and my agent could not find the announcement in *The New York Times*. Yet funders, accountants, my deans, friends I hadn't heard from in a long time, knew that I had spent thirty-five minutes on Air Force One.

VIII. THE AIRPORT IN BIRMINGHAM, ALABAMA

The plane landed in Birmingham. It had been a very long day, and I was still due to go to a revival meeting and do a couple of interviews. The airport was spanking new. I didn't expect it to be so modern.

Matthew met me at the gate. He was in a very good mood. I'd asked him to come to the South because he was completely dependable; I knew I could count on him to be meticulous, even anal, in setting things up. He had been in Birmingham and Tuscaloosa for a couple of days. He had driven all the routes we had to drive, had found places where we could eat fresh fish and vegetables, had even found a good swimming pool.

He knew about the *New York Times* pieces. As we walked from the gate to baggage claim, our conversation went something like this.

"They used that picture with your hat," Matthew said.

"You're right."

"Yeah, you had on a sort of weird hat. It's like they picked a picture that made you look kind of weird, like a performance artist, instead of more serious, like a professor."

"Yeah."

"Why'd they put in two pieces about it?"

"One is the straight man, one is the burlesque. They had to put the first one in to let people know who I am, and what I was doing there; otherwise Dowd's column wouldn't have made sense."

"You know," he said, "there comes a—there comes a time when we have to just be delivered from what other people think of us if we're going to be able to go forward and live our lives in the way that God would want us to."

The other reason I took Matthew with me to the churches in the South was that he was born again.

At baggage claim an old, thin, but very fit black man came up to us with a luggage cart. He looked like he had been carrying people's bags all his life. This was not a part-time job while he was waiting to make a million dollars. This was his job, his profession. I asked him about the church in Birmingham, the history of the four little girls being killed. He said he couldn't talk about it.

"You can't talk about it?"

"No, ma'am."

"Why is that?"

"Spike Lee been down here making a movie about it, and we not supposed to talk about it, till he done making his movie."

We waited patiently for my luggage, and it did not turn up. This was not good.

What would I do without proper clothes? I couldn't go to church that night the way I was dressed. In jeans. The old black man waited patiently with us while we tried to sort this through. I tipped him although no bags came. Or maybe he should have tipped me. I had done a remarkably restrained performance. Matthew doesn't like profanity, so, through the entire lost bags ordeal, I was very subdued. Without access to profanity, I had to be imaginative. My imagination left me silent.

IX. SHONEY'S RESTAURANT, TUSCALOOSA, ALABAMA

We drove past a huge Mercedes-Benz plant as we left the airport, on our way to meet Reverend Coleman, pastor of Rising Star Baptist Church. We were set to meet him at a Shoney's restaurant off the main highway.

Matthew had a gift waiting for me in the car. A Bible. He was very excited and gave me a detailed, and animated, description of a huge Christian bookstore in a strip mall. ". . . with these tacky handwritten signs. You know, the kind of signs that tell you what section you are in? Well, they were handwritten!"

We pulled into the Shoney's parking lot. Matthew sat in the car, staking out the parking lot for Reverend Coleman. We didn't know what he looked like. I went inside to buy an orange juice, and to get the benefit of air-conditioning. I remembered suddenly that I was supposed to call Maynard at *Newsweek* to "check in," so I did.

Maynard's vocal tones were melodic—the kinds of tones meant to make you think everything is fine. He said that he thought this thing with me on Air Force One and the *Times*'s response to it would not have blown up if it hadn't been for the Joe Klein story. "It was the two things together, you see," Maynard said.

Having "checked in," I hung up and saw a black gentleman with a huge smile. He came up and looked at me as if he had known me all my life. "Reverend Coleman?" I asked. He nodded and clasped my hand in a firm handshake.

He did not look at all like he was in the middle of a drama, that is, the drama of his church having been burned down. He looked strong and steady. His smile was familiar.

Suddenly I remembered my appearance. "I'm so sorry, you have to excuse the way I look. They lost my luggage."

"You don't need to worry about that." He, by contrast, was pressed and suited for the evening revival meeting.

We went outside to Matthew. We determined that I would drive with Reverend Coleman, and Matthew would follow us. I took out my tape recorder right away. "Okay. The church was sixty-five years old, and it was a brick building that had bricked over siding, and the siding that they had was that asbestos-type siding. Now I don't know exactly what year they rebricked it, but they rebricked it and they remodeled it. There is no elected official in the church. There's professional peoples as relate to education in the church. There's insurance peoples, and just your common everyday peoples that really love that church."

Coleman was not a full-time preacher. He had a "day" job.

"Personally, I did not recognize how many fond memories I had of the church until the building got gone. Then I reflected in my mind the many of times that I have had the visitation of the Holy Spirit in that building."

The church had burned around three or four o'clock in the morning. Reverend Coleman was clearly perplexed that Clinton and others suggested that the burnings were racially motivated. Perplexed because when the cases went to court, no one was tried as if there were racial motivation. To my mind, that didn't mean they weren't racially motivated, it just meant the courts didn't go there. But Coleman had his own ideas about the vandals.

"There is something wrong in their relationship with God," Reverend Coleman told me. "There are several times in the Bible that you see how Satan just motivate an individual."

"Oh?" I said.

"It's not all that black or white, just Satan motivate that person."

We pulled up as people were arriving. We got out of the car and went into the small country church. Matthew was in a suit and tie, I was in slacks. I felt so out of place.

Matthew and I were in a world entirely different from the one of the campaign trail. What went on inside there was the flip side of everything I was seeing in Washington. The droning voices, the sounds, the community. People were talking to Jesus, and they were talking to each other. The preacher, the Reverend Elijah C. Weaver, weighed about 350 pounds. A very dark-skinned man in a purple suit under his white robe. His preaching was more sounds than words.

"And they put Jesus in the lion den . . ."

"Welll."

"Can I get a witness?"

"Yes."

"And when dey put im *in* deah, Jesus wen in dere wif him and made du lion to lay down so they could be a pilla ta Daniel head."

"Amen. Amen."

"And he made du lion da lay down ta be a pilla ta Daniel head!"

"Wellllll."

"An only Jesus could a don it cause dose lion in the lion den
They wan tame like da lion in the circus
See we see a lion in the circus and they be trained

But these lion wan tame
These was *wiilllld* lions in the lions' den.
Am I right about it?" he sang.
  "*Weeeellllll.*"
  "Can I get a witness? Amen. . . . Amen."
  The drone of the music, the sweat of all of us.
"Aaaaaammmaaazzzzing grace!!!!!!!!!!
Howwwwwwwwwwww
Sweet!
The
Souuuuuunnnnnddddddd.
Thaaaaaat saavvveeeuuuuuuvvved aaaaaaah wretch liiiiiike me!"
  Matthew was beside himself. He was crying, I was crying, and laugh-
ing. We were both clapping, and singing. We were a mess. We had heard
the song many times, but not like this.
  He leaned over, thrilled. "I *knew* we would have an experience with
the Holy Spirit, I just *knew* it!"
  What if democracy felt like that? Why is it so entirely rational, even
in a time when we know the limits of our reason, even in a time when we
know we're so smart that we're not wise. Even in a time when we know
we have no proof that knowledge, knowledge alone, and material gain
alone, will not make us a better species. And it's dangerous, too, that the
right wing has grabbed ahold of the evangelical movement, and wants to
hold on to the truth of it. I'm not suggesting that we confuse church and
state—I'm just suggesting that we find other ways to talk to each other
than through reasoned discussion. Maybe even (God forbid) the arts,
which house empathy, if not spirituality, can be useful to us.
  I was enthralled with Reverend Elijah C. Weaver. When I went up to
meet him, I felt like a fan of a rock star. He had a white dot in one eye.
We begged him to meet us for breakfast the next morning. He was
amused by our enthusiasm, I think, and gave us intricate directions to a
gas station where we'd rendezvous early the next morning.
  "All right now," he said, as we went off into the night with our chorus
of thank-yous. That night we visited the oldest member of the church,
and turned in rather late.
  The next morning, I swam with great energy in an Olympic-size pool
Matthew miraculously found. We then drove to meet Reverend Weaver

at the gas station. From there we followed him in his long, old Cadillac to a diner, with only black customers. Over grits, biscuits, and bacon and eggs, we talked to him about talking, about how he talks to his congregation. He explained to us that he was talking for the Holy Spirit.

I would visit Reverend Weaver several times, and travel with him each time to another church, to watch him preach, and to hear the music of his congregations. The music of hope:

> *Oh it's another day's journey and I'm glad*
> *About it*
> *So glad*
> *So glad*
> *So glaaaaaaad!*

And the music of warning:

> *Iss gon rain*
> *Iss gon rain*
> *God tol Noah iss gon rain*
> *And when da watuh begin to pour*
> *Knock on da winda and knock on da dooor!*

I would call him on the phone, the way I spoke from time to time with Judith Butler, scholar of rhetoric. I would call him, as I had called her, to talk me through things that I didn't understand by looking at the surface. I realized I needed not only intellectual explanations but spiritual explanations. In neither case could I accept pure doctrine. Judith Butler's insights weren't the be-all and end-all, and neither was the Reverend's Christianity. But to understand "the words" I was hearing in Washington, I needed to look at words for their political potential and their spiritual potential. Most of the words I was hearing were flat compared with what they could be. I needed to understand what was, or was not, beneath the words.

AND THE SWING KEPT ON, ALL THROUGHOUT THE SUMMER. I WENT to both conventions, wrote for *Newsweek*—and just kept moving throughout America, with a few more stops in Tuscaloosa to get my battery charged.

Onward to see the end of the tale: Who would be the next president of the United States? No one seemed very excited. There wasn't much suspense. Few people thought it would be Dole.

MIKE WALLACE

60 MINUTES

"Proud"

You're going to believe Richard Nixon?
I wasn't sure what I believed about Jack Kennedy.
I remember that he was going to change the housing situation in
    this country, with a stroke of the pen
which stroke of the pen never
somehow never hit the paper.
Uh uh, Jimmy Carter couldn't persuade anybody to do anything.
He was well-meaning
But he didn't
he didn't make the country
he didn't capture the heart or the attention or the focus of the
    country
the way
certainly the way Roosevelt did and
to a certain degree
that way that
that Truman did
over great
the great skepticism
and people who were looking down their nose at
this haberdasher.
But eventually

but eventually
as far as
as far as Korea was concerned
I'm wandering all over the place
but
Yeah
Well, yeah
It
it's not quite awe.
I want to
I really want to admire him.
I want to say
"Boy am I proud to have that man sitting in the White House."
I, I want to be proud.
He's
he's the top
he's the president.
I want to be proud of my president.
It's as simple and straightforward as that.
And it's—
I can't be proud of Bill Clinton.
I can't be proud of George Bush.
I can't be proud of Jerry Ford.
Can't be proud of,
uh,
Jimmy Carter,
can't be proud of Richard Nixon.
That's a long time.

THEATER HISTORY

SUMMER 1996
LIBRARY OF CONGRESS
WASHINGTON, D.C.

AM SITTING IN A SMALL ROOM AT THE LIBRARY OF CONGRESS LISTEN-ing to tapes of the conventions dating back to the first recordings. They were raucous events. Someone with a gavel was banging away, asking for order, and the conventioneers did not heed. It sounded like an all-male affair. "Happy Days are here again, here again," et cetera.

NBC TELEVISION ARCHIVES
NEW YORK CITY

I am sitting in a small room at NBC in New York, watching the earliest television we can find of conventions. It's black-and-white. Huntley and Brinkley are anchoring. They are smoking on television as they speak.

Everett Dirksen is banging the gavel, trying to speak. He gets a few sentences into the speech, and the crowd begins to scream.

"Will you let me go on?" he wails. To no avail. The crowd has a mind of its own. They are clearly not there just to hear the speakers.

SUMMER 1996
REPUBLICAN CONVENTION, ARRIVAL
SAN DIEGO, CALIFORNIA

San Diego was a welcome sight after so many months in Washington. Everything looked so clean and new. *Newsweek* hires firemen to take attendees around the city. When I arrived, a fireman picked me up and took me to my hotel. He was a terrific-looking black guy, jovial and talkative. For a moment, I thought the convention would be fun.

I went to my room, got settled, and hooked up with Rob Maas, the photographer who was assigned to me. I did thirty-five interviews in three days. I never worked so hard in my life.

ON THE FLOOR

I was on the floor of the convention, in the middle of an interview. These kinds of interviews, standing up holding a mike in front of someone's face, can only yield sound bites. There was loads of noise in the background.

Mary Summers is screaming over the noise into my microphone. "I began working in the pro-life movement when I worked for Jesse Helms, and I began working for him after I graduated from law school in 1984. He is one of the most honest men I have ever met. He is one of the most courageous men I've ever met. And he's a very compassionate man. People don't know this, but, contrary to what the popular belief is about him, he is a great promoter of women.

"I think abortion is the greatest social evil in our society, because if we abandon the inalienable right to live, then we're going to lose the rest of our freedom, and if we abandon the right to life of the innocent unborn, then we are going to eventually lose the rest of our freedom and the inalienable rights that our forefathers fought so hard to keep."

Although I had to yell over the noise to continue our conversation, I was still able to do it. If I had been trying to have this conversation in 1932, not only would it have been politically impossible but it would have been technically impossible.

There was much discussion about the Republican convention as "too scripted" because the organizers of the convention were determined to bring the thing in under time. Much of the media complained, and Ted Koppel even left because of this. Television ratings were quite low. What was scripted was the speaking on the part of the stars. I wondered how a huge convention could be controlled. How could they control the crowd? Having listened to and watched several recordings and videos, I knew that audience response could add time to the event.

I asked one of the producers how he could have counted on the audience responses lasting only a specific period of time.

"It all has to do with the music. We told the bandleader not to play music that would get people riled up."

This was the antithesis of what I had been listening to at the Library of Congress. Who demands this control?

It was outside the hall that I found passionate discourse. There were Flip Benham and Rusty Thomas of Operation Rescue, who were holding funerals for fetuses outside the convention hall. There were the Mexicans who set off on a march on the first day of the convention down to the border and back to protest all the anti-immigration propositions. And there were all the born agains, Phyllis Schlafly, the evangelicals, camping out in the peripheries. People on the margins, trying to inch into the center.

The happiest people seemed to be the youngest ones. The Young Republicans became more and more sure of themselves as the week went on. I had traveled into San Diego with them on a train that had come from Chicago. I got on in Los Angeles. By that time they had been up all night for several nights singing "Proud to Be an American" and talking through their ideas about policy. They were carrying the future in their hands, and they knew it. There was no studied nonchalance here. All passion. Just free, wild optimism. As I ran into them in the course of the week, they became hoarser and hoarser. They, it turned out, were responsible for most of the cheering and passion that was felt on the floor.

A scholar at Stanford had told me, "There is a slow glacial move in this country to the right." If I were to go by the health and spirit of the Young Republicans, I would have to believe that was true. It was the older folk who were dissatisfied.

One day I was walking through a parking lot, and I saw a very disgruntled Jack Germond sitting on a crate of some sort.

"How about breakfast?" I asked. "I eat a real breakfast," he said. We'd have to go someplace where they were able to roll out the bacon and eggs and biscuits. I had melon, he had a real breakfast. He was mourning the death of politics as he had known it.

"This is—this is all—this is all showbiz now. There—there's—there's nothin' for them to tell ya. I mean, 'cause it's—the decisions are made in a different way."

It was all very clean in San Diego, all very neat. The only unbridled emotion I saw was inside the hall when the tribute was played to Ronald Reagan. I was right in the middle of the Minnesota delegation. There wasn't a dry eye in the place. Men and women both, weeping.

SUMMER 1996
DEMOCRATIC CONVENTION
CHICAGO

The ambience in Chicago was remarkably different. There was a lot of music. And it wasn't the kind of music to calm a crowd down. Bonnie Raitt was in town. Jessye Norman and Aretha Franklin both sang inside the hall. When Aretha sang "America the Beautiful," people were dancing in the aisles. The convention room floor smelled of french fries and hamburgers. There had been no food on the floor of the Republican convention.

The fringe events at the Republican convention seemed to be about passion held back. The fringe events at the Democratic convention seemed to be about a dying left. Many of them were half empty. What was more remarkable was that there were very few young people at the fringe, progressive events. I got the feeling that it was hard here to figure out where passion should come from, other than the music.

The 1996 Democratic convention didn't really need anybody to monitor the music, because even if they had gotten riled up, it would not have been about an issue.

Something else was lurking underneath the Democratic convention, though. It was a vivid memory of another time. It was the memory of the convention in Chicago, 1968.

There is a kind of political theater that happened in '68, that burst up like flames, but was put out just as quickly. It was so "hot" that even the Beat poet Allen Ginsberg and the French writer Jean Genet had gone to it.

Passion is dangerous. Passion leads to theater, or to a make-believe world. You can begin to believe what you are fighting for is possible. And if you get too wrapped up in that reality, somebody is sure to come along and let you know what reality actually is.

Nobody today needs to worry about getting carried away. In fact, I'd bet we're actually still smarting from some kind of a death blow that was struck in the seventies. That's what it looked like, at the Democratic convention, on the fringes. The tried and true were gray-haired and tired, and I didn't see any descendants.

We are not in political theater right now. What is happening in public life is not theater at all. It is fraught with imitation—true. It is fraught with design—true. But it is not theater at all. It is a series of commercial breaks. And it's hard to hang on to those breaks.

ARIANNA HUFFINGTON

COLUMNIST, COMMENTATOR

"Grace"

It occurred to me in the course of writing *After Reason*
that we, we had looked at human nature in a very
again, shrunken way, to use the—a term I've used before
in terms of three instincts
as a survivor
sex, and the instinct for—to assert ourselves
power
the ego instincts.
And that we had missed out on what I call the fourth instinct
which was the spiritual instinct.
And I call it an instinct because I believe that it is genetically
    encoded in us

and that if we don't honor it we pay a heavy price.

We pay a heavy price as individuals and we pay a heavy price as
a culture.

And, interestingly enough

when I was writing that book

After Reason, I—the one question I kept asking myself

and I had no answers [was]

but how do you—how do you honor it?

How do you get people to make it part of their lives because you
can't tell people

"It would be a good idea if you believed in God."

[Laughter]

I mean it's grace.

You can't make yourself believe in something.

So, that's when for me it's come full circle now

with the work I'm doing now

getting all of us to be involved in service

because I believe that that's something that we can do and that can
get us to God.

That we can't sort of get from here to God directly.

Sometimes we have to really serve his children and get to him
indirectly.

And this—and the question of how do we get to the critical mass

is, is a constant preoccupation of mine

and it's hard sometimes to do it through prose.

You have to get it

because what we are talking about is not just rational.

So, when you do it through poetry and through the theater

you can get to a part of us that is not as barricaded as if you do it
through columns or speeches.

You know

people in a, in a dark theater are more vulnerable in a positive
way

and a lot of politics is performance in the negative sense.

It's interesting that we have—we have now taken performance to
mean something very different than, say, when in *Hamlet*

you have "The play is the thing"

you know, through the play you get to the consciousness in a way
    that you can't do it through
ah, preaching or prose or this or that.
But now performance has come to mean something that is a lie
in the same way that the word *myth*
has come to mean something that is a lie.
And, you know
and myth is something which is so profound because it's beyond
    what we can express in rational terms.
It expresses deeper truths.
And, yet, what does it mean today?
It means a lie.
That's part of the, of the modern tragedy
of thinking that we can understand and live everything through our
    minds.
Shrunken humanity
shrunken view of nature.
It's like it's desiccated
and we don't even know we're not wise because we're so smart.

PERFORMING FOR THE
PRESIDENT

ELECTION DAY, 1996

THE CAMPAIGN WOUND TO A HALT, AND AT SOMETHING LIKE 4:00 A.M.
we, who were on that last mad swing to eight cities in two days, pulled
into Little Rock, Arkansas. We piled into an Arkansas hotel. I wouldn't
have to be awake early in the morning. In fact, I wouldn't have to get on a
press plane anymore. And that was it. I was exhausted. Richard Ben
Cramer had been right. You had to be in good shape to make it through.

In less than ten days, I was going to have to be onstage, playing, in a
two-thousand-seat house, my one-woman show *Twilight: Los Angeles,
1992*. It's about the Los Angeles riots, and in it I play forty-six characters.
It takes a lot of stamina. I'd be leaving Arkansas after the election results
were announced and heading to a spa.

I was glad for a bed with clean sheets, and the possibility of lying
down flat. I had spent several madcap days sitting up straight between
journalists on an airplane. Two male journalists, one of them a photographer, almost got into a knock-down-drag-out fight in the aisle. I was extremely tense myself from being around this less than happy bunch of
people. But a couple of levelheaded people broke the fight up, and everyone went back to naps on the plane, or to clicking away on a laptop.

When I woke up and went outside, Little Rock looked like it was set
up for a carnival. People could buy alcohol right out on the street.

I was hoping to find some kind of way to be near Clinton as the vote was coming in, but I knew there would be no such luck. Two of my friends, Diana Walker, a photographer for *Time,* and Karen Breslau, a correspondent for *Newsweek,* had figured out how to get behind the scenes. I knew from watching them that this required a very special skill in relationships, to go, as it were, behind the lines.

I learned that my friend the opera singer Jessye Norman was in town, and left word for her that I was too. We made a plan to meet. I was in the thick of the crowd at the Excelsior Hotel. People were getting drunker and drunker, and the human sea was getting denser and denser. I was to meet Ms. Norman by the elevator. There was no space to move. She got off the elevator with a friend, and they both immediately registered the impossibility of the situation on their faces. How, without an escort, would she ever get to where she needed to be, behind an outdoor stage? In the thick of this crowd appeared Vernon Jordan.

She asked him what she should do. He looked around the crowd, beckoned, and men came forward, almost like out of the woodwork. There were several aides to the president who looked as if they were just part of the crowd. Quickly one of them was assigned to Ms. Norman by Vernon Jordan, who just happened to be passing by.

The aide told us to hold hands and began to lead us through the crowd. A black woman in her early twenties passed by with friends. She suddenly blurted out to Ms. Norman, "Hey, ain't you somebody?"

Hey—ain't—you—somebody?

You get the feeling that people cruise these situations just to see who they can see. And that would be something to call home about.

Ms. Norman was taken to a big, old house that had almost no furniture. It had the look of a house that had once been wonderful, and then was turned over for an army headquarters of some sort. She went upstairs to prepare to sing. The room looked like an abandoned office. Strange to see a diva placed in such a spot to prepare to sing for the president and the nation.

I sat downstairs in another empty room, with a man who was watching the returns. It was over for Dole. We waited to see the concession speech. The room was very red, and disorderly.

I walked out back, behind the stage, and watched Jessye Norman sing. I watched the crowd who were cordoned off, and watched from behind as the president and Mrs. Clinton came out to wave at the crowd in the president's moment of victory. His second victory.

There was an anticlimactic feel to the event.

INAUGURATION EVE, 1997

We were told that it was going to be very, very cold on inauguration day. I got there the night before and went to the pre-inauguration celebration. This was followed by a party at the Jockey Club. I was shocked at how small the restaurant was at the Jockey Club and at the condensed mixture of movie stars and political folks. It reminded me of the small outdoor departure area at the old Martha's Vineyard airport the summers that Clinton was there. I suppose people in that circle could easily believe that there really are only two people in the world. The crowd was almost identical to the post–Academy Awards crowd at Mortons.

I had come to the party with a costume designer who was working with me on my play. She did research. We spent most of the evening standing at the bar, talking to the model Lauren Hutton about everything from politics to crocodiles. At one point, my designer turned to me and said, "You have no idea how much plastic surgery is in this room." I took a look around, and she was right. You could probably redo all of the nation's schools with the money reflected there in jewelry, cosmetic surgery, clothing, and appearance in general.

INAUGURATION DAY

I was in a group with Kevin Costner.

We were trying to get to our seats and were walking through the Capitol. The area was restricted—we weren't really supposed to walk through the building—but one of the guards noticed Kevin Costner. Security restrictions do not apply for movie stars.

The ceremony itself went without event. Ruth Bader Ginsburg said, "Every good wish," to Al Gore. To Clinton, she merely said, "Good luck."

We were leaving. A group of soldiers in formal dress and in formation were marching by. One of them noticed Kevin Costner and broke out of formation, gesturing wildly, pointing, and mouthing, "That's Kevin Costner!"

This soldier, and the guard who let us walk through a high-security area in the Capitol, are both supposed to be performing an important service for the president and the country. Yet celebrity caused them to leave their posts.

That night I was talking to Sidney Blumenthal. "It's form over content," he said, "everything is form over content." Clearly not the case for those soldiers. They abandoned form to recognize a movie star.

1997

WHEN CLINTON CAME TO SEE ME PERFORM

FORD'S THEATER

THE WATERGATE HOTEL

Soon after the inauguration, I was scheduled to perform *Twilight: Los Angeles, 1992,* at Ford's Theater. The show was a success and played to sold-out crowds.

On the Saturday before my last performance, I had only an evening show. No matinee. I was in my room at the Watergate Hotel, and the phone rang. It was the theater. They had just gotten word that President Clinton, Mrs. Clinton, and Al Gore were going to come to the last show. I was with my best friend of twenty-five years, a friend I see only once every five, sometimes ten, years.

I was not immediately ecstatic about the president coming. In fact, my reaction was the opposite. That certain dread hit me. That dread that I knew so well. It was the first-day-of-school dread magnified. It was the dread on the three days or so that the critics are coming to a show. It was the dread about performance. There's the thrill, but there's also the dread. The dread comes because there's a part of you, no matter how calm you try to be, that believes that performance—the taking on of personalities, of other personalities, and of staying in that state for nearly three hours, alone onstage—is a feeling of life and death.

It's an intense state of aloneness. Although the audience is there, what goes on inside is an intense aloneness. You fear you could lose your lines, lose your moments. But you have to go through till the end, and you never understand *really* how you get through. And no one can really help you except to say, "You're going to be fine." I always feel before a big performance, an opening, or a performance such as the one I was about to face with the president, that I am in the hospital, and that friends backstage are visitors at a hospital bed.

I also feel a big responsibility to the people I am portraying in the play. They are real, their words are real, and I have a responsibility to live up to their words. I am never as critical of the people I am performing as the audience thinks.

"What if I get stage fright?" I said to Jane.

We couldn't dwell on it. I had to perform that night. When I got home from the show, I got a call from Jane. "How are you feeling?"

"I'm worried I'll get stage fright."

Stage fright is not just nerves. It's much worse. I am told that Sir Laurence Olivier had such bad episodes of stage fright that he would have to have someone standing in the wings that he could see. I don't usually get a bad case of stage fright, but when I do it's memorable.

"You have to think of the thrill," she said. "The thrill of it. It's all an adventure. It's like going through the jungle. The thrill that anything can happen is what you have to think of."

In a way I felt like I were preparing for a big boxing match. It doesn't matter how many times you perform. The only thing that matters is your ability to be in the moment of the doing. It takes a tremendous amount of concentration and spiritual energy. The most important thing to have intact is your will to communicate, your lust to tell the story, as if every moment could fail, or every moment could soar. It's hard.

"You never know about these things. I could go through all this preparation, and he could cancel."

"What are you doing right now?" she said.

"I'm writing a recommendation for a student."

The night before I performed for the president of the United States I was sitting in bed in the Watergate Hotel, with my laptop, writing a recommendation for a student to get into graduate school.

1997

FORD'S THEATER

On Sunday morning I went to a spinning class, swam a mile, had a massage, and headed to the theater for the matinee. When I approached

Ford's Theater, I could see police cars and security tents. It looked like the president was coming after all.

When I got to the backstage entrance, my stage manager came out to meet me. He was a redhead with peachlike skin that was now flushed. His pace was swift. "The place is crawling with security," he said. "You're not going to believe this."

He took my bags and we entered the stage door.

There was a human wall. On both sides, against both walls, all the way down the hall, and all the way up the staircase, there were Secret Service. My stage manager and I recall that they seemed to be standing elbow to elbow. On both sides. Literally, there was a human wall. There were both men and women Secret Service. The women were very ordinary looking. When we got to my dressing room, there were Secret Service outside of it.

My press rep was waiting in a dressing room next to mine. He is from Los Angeles, but by coincidence he was there.

"You okay?"

"Yeah."

"The president will want to see you afterward."

"Okay."

"Need anything?"

By another coincidence, my mother, who lives in Baltimore, and who had seen the show several times already, had come with a busload of friends. I mentioned this as an afterthought.

"Your mother is here?" He paused.

I nodded.

"I'll take care of it." He went off to organize having my mother meet the president too.

I went in to work with my vocal coach, warmed up, and waited for the delayed curtain to finally rise. The theater had to move thirty people out of their seats, so the president could be surrounded by thirty selected, known people.

As I stepped onto the stage I was supremely aware that I was performing where Lincoln was shot, April 14, 1865.

The play is about the tragedy of the Los Angeles riots.

The audience was different that afternoon. They were almost raucous. Almost bouncing off the walls. But there is quite a lot of humor.

When they laughed, they really laughed. They often applauded inside the acts. It was wild. It was a very wild feeling, like being in a coliseum. I looked up often at Lincoln's box.

One of the characters in the play is Professor Cornel West. He is a very hard character to portray. He speaks a very complex English, with a lot of words, constructed, designed like an intricate musical score. It was the hardest thing I ever had to learn, and among the hardest to speak. You can't really go back and get a word in if you miss it because the construction is so tight. It takes a tremendous amount of concentration, and for that reason I put it at the top of the second act, so that I could prepare for it during intermission. I usually lie on the floor during intermission and breathe, or meditate, in preparation.

I went out to begin the second act. There are slides that announce the characters. When Cornel West's slide came up, a very vocal black woman in the audience yelled something out. I added a line to the show: "Don't rush me now." I had learned that from Reverend Weaver. "Don't let them rush the spirit."

Then it hit me. The audience was so wild because *they* were performing for the president too. They wanted him to know what they thought about these people, all of whom were saying racially charged things. This audience was the exact opposite of the audience who passively observes. This audience was proving itself to be a thoughtful citizenry. In its way.

The president's presence can convene a civic dialogue. In that way, I wish I could perform for the president all the time.

After the show, I was taken under the theater, through the museum, with its gory evidence of the assassination of Lincoln, and up the stairs to a holding area to meet the president. Just as I came up, I saw the first lady. She was leaning on a counter. She looked like a teenager who was waiting for her parents. When she saw me, she stood up and congratulated me.

After a while the door opened and the president burst in—with my mother on his arm. He had walked her up the aisle. There was a burst of energy when he came through. He was smiling, and wearing a blue shirt and a yellow tie.

Then my entire family arrived. I hadn't expected my sisters and brothers and their mates as well as my mother, so it was rather overwhelming. The president, the first lady, Al Gore, his son, and their entourage were all crowded around. We were bunched into a crowd, and several photographs were taken.

Finally the crowd began to dwindle. I stood at the door as people took off for the motorcade. I felt like I was saying good-bye at the end of a party at my own house. I was only a visitor at Ford's Theater. Yet theater has the possibility of providing a "house" in the course of two hours, and it was with that feeling that I saw them off.

The president and I had a few exchanges about his upcoming race initiative. He said slowly, "I . . . think the country is ready to do something about it." I was surprised that he wasn't more optimistic.

I turned to go. Someone from the theater said, "Don't go through that door!" Behind the door was the entire audience. They had been waiting for about half an hour—unable to move because the president was still in the theater. As I was taken another way, I could hear the explosion of people being released.

Afterward, the stage manager told me that a member of the SWAT team with a machine gun stood behind him in the small booth the entire time he called the show.

SPRING 1997
NEW YORK CITY

On Monday I was in New York. An article about the president's presence at my show came over my fax machine. I don't read reviews, and everyone who works with me knows that. Since it's unlikely that anyone would send me a review, I didn't expect the article to be a review. It wasn't, but there was a line in it that went something like this: "Her show, which was laced with profanity, brought a standing ovation at the end. The president laughed often." *Which was laced with profanity.*

I was absolutely amazed. This is a show about a tragedy in our country. It has forty-six Americans who testify, witness, expound on what happened to them in that tragedy. It represents a variety of cultures and social classes. Audiences laugh and cry. Sometimes people who are laughing will notice that the person to their left or right is crying at the same thing they found humorous. The language of these people, which is all verbatim, is in its way a gorgeous libretto of their American experience. To reduce it to "laced with profanity"? I was speechless.

1997
A FEW WEEKS LATER

The president was in New York. I had requested an interview. I was told it "might" happen. It was obvious I would be "on call." It's like being in a movie. You arrive in the morning and get ready for the scene. There's a chance that you won't get to the scene. Something could happen, so you're just held, possibly for nothing.

The rule was, the president would meet with me off the record.

He was at the Waldorf. Because I was working in New York at the time, I had taken an apartment on the West Side. I was working on the East Side, but I knew that there was no way I could get home to the West Side and change before meeting with the president. Traffic is impossible when he is in town. It was also clear that I was going to be "slipped in." This meant that I had to be very nearby when I got the go-ahead.

The logistical solution was that I got a hotel room right across the street from the Waldorf, and got dressed and even asked someone to help with my hair and makeup. This was really like being in a movie.

I waited, and at a specific time I called a special number. The man on the other end of the phone told me he would call back. I could look out the window at the Waldorf. The phone rang.

"I'll meet you on the Lexington Avenue side." He described what he looked like.

I went across the street immediately. The rendezvous was successful. I was taken up to the president's suite. I waited in another room, which had been turned into headquarters for the Secret Service. Everything was put to some sort of functional use. There were cables and wires every-where. The room itself was a mess. The "hotelness" of it was gone; it looked like a movie set or a combat headquarters.

I was called in to see the president. I met with him and with Sylvia Mathews, his deputy chief of staff. She sat quietly with a pen and pad. I was told that I could take nothing into the room.

The president spoke about his experiences with the press, because my play was going to be in part about the relationship of the press to the president. "Well, I'm only talking to you because I thought I perhaps I could be useful, by telling you what this is really like. I thought I could give you a feel for it."

The conversation was off the record. He talked for about an hour.

He walked me to the door.

"You were very lithe when you took your bow. Do you practice that a lot?" he asked.

"My bow?" I said. Did he actually mean my bow at the end of the show, as in "take a bow"?

"Yes, I was wondering if you practice that."

I didn't know how to answer that. "Uh, yes."

I said good-bye to the president and told him how grateful I was that he had seen the show and that he had met with me.

Do I practice my *bow*? I thought, as I stood at the elevator. What a *strange* remark. And then I realized that I did have to learn how to bow. Arthur Mitchell, the director of Dance Theatre of Harlem, taught me how to take a bow. It was a simple lesson.

"Watch me," Arthur Mitchell had said. "Bring everything together like this." He stood perfectly straight with his feet perfectly together, his body centered, and his torso tall.

"That's it," he said. "Bring everything together, because you're ending the evening, closing it down." Then he said, "Now, would you like a standing ovation?"

"Sure," I said.

"Then do this." He bent forward, and when he raised his torso, he lifted both of his arms out to the sides with his hands turned up. "You see," he said. "Try it."

I tried.

"That's right, you lift your hands up, you *instruct* them to stand," he said. "And they will."

I had an impulse to go back and tell the president how to take a bow. I couldn't have gotten back in. I also realized, Presidents don't really bow, they wave.

And there we have it. Presidents are not *performers*. Performers bow, and subjects bow. Performers bow because we understand that we are *subjects* of the audience. We do not, as performers, really *rule* the audience. It's a dance, but deep down we *have* to bow, because the audience demand that of us. They understand that, in some kind of odd way, we are speaking only with their permission. Presidents don't bow. They wave, and make victory signs. The presidency has so much to do with winning, and staying in the "win" position. I would imagine it's difficult to find the subject position. Of course, a president can be forced into a subject position by those on the other side who are very interested in turning him into a loser. So where does service happen?

Performers are not winning and losing. We are serving an idea. We are serving a feeling. We are bowing in recognition of those few special moments when we actually touch or feel humanity in its varied aspects. The audience, ideally, is a witness and a participant.

GEORGE STEPHANOPOULOS

FORMER AIDE TO PRESIDENT CLINTON

"Celebrity in Chief"

We're a celebrity culture
and the president is the celebrity in chief
and also there's this *weird* thing with the press
which was *not* true as much before
but this deathwatch has gone out of control
you know the idea that they have to be with him every moment
every second of every day
just in case something happens.
I think the only private time a president has
is when he's in the oval
and he walks from the oval
to either his private study or his private bathroom
that's it.
Once he's in the residence he can move between rooms
but there's still some servants around.
As far as officially, the only truly private time he has is
within that small

sweep
which is one
[he counts]
it's four rooms plus a terrace and one of those rooms is a
     bathroom.
He's sitting at a desk with one of the best views in Washington
certainly the best morning light I've ever seen in my life
but it's got glass this thick
that can't be touched
you've got a s——
two secretaries on the outside,
and two Secret Service people between them,
as you move across the hall in the oval
there's another room to where
there's a tiny little pantry and there's another Secret Service agent
     there
and then you get to my office—
And every door
is wired.
Like if I
moved in the back door
between my office and the oval—
the Secret Service would know because it was wired.
And
I've never thought of it this way before
either.
What happens? When you juxtapose incredible, immense, power
but the price—
I mean it's a different
um.
It's a different devil's choice
The price is
transparency.
Everything you do is known.
You can be the most powerful person in the world.
You're going to uh
have every privilege known to man.

Every whim! Is going to be catered to.
[he's chewing something]
The *deal* is
you can do whatever you want.
The price is that everybody is going to know *everything* you do!
It's beautiful!
And actually I've never thought of it before
but that's it!
A corollary to the rule
everything will be known—
but all that will be remembered in the short term is the bad.
They all feel that none of their good is acknowledged and that all of their
bad is exaggerated.
And,
and every one of them would do it again.
You have more power in
a second to help people
you could have never
thought of helping
than most people will have—
not most people—
than most
countries will have in twenty years.
The less noble things are—
I mean all that power
and you'll never be forgotten
at some level.
Not a bad gamble if you're in the position to accept it
if it was a locked deal.
[Pause]
I would be scared to death
To know there's no such thing as a private moment in my life . . .

CULTURE WARS AND
DOMESTIC BEATINGS

THE CULTURE WARS ARE NOT NEW. ANY OF US CAN GET CAUGHT IN the middle of them. If you are moving in the middle of the war zone, you might get hit. Be prepared.

CIRCA 1850
IN ABRAHAM LINCOLN'S TIME

I learned a lesson from Elizabeth Keckley, who was the dressmaker for Mary Todd Lincoln. She wrote an autobiography called *Behind the Scenes, or, Thirty Years a Slave and Four Years in the White House.* A large part of the book is about her taking care of Mrs. Lincoln after the death of Abraham Lincoln. Mrs. Lincoln was nearly penniless, so Mrs. Keckley accompanied her to New York to sell some of her dresses. There were those who felt that she took advantage of her closeness to Mrs. Lincoln in writing the book.

There was a takeoff, or burlesque, written about Mrs. Keckley's auto-biography. It was called "Behind the Seams: by a Nigger Woman Who Took in Work for Mrs. Lincoln and Mrs. Davis." The work did not list an author, and it was signed with an X, said to be the mark of Betsy Keckley. It was published in a newspaper.

I read both Mrs. Keckley's autobiography and the takeoff. I was amazed at the time spent on the takeoff. It was a vulgar translation, word for word, of the original. For example, Mrs. Keckley's book begins, "My name is Elizabeth Keckley, my life has been an eventful one. I was born a slave, was a child of slave parents. The twelve hundred dollars with which I purchased the freedom of myself and son, I consented to accept only as a loan."

And the burlesque begins, "My name is Betsey Kickly, and I am a most extraordinary nigger. As this is the case and as a large number of people who know me have often requested me to write my life for the benefit from a pecuniary point of view, as I am hard up, and the pension of eight dollars a month does not suffice to pay my board, I am going to try an experiment and see if I can't make more money by writing a book than by taking in sewing."

We have talk shows and late-night comedy shows to take the place of such newspaper burlesques but, from as far back as Jefferson's time, in respected papers, we find forms of these burlesques in the attitudes that journalists have toward their subjects.

It may be that public life simply cannot have civility. I noticed a strong similarity between the narratives of slave beatings and the narratives of political beatings. Compare the following account of a beating from Elizabeth Keckley's narrative, and the story of former governor of Texas Ann Richards, who endured a political beating.

It was Saturday evening, and while I was bending over the bed, watching the baby that I had just hushed into slumber, Mr. Bingham came to the door and asked me to go with him to his study. Wondering what he meant by his strange request, I followed him, and when we had entered the study he closed the door, and in his blunt way remarked: "Lizzie, I am going to flog you."

"Whip me, Mr. Bingham! What for?"

"No matter," he replied. "I am going to whip you, so take down your dress this instant."

Recollect, I was eighteen years of age, was a woman fully developed, and yet this man coolly bade me take down my dress. I drew myself up proudly, firmly and said, "No, Mr. Bingham, I shall not take down my dress before you. Moreover, you shall not whip me unless you prove the stronger."

He seized a rope, caught me roughly, tried to tie me. I resisted with all my strength, but he was the stronger of the two, and after a hard struggle succeeded in binding my hands and tearing my dress from my back. Then he picked up a rawhide and began to ply it freely over my shoulders. With steady hand and practised eye he would raise the instrument of torture, nerve himself for a blow, and with fearful force the rawhide descended upon the quivering flesh. It cut the skin, raised great welts, and the warm blood trickled down my back. Oh God! I can feel the torture now—the terrible, excruciating agony of those moments. I did not scream: I was too proud to let my tormentor know what I was suffering. On the Friday following the Saturday which I was so savagely beaten, Mr. Bingham again directed me to come to his study. On entering the room I found him prepared with a new rope and a new cowhide. I told him that I was ready to die, but that he could not conquer me. In struggling with him, I bit his finger severely, when he seized a heavy stick and beat me with it in a shameful manner. Again I went home sore and bleeding. The following Thursday Mr. Bingham again tried to conquer me, but in vain. We struggled, and he struck me many savage blows. As I stood bleeding before him, nearly exhausted with his efforts, he burst into tears, and declared that it would be a sin to beat me more.

JUNE 1997
RESTAURANT NORA
WASHINGTON, D.C.

I was having dinner with Ann Richards and one of her previous campaign organizers, Jane Hickie. The subject got around to her campaign for governor. Her opponents did all manner of things—they brought up the fact that she had been treated for alcoholism, and accused her of drug addiction. She was toughened by the time she met this opponent by her campaign for treasurer, during which she was accused of being mentally ill, and of beating her children. So she had learned how to fight back.

ANN RICHARDS: Well, I remember them telling me what I had to do. I remember that—the campaign saying, Okay, you've got to go in there and you've got to let these guys have it. In honesty, I think that they thought each other was the opponent. I don't think they thought I had a hoot in Hades' chance of winning, and as a consequence, when they discovered that, really, I was the one they had to beat, they were both kind of tacky. But the campaign told me I had to go out there and I had to let them have it. And I can't even remember what all—I can't remember what all I said. All I know is that I felt very very cool. I was very self-possessed. I was very cool. I was very cool. In fact, I can still feel the power of it. It was real—because I know that's what I know how to do. I know how to, I know how to walk out and communicate. I mean that's really what I do best. So going out to a press conference and cleaning somebody's clock is no challenge.

JANE HICKIE: There were people packed in that room and you couldn't move. It was a full-scale—you know they're talking about the wrong thing, and "what's important here is"—I mean, she took charge. She used the attack on her as leverage.

ANN RICHARDS: I changed the focus of the campaign.

JANE HICKIE: And I mean there were people hanging out. You couldn't get in the doors. You couldn't get in the room. We were in the campaign headquarters, and Ann walked out, and I mean there were—it was just like this, and nobody was breathing. And she hit it and she was on it, and she was in charge, and they hadn't beat her. She beat them. And it was—everybody knew it. I mean, it was just—the place blew up.

The dialogue of campaigning is the dialogue of beatings. It is perhaps naïve of us, in the general public, to believe that civic discourse can take place while a beating is going on. As it turns out, these beatings can go on after a candidate has won. If there is no room for us to talk while they are beating each other, when shall our discourse occur? We have to carve out other spaces. People say that we fight because we are at peace. We give lip service to the need to make use of peacetime to get further ahead in making domestic life more civil in all ways. The danger of trying to find a way to talk to each other in the atmosphere of culture wars is that, inevitably, the fight "they" are having takes all the attention. But their fight is half performance, half bluster, half an adrenaline rush. We end up as mere spectators. There's a price to our spectatorship too.

PAULETTE JENKINS

INMATE,

MARYLAND CORRECTIONAL INSTITUTE FOR WOMEN

"Mirror to Her Mouth"

This is like when you bein abused you know and you don't tell?
Then somebody tell?
Then somebody
tell.
[she laughs]
I think he's a damned good president
how he conducts his job is one thing
it's just like
someone can have on two hats.
In some homes you would never think
that father abused that child
because look how well
dressed the child is
look how
the home is and
know what I'm sayin?
He got a good job,
but
you never know.
And that's how it start
that's exactly how it start.
When he becomes jealous
and want to be with you all the time.
You know.
And want to know why you're not doing this.
And why the children are making so much noise.
And can you keep 'em quiet?

And it began to escalate.
And it escalated.
I began to learn how to cover it up.
Because I didn't want nobody to know that this was happening in
    my home.
Ya know
I wanted everyone to think that we were a normal family,
and I mean
we had all the materialistic things.
But that didn't make my children pain any less.
I ran out of excuses about how we got black eyes,
and busted lips and bruises.
Me and the kids.
I didn't have no more excuses.
But it didn't change the fact that it was a nightmare,
for my children
it was a nightmare.
And I failed them,
dramatically.
Because I allowed it to continue on and on and on.
And the night that she got killed—
and the intensity just grew and grew and grew.
Until one night,
we came home,
from getting drugs,
and he got angry with Myeshia,
and he started beating her,
and he just continued to beat her.
He had a belt he would use a belt.
Because he had this warped perverted thing that Myeshia
was
having sex with her little brother
or
they was fondling each other.
That would be his reason.
I'm just speaking of the particular night that she died.
And he beat her.

And he put her in the bathtub.
And I was in the bedroom.
But before all this happened—
four months before she died—
I thought I could really fix this man.
So I had a baby by him.
Insane?
Thinking that
if I give him his own kid
he'll leave mine alone.
But the night that Myeshia died,
I stayed in the room with the baby
and I heard him
just beating her
just beating her
like I said he had her in the bathtub
and every time he would hit her—
she would fall.
And she would hit her head on the tub.
I could hear it.
It happened continuously,
repeatedly.
[whispering]
And I dared not to move.
I didn't move.
I didn't even go see what was happening.
I just sat there and listened.
And then later
[she sucks her teeth]
he sat her in the hallway
and
told her just set there.
And she set there for bout
four to five hours.
And then he told her to get up,
[crying]
and when she got up she said she couldn't see.

[whispering, crying]
Her face was bruised.
And she had a black eye.
All around her head was just swollen.
Her head looked like it was two sizes of its own size.
I told him let her go to sleep, and he let her go to sleep.
[whispering]
The next morning she was dead.
He went in and checked on her for school.
And he got very excited.
And he said
"She won't breathe."
I knew immediately that she was dead.
Cause I went in—
I didn't even want to accept the fact that she was dead.
So I went and took a mirror to her mouth.
There
was no-thing, coming out of her mouth.
Nothing.
He said
"We cannot let nobody know about this,
so you got to help me."
And we got the baby
and we drove like out to
[hear her getting the slightest bit tired here]
I-95.
I was so petrified
and so numb
all I could look
was in the rearview mirror.
And he just laid her right on the shoulder of the highway.
My own chile.
I let that happen too.

"THAT'S NOT MY JOB"

Diana Walker, the photographer for *Time* magazine whom I had met on the '96 campaign trail, gave me a small dinner party at her house. I was seated between Art Buchwald and a correspondent from *Time*.

I struck up a conversation with the *Time* correspondent. I asked him if he liked the president. He said, "That's not my job." That was during the first course.

He said that liking the president wasn't the point. You don't like the man, in fact you try to stay as far away from the man as you can. You're trying to look at the man in the office and at the degree to which he lives up to the office. He was very expressive when he talked, moving his head a lot. He said that my questions were as discreet as my answers.

I suddenly saw the president and the presidency as a man and a shadow, the shadow being the office. What's odd about shadows is that they change according to where the sun is at any given time of the day. Ann Lewis had talked to me about the president as wearing a "cloak." The cloak is the presidency. So there's a difference between the president and the presidency.

I offered up that you don't just look at a movie star as who she or he is. You are always looking at the movie star against the backdrop of something called movie star–ness. I gave an example of a movie star. He didn't agree that my example was really a movie star and offered up his idea of a real movie star—Holly Hunter. People—including journalists—have very personal reactions, very nonobjective reactions to presidents, movie stars, and more. Objective as they claim to be, I found journalists to be among the most opinionated people I have met—more opinionated than academics.

The correspondent then said that Washington was a city of fear. I told him that John Lahr had once described L.A. as a city of envy. Fear and envy, each in a capital of the nation's discourse. Then another guest said from across the table that Washington is a city where you delight in other people's failures. The conversation held little optimism.

When we were eating dessert, the same woman asked me, "Do you like the president?"

Taking a deep breath, I said, "That's not my job."

I said, "I hate to use a four-letter word here, but I'm an actress. My job is to love the character, to love the president."

The actor's love, of course, is a kind of greed, a greed to be the other, to know the other by being the other. The journalist, it seems, knows the other, in part by being skeptical of the other. Neither way of knowing is necessarily a "nice" way. In both cases you are crossing a threshold, invading, occupying an area where, in reality, you don't belong. Caution, perhaps, is the best approach.

TALKING TO THE

PRESIDENT

FALL 1997
THE WHITE HOUSE
WASHINGTON, D.C.

I HAD BEEN TRYING TO GET AN ON-THE-RECORD INTERVIEW WITH THE president since 1995. This had entailed going to a variety of events where I had twenty-second interactions with him, getting him to my show *Twilight,* and having had an hour off-the-record conversation with him.

I was in rehearsal at the Arena Stage for the first workshop version of *House Arrest.* This was all pre–Monica Lewinsky.

The call came. This meant that everything else I was doing had to stop.

I was told that I should come to the press conference that Clinton was doing with the president of China. I was instructed to arrive about an hour before the conference began. When I arrived, no one was there except the photographers, who always arrive early to stake out their positions. I was taken to a seat near the side door. I was told that just before the president was finished with the press conference, I would be escorted to where he was, and, depending on a cue from Mike McCurry, if all systems were go, I could speak to the president for about five minutes, while he was in a kind of holding pattern. I was warned that this could all change, but that this was what we would aim for.

I sat on the side of the room during the press conference. The president seemed very calm throughout, and less expressive than usual. As the press conference was coming to an end, one of Mike McCurry's assistants beckoned to me from outside a door that led into the hallway of the

Old Executive Office Building. I gathered my tape-recording equipment and followed her. The president was just coming out. Mike McCurry met me. "We'll walk with him and see what's going to happen."

Everything was in motion, and it was not what I expected. I had imagined I would be in a small holding area for a few moments. This was moving. I had never been with the president when he was "moving." I knew what it was supposed to feel like from scenes I had been in in *The American President*. The blocking was the same, but there were lots more people, and real Secret Service up the ante in a way that anchors can't. It felt like I was on a kind of moving sidewalk—or a bit like when I was on-stage with the Alvin Ailey Dance Company. You have no choice but to move with them, it's amazing the first time you do it.

McCurry did a kind of a narrative as we walked along, sort of explaining to me what was happening. The way he talked was a striking counterpoint to the ambience of what was happening. His manner was very low-key, whereas the activities around me were extremely high-powered. The president was walking in front of a small crowd with the president of China. There were Secret Service behind him and all around him. It was like a small parade.

"Let's walk with the president," McCurry said at one point. So we moved just a little ahead, and I found myself standing right next to the president, with McCurry on my other side.

He said, "Mr. President, remember, we were talking about maybe you would talk with Anna for a few moments. You think that will be okay?"

"Sure," he said.

I was stunned at how this sounded. It was as if they were making this decision on the spur of the moment, when really, my ending up next to the president had taken several phone calls, security clearances, and four years' worth of other efforts. "Thanks a lot," I said. "I really appreciate it."

Although I wasn't acting, it had the feel of saying your lines onstage or in a movie when it's your first time. And I had spoken to the president on a few occasions now, but this time he was flanked by all his "motion." When you're acting with a big movie star, or in front of the camera for the first time—you are prepared, and you know your lines, but there's still something that feels very staged. The simplest line causes you tension.

The president was walking alongside the president of China. He did an introduction. "This is Anna Deavere Smith," he said to the president of China. "She is a great actress and a wise woman."

When I listen to the lines of this conversation on tape, my language sounds very "fake"—something that a director would make me redo. Yet I wasn't acting. I was simply being me in a very unusual experience, in fact, in a "bigger than life" experience. That's how some people would define acting. I actually think it's not enough to "just be you" in a bigger than life experience. In life and onstage, I think you have to rise to those occasions.

McCurry, somehow, very smoothly veered us away from the president, and we walked behind him as he continued to talk to the president of China. I now found myself walking between Madeleine Albright and Erskine Bowles.

"Anna, do you know Erskine?" McCurry said, as though we were all on a first-name basis.

I said how glad I was to meet him, and I smiled at Madeleine Albright.

McCurry continued to me, "I'm not sure exactly where you'll talk with him, but we'll just follow."

It was like being on a small ship. There was the sound of all the feet moving down the hallway of the Old Executive Office Building. I kept waiting for someone to call "cut."

We followed the president out of the building. He said a public goodbye to the president of China and went into the side door of the White House. The two presidents had a further about thirty-second conversation. And that was it. The president of China took off.

We went into the White House, which from that entrance in particular has no grandeur at all. The offices are sort of tacky. It would remind you of a side entrance to any suburban home—like entering a house through the den, or the most used part, a recreation room, for example.

McCurry said, "I think maybe you're going to do this in the Oval. I'm not sure."

We kept walking, and I found myself standing in the middle of the Oval Office. The president disappeared for a moment.

I had been in the Oval Office before, after one of the president's radio addresses. I had my picture taken with the president and the vice president. Having been in the movie *The American President* also took some of the once-in-a-lifetime feeling out of the event. The set design had been so accurate that I felt as though I had spent a lot of time in this room already. The scenes I shot in the Oval Office on a soundstage in Los Angeles are merged with my sitting with the president in the real Oval Office.

For a second, I flashed on a conversation I'd had with Nell Painter, a biographer of Sojourner Truth, in which she described Sojourner's visit with President Lincoln. She described the effort it took to get Sojourner Truth there, and pointed out that although she made it sound as if it were a wonderful meeting, in actuality Lincoln had kept her waiting for a long time, while he talked with some white male visitors, and addressed her as Auntie, which was a diminutive way of referring to black women. My interaction with Clinton was quite different from Sojourner Truth's interaction with Lincoln.

Clinton sat down, leaned over in his chair as if he were speaking to an old pal, and, sounding like a black woman really—a "girlfriend"—said, "How you doin', girl?"

One of the White House photographers snapped a couple of pictures. One of the aides said, "Mr. President, what do you think? About ten minutes?" He said yes, they shut the door and left.

It was just me, the president, and my tape recorder. I was later told that this was unusual. He is seldom left unstaffed, and they normally also do their own tape recording if he is being recorded.

Since I was to have only ten minutes, I jumped straight to questions I thought would get him to really speak. I began by asking him if he felt he was being treated like a common criminal. This was four months before the Monica Lewinsky story broke, but he had already been through the wringer.

He paused, and said thoughtfully, "I think George Washington said that. I don't know about that. No, I wouldn't say that."

He then took off on a jazzlike riff on how unfriendly his relationships with the press were. "I think that the political press has this image that the presidency is so all-powerful that none of the presumptions should apply, no presumption of innocence, no presumption that some techniques and things are off balance."

He is a very expressive man.

"I mean, it's really chilling when you think about what happened.

When Hillary's legal, uh, bills were found, Oh! It was all over the papers, right? She had to go talk to the grand jury. *First lady*, going to the grand jury . . . *big* pictures." He was sitting on the edge of his seat.

I had also met with George Bush, and with Jimmy Carter. Clinton was playing a whole different kind of music. Carter, sitting in his chair at the Carter Center, was very relaxed and comfortable for the entire interview. He was warm and gracious, but, although he was out of office, he seemed significantly careful, watching every word. Bush and I had met across the street from the White House in the summer of '97, on a sweltering day. It was so hot that nobody could move. Bush was upstairs in an elegant room with a table. He had taken his jacket off, loosened his tie. He drank Orange Crush soda on ice and ate two huge chocolate chip cookies, which had been made especially for him by the White House chef. He spoke very informally, with long, easy tones, and with a surprising irreverence for the press. He hadn't appreciated the way they tried to make him look as though he were without guts—and talked about how he'd just jumped out of an airplane. He made it sound easy, and had a sense of humor about some of the things that had happened. His sounds were those of "Oh it's all right, it'll be all right."

Bush gave what for me was a memorable warning when I said, "Some people say maybe we don't need a president."

"As long as we're fat, dumb, and happy, that may be right. Long as the economy is good, people say, 'Get the government out of my life, we don't need it.' Economy goes down, people get thrown out of work, that'll change. But as long as the economy is good and people are happy, you're not gonna have any great worrying about the White House."

He said all this as he easily broke off a chunk of chocolate chip cookie and took a swig of Orange Crush. He was perfectly happy to pass the time and do someone a favor. He had nothing to lose. Dana Carvey had imitated him already.

Nora and I and all the interns working on the project had thought of several questions to ask Clinton. His dossier was understandably pretty hefty. Yet I didn't have to ask very many questions. He held forth nonstop. "Today you have all the power in the world, and you can do everything but protect yourself. And the people you love."

People would come in to try to stop the meeting. "Uh, Mr. President, you're supposed to be speaking tonight, and I want to make sure everything's okay, you should rest your voice."

"I'm fine."

The door shut. Exit.

He spoke as though he had everything to lose, but they were trying to take it all from him anyway, so what the hell, let it rip. It was nearly absurd at this point. "It's like *Darkness at Noon,* Koestler's book, the Stalinist show trials. They decided what the truth was and told people to tell it."

Clinton's sounds were jagged, even sharp; sometimes he was barely getting his breath. There was an urgency—even though it was just he and I.

Someone abruptly opened the door, took a look, and left.

"There are elements in the press that believe that the only way that people who talk about politics matter is if the president's being weakened, shown up to be a bad guy. Somehow you have to prove yourself innocent, and if you can't it's your fault."

He laughed for a moment, and sat back. "But the country's done well. It seems for some of 'em, the better the country does the madder they get. The more they want—" He was laughing. The laugh had a squeak to it, and the sounds he made would have concerned a good vocal coach. He was getting very hoarse. I was surprised to hear the door open exactly at that moment, the moment he was laughing.

This time a slender white woman with a southern accent walked in. "You really ought to rest your voice. It's really, I'm sorry," she said, with a very concerned look on her face.

The president did not turn around to look at her. He merely said, "Okay. Go 'head. I'll be right there."

She held her ground. "But you're really straining it, and Mike had said five minutes and I've let it go about ten now."

The president didn't even look in the direction of the door. He waved her away. "Okay. Bye."

She left. The door shut.

He was on a roll. He had a wider range of expression than most of the people I had interviewed.

When I was in rehearsal, preparing to perform some of the people I had interviewed, my vocal coach listened to the tapes of interviews. She was struck, as I was, that the incarcerated women were oddly freer vocally than the press people I had interviewed, and the people who worked in the White House. Whereas the voices of the Washington insiders tended to be constrained in one place or another, the prisoners had full range, and especially full use of the lower parts of their bodies. Perhaps the inner workings of the voice are a rare place to find freedom when you are bound. African Americans have explored that area in song and in oratory during times of restraint.

As I watched the president I marveled at how uninhibited he was in the ironically small space he had. We're told that the only space he has is the Oval Office and a few rooms surrounding it. During the interview he sat in his yellow chair, but he moved forward, he moved back, he moved to the side, he gestured, he came all the way to the tip of the chair, and then sat all the way back. Only very expressive people do this. How could this be? Wouldn't the most observed person be the most inhibited?

People say that Clinton performs, that he is very aware of the picture he is making. In this case, that did not seem to be so. He was being led by his passion. He was telling me about what happened to Mrs. Clinton when, during Whitewater, they found her legal bills. Very exasperated, he said, "We said, 'We're glad they turned up because they support her story.'" He moved forward in his chair, gesturing expansively. "*Why would we cover up records that support her story?* That's what we said, that was down in . . . paragraph ten here."

Then he talked about how a Republican law firm had spent $4 million looking into all the documents of the savings and loan investigation. "You know what it said? No basis for criminal action! No basis for a civil suit! The records—support—Hillary's account!" He stopped short, as if he barely had the breath to finish. Then he leaned forward, whispering intensely. "Did all those people who [here he raised his volume] *blared* the record discovery, who *blared* the grand jury testimony bother—to—tell—the—American—people—that—that's—what—this—report—done—by—a—Republican—law firm, after they spent almost four—million—dollars, said?"

And then he bounced forward further, like Ali out of the rope-a-dope. "*No!*"

And he made a very raspy sound. "Little bitty notice made!"

Little bitty notice made? When people start talking like that is when I normally say in an interview, "Now you're talking." By *now* you're talking—I mean, now you are past language as information. I don't need information, I only need you to come out of the confines of presentable sentence structure, to bust right out of grammar to show me who you are.

It was jazz. Clinton was in a class by himself. Yet, I wondered why he was so aggravated. I wondered why his voice was so raspy, beyond allergies, beyond overuse.

Whatever it was, I'm not a judge. I'm not a jury. I'm not the IRS. I'm not the press. I'm not a special prosecutor. I don't think any of those perspectives would get me any closer to the heart of America or its soul. What I'm looking for is not what is right or wrong, I'm looking for what is right *and* wrong, and more than the sum of both.

I wasn't there to indict the man. I wasn't there to expose him. I was there to listen to him, and to try to get him to talk to me with "litty bitty notice made." My mind catapulted back quickly to that linguist who had given me the three questions at the beginning of my work on language.

The president was answering, without my asking him, one of the three questions. He was speaking as if he were answering "Have you ever been accused of something that you did not do?" Sometimes we find ourselves in a position where we speak as though we are always answering one of those three questions, as if one of those three questions is the very foundation of who we are.

"I think the thing is totally—out of . . . whack!" he said and sat back on "whack!"

Then a pause, and then out again. "I mean it's really *chilling* when you think about what happened! I was stupid enough to believe 'em when they said if we were honest, and forthright, it would clear the air!"

I had to do a very intense kind of listening to absorb it all. My tape recorder would never absorb this. Technology makes flat renderings, and it requires that we deliver a flat performance. You don't want to be too big for television. Television diminishes the humanness of our presidents, of our actors—of all our public figures, who by nature are *bigger* than life. Television, by its nature, likes people who are *smaller* than life. It's a little screen. It is intimate. Just you and me in your living room. It would be healthier to create technology that allows us to be as big, as heroic as we are.

After about thirty-five minutes, the door opened for the last time. Rahm Emmanuel walked right into the center of the room, around and in front of the president, and said, "I'm gonna do one thing. He's got to do a toast tonight. And I don't want im ta lose his voice."

I said thank you, shook hands with the president, and left.

GOT BACK TO REHEARSAL. SOME OF THE ACTORS OF COURSE WERE dying to know. "How was it?"

"It was fine," was all I said.

I couldn't have been back in the rehearsal hall for more than fifteen minutes when an intern came over to me and said, with alarm in her eyes, "It's the White House!"

I went to the phone. It was Mike McCurry. "What did he *say* in there?" he asked.

I gave a general summation.

"He was worried that he might have gone too far."

I tried to allay Mike's fears.

As I hung up the phone, I thought to myself, There is no going too far, if all you're listening for is rhythm and music. In fact, I wish more people would go further.

BILL NELSON

LEGAL SCHOLAR
NEW YORK UNIVERSITY SCHOOL OF LAW

"These People Rich and Those People Poor"

They [the press]
are enormously valuable, effective uh and I think important in
    bringing to light certain key scandals
such as Watergate,
I mean uh
the idea that we have to fear the press more than we have to fear
    government is absurd.

I think we have to fear the government immensely and uh
I think the uh, the uh, the opportunities and incentives for corruption
    in government are
huge, and the opportunities
and incentives for corruption on the part of the press are relatively
    small.
Uh the
uh uh
I think people who want to maintain private lives do not have much
    difficulty
maintaining private lives
and I think the press is indeed
I've never felt
I
I've never felt the press
of reporters upon me.
I'm sort of constantly battling the handful of real graduate students
    around this place who take Foucault seriously.
I understand that there are a lot of mechanisms creating culture
and it's important what those mechanisms creating culture are.
But the ability of government to come in and take your money
and to do it through the withholding tax
and then the ability of government to decide how to spend that
    money
and then it's my understanding that anyone who has ever made big
    money in the United States has done it as a result of receiving
    government subsidies in one form or another.
I'm,
there are exceptions
but I mean
the decision of government to let the money go this way rather than
    that
has an extraordinary tendency to make these people rich
and those people poor.
They certainly create the mind-set
uh
but they don't interfere with people's lives

the way that government does.
Uh the
I mean one has the uh
you know
occasional things come to mind
like there was this gay magazine outing people a while ago.
That seems to me
uh
very intrusive,
but I suspect the uh
the New York City Police Department outed a lot more gay people
    than that magazine
ever did.
I think the move away from fearing government
the move away from appreciating how much harm government can
    do
and how much good government can do
uh
has diverted people's attention from politics and from elections and
    has produced a lot of
the worst elections that we you know
uh uh
has produced
and God knows what it'll produce in the year 2000.

THE DEATH DRIVE:

IT'S THE MAD HATTER'S

TEA PARTY AND

TOM DeLAY IS POURING

WINTER, SPRING 1998
WASHINGTON, NEW YORK, LOS ANGELES,
SAN FRANCISCO, PALO ALTO

THERE WAS A TUMBLE OF TALK. I WAS REVISING MY PLAY *HOUSE ARREST.*
It had had a "work in progress" performance in Washington. The idea
was, I would revise it for a second performance scheduled for spring '98 in
Los Angeles. I was on a plane from New York to San Francisco. The beginning of the story of Monica Lewinsky was in *The New York Times.*

Rather than going right to my computer when I got home, as
planned, I went right to my tape recorder and plugged it into my telephone. I began immediately doing interviews over the phone. It was like
starting all over again. Yet at that point no one was sure how far this
would go, or not go. It went, as you know, very far. Too far.

SPRING 1998

Was Clinton lying? The press could not deal with it. I'm not saying they
should have. They seemed significantly more distressed about it than the
rest of the nation.

In the midst of this I began to wonder when we, as human beings, begin to learn about truths and lies. I called my sister, whose little girl was
two at the time.

"She does know what it means to tell the truth."

"Does she know what a lie is?"

"I don't think she understands fully what a lie is. She makes up stories. She doesn't tell the full truth about some things. For instance she might hide her shoes somewhere and when I ask her where they are she says she doesn't know and will say that her daddy hid them or she'll blame things on Jessica you know the cat."

SUMMER 1998

Monica Lewinsky's semen-stained blue dress was found and displayed to the world. The DNA labs had gotten hold of it and showed that the president had not told the truth. I did another rewrite. The day we performed that rewrite turned out to be the day that Monica Lewinsky went before the grand jury for the first time.

Then, on August 17, 1998, Clinton confessed to the nation. I was on Martha's Vineyard at the time and soon saw the president at a party. He looked, as they say, "terrible." Yet I marveled at how he and the first lady had the stamina to show up in public at all. Every conversation had such an enormous subtext. The president caught my eye and said, "Let's go listen to the music." It meant nothing, but carried the weight of his reality. The first lady and I talked about the lack of women of color on the faculty at Stanford, where Chelsea was at school. Anything she talked about would seem to be an avoidance of the circumstances. But did any of us think that she or the president would talk about the real circumstances? Of course not.

The next morning I went to the president's radio address held in a school library. A young woman stood in front of a microphone, like a human clock, saying steadily, "The president's radio address will begin in exactly ten minutes from your mark. Mark. The president's radio address will begin in exactly nine minutes from your mark. Mark." I thought I was in a shooting gallery, or on an archery field—somewhere where there was a target. The president appeared, did the radio address, and had his picture taken with everyone who wanted a photo. We all had to fill out index cards with our addresses. The president looked tired, many of us said knowingly. But what did we know, other than the obvious.

I wrote another draft in September. I was waiting for FedEx to come pick it up, and television was broadcasting nonstop coverage on Congress's vote on whether or not to release the Starr Report. The draft went via FedEx. I took a flight to New York the next day. Everybody on the plane had *The New York Times* wide open reading the excerpts. Never had I seen such a flood of open newspapers on a plane trip.

This was a very difficult time to do theater, which likes to have nailed down, finished stories. The theater is not designed, just on the level of logistics, to keep up with real life. Perhaps theater is meant to be a more leisurely assessment of life as it goes by. I have been trying to create theater that reflects my time, as I live it. The story of the president was a marathon.

Even my classroom at Stanford held surprises.

FALL 1998
STANFORD UNIVERSITY, PALO ALTO, CALIFORNIA

It was the first day of class. I asked my students to do an exercise in which they portrayed one another's dreams. One dream was very strange. I asked the student for an explanation. She explained that the dream was about Chris Rock accusing her father of all kinds of things on the radio. She went on to say that Chris Rock in reality had accused her father of things on the radio. There was whispering in the class. "Who's her father?"

As I left the classroom I saw two grown men dressed in slacks and golf shirts just outside the door. The department administrator was there too, with revised class lists.

I took the lists and said, "Starr? Is . . ."

"I should have told you," he said.

Yes, he should have. Caroline Starr, Kenneth Starr's daughter, was in my class. Chelsea Clinton and Caroline Starr were at Stanford. Caroline stayed in the class for the semester. And the federal agents stood outside all semester.

To teach acting with something as dramatic as the Starr Report permeating our culture was an interesting predicament. I did not discuss the report or my work in class because of who was in my class. Caroline volunteered to keep attendance and a record of who was late for class when no one else would. She was also very well prepared all of the time. And although she was a freshman in a class of mostly upperclassmen, to some extent she "ran" the room. Celebrity power. No one ever contested her views or opinions. The class was strikingly apolitical.

The other class I taught was reading the writings of Konstantin Stanislavsky, the "father" of the acting "method." He was the main force behind what we know acting to be today. He brought naturalism to acting technique. One of my students came to office hours flushed in the face.

"I can't believe this book!" she said, speaking of Stanislavsky's text *An Actor Prepares,* which was written in Russia in the nineteenth century. "I am a student of Russian history, and this book is written as if he has no idea what is going on in the world around him!"

I understood his predicament. Sometimes it is impossible to get art to catch up with life. Then again, some of us don't try to get it to catch up. I taught simple, basic acting with no reference to the odd theater of our time. But then again, acting is not about truth and lies in the ordinary sense of truth and lies. Acting is not reality, but sometimes it is more about reality than reality.

FALL 1998
MY APARTMENT
SAN FRANCISCO

Suddenly history was no more stable than the present. A retired scientist named Eugene Foster did DNA testing and came up with further evidence that it was most likely the case that Thomas Jefferson was the father of Sally Hemings's children.

The people at Monticello were giddy with talk. The black descendants of Sally Hemings and Thomas Jefferson were on *The Oprah Winfrey Show.* There was a flurry of talk. The scientist, of course, could not get some of the finer points across.

"I have emphasized strongly, and in a loud voice, in many statements to the press that we would not be able to prove anything either positively or negatively with a hundred percent certainty."

I asked him what he thought the public believed.

"I think the general public has come to believe that we proved the relationship. We absolutely cannot say that!"

He was stuck on the idea of probability. Which is fundamental to science, but nobody cared about that. "They want to know, well, is it or isn't it?"

The press and everybody else, including Monticello, was off and running. The debate about Sally Hemings and Thomas Jefferson had been a part of the play. Now it looked as though there was no debate.

I visited the DNA lab at Stanford, which does some of the best work in the world on the human genome project. For all the seriousness of the work, I found the place to be refreshingly lighthearted, perhaps because it's all about evidence. As I entered, I remarked, "This place smells like egg salad."

"That's Ralph's hair," the postdoc who was my guide said, alluding to his wiry colleague.

They were in the process of "spinning" DNA. Literally.

My guide took me to a blackboard and showed me a complicated equation of X and Y chromosomes that displayed the relationship between Jefferson's DNA and that of his presumed sons.

After an intense hour in the lab, I thought back on the equation and said, "Now, wait a minute. All of this information is about Sally Hemings's *sons,* is that right?"

"Right."

"So, if she had had only daughters, we wouldn't be here, is that right?"

"Right."

Even in science—that which is thought to be real truth, real fact—the patriarchy reigned again.

Knowledge itself is so dependent on human achievement. Inherent in knowledge is ignorance. What, then, are "facts"? Temporary truths?

I was reminded of something David Broder had said at breakfast during my first year in Washington. "Instead of the *New York Times* thing about all the news that's fit to print, we would say to the people on the front page every day, 'This is a partial, hasty, compressed, necessarily distorted version of some of the news yesterday. We'll be back tomorrow and try to improve on the quality of the information we're giving you.' Because that's the truth."

The Zuni Café sits on a sunny corner on Market Street in San Francisco. It has gourmet food, often organically grown, always correctly served. I'm told the shoestring potatoes are terrific. There's an oyster bar. I know the owner, and there are a couple of pocketed tables that are perfect for tape-recorded interviews. I was interviewing Judith Butler, scholar of rhetoric.

"This was the second thing that interested me about the transcript. Is the sexual ambivalence. Why he could pursue pleasure to a certain degree and then he couldn't really uh let her—"

I chimed in. "But we weren't actually there ourselves. So this is according to Monica Lewinsky. According to *her.*"

I regretted saying that. I couldn't stop myself from thinking of things as though I were going to "play" Clinton. In which case I would have to try to see things in his best interest.

In the course of the past four years, I had interviewed Butler about eight times. She was always, for all her black-leather-jacketed, sometimes tough exterior, very gracious.

"Well, according to *her.* That's right," she conceded. "He pursued it to a certain degree. He maybe once or twice allowed her to bring him to a climax, but otherwise he didn't allow that to happen. We assumed he either gave himself that satisfaction or went without it. I do think there was a certain moral moment. 'I can't go that far.' 'I'll get addicted to you.' 'I won't be able to stop . . .' " Her voice was reaching a singsong.

We had known about Monica Lewinsky for a full year. At Christmastime Clinton had bombed Iraq. I was in San Francisco, holed up in its rainy season, working on the seventh or eighth draft of *House Arrest.* Butler continued:

". . . And I gather it's part of southern white baptism that a whole lot of those young boys grew up thinking you can do a whole lot of things with a girl but it's not sex until you've actually had intercourse. And of course I have a problem with that because it means no gay sex is ever sex. I mean that's so ridiculous."

To me there was nothing ridiculous about any single inch of this saga. Nor was it a farce, or a burlesque, or any of the many things that some of the smartest people I knew were calling it. To me, the whole thing felt like a funeral.

DECEMBER 1998
THE CONGRESSIONAL CHRISTMAS BALL
THE WHITE HOUSE

Amo and Priscilla had invited me to the Congressional Christmas Ball at the White House again this year. I have now two or three sets of pictures of going to that ball—pictures of me with Clinton and the Houghtons (two different Christmases), pictures of me and Priscilla in front of the White House Christmas tree, pictures of all of us dressed in our black-tie finest on P Street lining up to go. I have a veritable gallery of photos of myself with the president because somehow the president's presence is connected to a camera the way a car key is connected to a car. I also have a few wonderful photographs of the president "behind the scenes," courtesy of Diana Walker at *Time*, who manages, miraculously, to capture one of the most photographed men in the world "candidly." This year was an entirely different matter. Christmas in the White House on the eve of a possible impeachment.

We gathered in the living room on P Street with the Houghtons' other houseguests, then Senator Michael Castle of Delaware and his wife. Spirits were low.

Amo and the senator struggled with what they were going to do. They didn't know, they said, how they were going to vote. Senator Castle was most likely going to vote for impeachment. His constituency wouldn't have it otherwise.

"This is going to be some party," Amo said in his generously volumed voice.

"A lot of people aren't even coming," Senator Castle said.

"I think it's just *terrible*," Priscilla exclaimed.

Both Amo and the senator were in cummerbunds and suspenders, not yet having donned their tuxedo jackets. Amo was holding a folded piece of paper in both his hands. It was an op-ed. The rest of us were holding drinks—varying from Perrier to Scotch.

"Amo. Read your op-ed for Anna," Priscilla instructed.

"Well . . ."

"It's *wonderful*."

"Well Idunnoaboutall *that*."

"*Amo*," she insisted. "*Amo* has written the most wonderful piece for the *Times,* and he's *got* to send it."

"Is there a problem?" I asked.

"*Well,* I dunno," Amo continued.

"You *have* to," said Priscilla with urgency, making quick eye contact with each of us.

The senator seemed to understand Amo's predicament, and so did his wife. It was Priscilla who was showing that she was from a long line of Bostonian abolitionists, and was pulling out all the stops to insist that Amo stand up for what, at least in her mind, was right. She was possibly the most liberal of the bunch.

Finally, Amo read his op-ed aloud to us. He was asking his colleagues to think of Christmas as the spirit of forgiveness, and to avoid impeachment. That doesn't sound outrageously progressive, but it was considered so among Republicans who felt that "forgiveness" was out of the question. The stakes were high for Amo, a Republican, given the fact that this vote was expected to be a completely partisan affair.

Throughout the evening, Priscilla would enumerate the reasons why he needed to send the piece to the *Times*.

"Time tago," Amo called out.

The men rose and put on their jackets. Amo stuffed his op-ed in his breast pocket.

Amo and Priscilla are not ostentatious. Amo had a driver who drove a simple American economy car. We piled in. When we got to the White House, we left David, who had driven us, smoking his pipe in the little bit of snowfall that there was. As we approached the walk to the White House, we met an assemblage of young women and men with notebooks to check our names.

"Anna Deavere Smith," I said, for the umpteenth time upon reaching the White House.

"Spell that?"

"D-e-a-v-e-r-e. Sometimes they leave the *a* out," I said, by rote now. "You might want to check under Smith."

"I'm sorry, ma'am . . . I don't . . ."

"It's Anna Deavere Smith," Amo chimed in.

"Oh, here it is under Smith. Okay, that's easy. Welcome to the White House."

This was almost like doing your combination lock at the gym. I would imagine that, even if you entered the White House with the president himself, you'd be checked for clearance. As we came to the door we were greeted by Marines in full-dress uniforms.

FEBRUARY 1999
THE ZUNI CAFÉ (continued)

Judith Butler is more agitated than I've ever seen her. These are not the vocal tones of someone who finds a bit of humor here and there, who left philosophy for rhetoric because she was too expressive for her philosophy colleagues. This is not the Judith Butler who looked at me with pity when I said I believed in an "authentic voice." There is absolutely not a grain of nonchalance in her voice. She was on a verbal mission.

"He produces a certain mental story for himself where he's not quite acting, not quite fucking, he's not quite taking his pleasure. Cuts himself short, undermines his own constituency."

A waiter, prepared to perform, stands at the table with his palms together at his torso as if he were going to sing an aria. He stands with yet another version of our society's "studied nonchalance." The waiter's "studied nonchalance."

The waiters at Zuni are noticeably pulled up from the abdomen, pulled up from the torso. It's a nice line to look at. Our waiter recites the specials: ". . . and that's topped off with beet juice and truffle oil. What kind of water may I bring you?"

I gesture to Butler. She shrugs.

"Will you be drinking wine?" he asks.

I extend my hand to Butler, who shakes her head no. I shake my head no to the waiter; he sweeps up the wineglasses and leaves.

She launches again:

"He's devastated welfare! He's reneged on gays in the military! He's done a lot of horrible things. But I heard people who I've never heard before say, 'I've never been able to support what they've been doing in the last fifteen years, but this time I'm going to write to my congressman and say, "Don't impeach him," ' so he's got massive leftist support."

I sit up totally straight, to give myself plenty of room to absorb the punch line, which I know is coming any second. "At the very moment in which he has that, for the first time, the first time we've seen that in this country for fifteen years, twenty years, he starts bombing Iraq!"

I strike the table with my hand. "Now you're talking," I mumble. My utterance is not meant to applaud her *opinion* (which is what happens on a talk show). I applaud her linguistic achievement.

Usually when Butler gets an entire thought out—and they are long but clear thoughts—she giggles at her own linguistic achievement. This time she did not giggle.

DECEMBER 1998
THE WHITE HOUSE CONGRESSMAN'S CHRISTMAS BALL
(continued)

Normally, Priscilla, who is a great enthusiast, would say, as we entered the White House, "Doesn't the White House look *wonderful?*" This time she said, "There don't seem to be as many decorations. Amo, I was just saying to Anna, there seem to be less decorations."

"There's Barney Frank!" Amo said.

Amo scurried us over to Barney Frank and introduced me.

As I looked around the hallway of the White House, I was filled with a sudden anxiety. First of all, there's something about the place that makes it feel like a part of the National Park Service, or a bit like a museum, but not a very nice museum. Some of the furnishings seem almost shabby. There's a certain coldness to the place, and under the circumstances, it seemed particularly cold. I was looking at the portraits of presidents who had come before Clinton. I empathized immediately with what it would feel like to fail, big. To be dismantled from that powerful assembly and, in fact, to have never really fit in. Total, flat-out failure. What would it be like to wake up the morning after? It would be like having a leg amputated.

As before, we stood in a line of people to meet Clinton. In the few years I had been on the project, I had stood in those lines many times. They were always created with velvet ropes. The president meets his guests all in the activity of taking photographs. Young women staffers in pearls and Papagallos and carrying white file cards would come along to get our names and addresses, so that copies of the pictures taken with the president would reach our homes.

I never understood what would cause people, nearly all of whom were winners in a big way, to stand on line like this. Most of them had "made it" in business, politics, art, or intellectual life. Many of them are the kinds of people who would steal a cab right from under your nose in New York, and who metaphorically have gone to the head of most lines in their lives. This was easy to tell, just by their posture, the confidence they had. Many of the "members"—congressmen—brought their daughters to these balls rather than their wives. The daughters were girls of about thirteen or fourteen, in braces and dressed, no doubt, in their first evening gowns, usually red or teal blue velvet. When you reached the president, you would exchange a few words. This was meant to be a conversation, and, whether it was truly a conversation or not, it would undoubtedly be quoted—exactly what the president said, and how Mrs. Clinton looked, and what she said.

This year the line was rife with another kind of anticipation.

A woman at a free-standing mike with cards in her hand, announces: "Congressman Amory and Mrs. Priscilla Houghton." "Anna Deavere Smith."

We step up to the president and Mrs. Clinton.

I couldn't think of anyplace I would less rather be than in his shoes at that moment. I usually have a very clear memory of every time I have interacted with the president. He didn't seem to be present this time, and it was almost as if he were not there. Mrs. Clinton was more alive. He's a dyin' man, I thought, echoing an interview I had done with a member of FDR's press corps, who told me about Roosevelt's last days.

As we left, one among us whispered, "He looked awful, don't you think?"

And then the expected: "Hillary looked great."

One among us disagreed: "I could see the strain."

And another: "Looks like he's put on weight."

I remembered a cancer surgeon telling me, "When you tell people they've got cancer, the first thing they want to know is, 'Will I lose my hair?' And here they are—dying." We are a society obsessed with looks to the point of absurdity.

Senator Castle remarked that it was "a shame to bring all these people here to eat your food and drink your booze and tomorrow they're gonna stab you in the back." We could hear the music of one of the many bands playing that night and moved upstairs to the party.

FEBRUARY 1999
THE ZUNI CAFÉ (continued)

"You know the French call orgasm *le petit mort*," Butler was saying.

"The little death?"

"The little death. And I think the idea is that orgasmic pleasure can be a kind of self-loss. It can, it can be a moment in which you lose yourself, when you no longer have a sense of who you are and you lose your sense of individuality and you can have a sense of losing yourself and it can be quite terrifying in the sense that it can threaten you with a sense of obliteration. I mean, Freud developed the death drive . . ."

DECEMBER 1998
THE WHITE HOUSE CONGRESSMAN'S CHRISTMAS BALL
(continued)

We had now gone upstairs.

There was a huge table with food—never enough, however. People stood in line to get a plate and wait for food. If there was food, there were no plates. I did think that given that this was the "home" of the most powerful man in the world, the food part could feel a little less like cattle grazing.

"I'm just *starving*," said Priscilla. "Aren't *you*? Amo could care less about food! We'll have to fend for ourselves."

Amo had taken someone by the elbow and was obviously telling a joke. I saw him give that person a punch in the arm and burst into peals of laughter. I marveled at how he could do that, with what he had on his mind.

"I always tease Amo," Priscilla once said to me. "I think he's had that tuxedo for thirty years. They don't even make them like that anymore!"

"How many women can say that their husbands can still *fit* in a suit that's thirty years old?" I asked.

"Well, that's true," she conceded.

Amo's father had been, among other things, the ambassador to France, and his mother apparently could manage to know everyone at a party by the end of the night. She had passed on her charm and gregarious spirit to Amo, who was moving around the room in a way that was certainly "working" the party, but it didn't look like work. He was used to holding up his end of a conversation and doing a little soft shoe with it. It was like watching Fred Astaire, watching him move around that huge room.

Once when we were driving home from another one of those parties, he had quietly said, "When I was a kid . . . we—had—to—wear—a suit and tie, ta dinner every night."

FEBRUARY 1999
SAN FRANCISCO
ON THE PHONE AT MY STONE-TOP DESK

I was talking to Patricia Williams, who is a legal scholar. She also writes for *The Nation* magazine. She has a little boy named Peter, who was seven at the time. She told me about the time that a friend of his was over, and suddenly one of them called out, "Let's go play Monica and Bill." With that they whizzed by Patricia and her mother, who was visiting. They went into Peter's bedroom and slammed the door.

Patricia was stunned and horrified. Her mind immediately went many directions about what would or would not be good parenting under the circumstances. She didn't know what to do.

Her mother rose without a word and went to the door. She knocked. "Boys, boys? What's going on?"

Then they heard the boys making the sounds of war: "Kerblash, kerboom!" It turned out, Monica and Bill was a game of "bombing the Monica."

They had conflated various parts of the news into one thought. They had heard talk of Monica and Bill, and they had heard language about bombing. The Monica to them was a ship of some sort, or an area of land. Another riff on Freud's "death drive," from a seven-year-old.

FEBRUARY 1999
THE ZUNI CAFÉ (continued)

Butler is eating salad. Her face is full of expression as we proceed. Her eyes seem to be moving to read her own thought as the thought comes out of her mouth.

"Actually, Freud developed the notion of the death drive when he started asking why people repeat some of the same patterns in life. And at first he thought, oh, they repeat them because they're just trying to do them differently? Right?"

"Okay."

"So they keep getting involved with the same kind of people or they keep producing the same kind of problems on the job because they are looking for satisfaction they can't quite have."

"Okay."

"And finally he decided, well, there are certain kinds of compulsive repetition that don't seem to be about finding satisfaction at all, they seem to be about repeating traumatic events where there, there's no possibility of achieving satisfaction."

"I understand."

"And that's where he decided that there were certain people actually in the grips of something much more self-destructive, and he decided that, in addition to libido or sexuality as a primary desire of humans, there's also the death drive."

"That's a dreary thought, to say the least."

"And they can work together. One has to ask about Clinton. I don't think that Clinton is the only one with the death drive. I think his colleagues certainly revealed the depth of their own death drives."

I told Judith about Patricia Williams's son "bombing the Monica." "My God!" she exclaimed, with a mouth full of salad. "Oh, my God! There you go, there you go! You don't even need to read Freud." The "death drive," is seems, is pretty basic.

Amo was chatting away. Priscilla was eating a "finger food" dessert. I perused the room. I stopped at the Clinton staff who were camped out on one side. No matter how dressed up they were, they always looked like they were working.

In fact, everyone at that party was working. It didn't matter what they had on, the fact of their work, their politicking work, was ingrained in every vessel. They could have been wearing Chanel, Armani, it didn't matter, the work seeped through.

I wandered over to the periphery, where members of Clinton's staff, each year, were stationed. I approached Sidney Blumenthal. "How are things?"

"Keep your eyes open for the next few days," he said. "It's going to get worse. Stop by." I never did. Maybe the whole thing was just too deadly.

I moved on to Ann Lewis. "How are things?"

Looking straight ahead at the party, with a huge smile on her face, she said, "It's Alice in Wonderland. It's the Mad Hatter's tea party, and Tom DeLay is pouring."

I wandered off and connected up with Amo. "Let's go hear the jazz band," he said, taking me by the arm. We went to where the music was, and found it a near-empty room.

"Look!" Amo pointed in the direction of the band. "Strom Thurmond is dancing!"

We gave up, finally, on the idea of a traditional play and decided in fact to leave room for the expression of a possible theater of our time. In the end, when *House Arrest* was produced in 1999, we played one act as in a play and left the second act completely open for audience discussion of what was happening in our country. According to a *Los Angeles Times* critic, the audience is said to have been more engaged than it had been for

a long time at that theater. At least it was a more truthful way to engage.
If engagement is the goal. And I believe it is.

MAGGIE WILLIAMS

FORMER CHIEF OF STAFF TO THE FIRST LADY

"Lie Detector Test"

I don't know if you've ever taken one.
Well
you know
it's like going to the electric chair.
[she laughs]
I mean
they strap you
in
and put things all over you
little wires that are connected to
your arms
like a blood pressure thing
and uh
you sit there and uh
I mean I kept thinking you know the whole time
when I was taking the lie detector test—I thought this was it
then they wanted me to take one that was given I guess by the FBI,
I don't know, Justice, I'm totally mixed up on this—
and you sit in a chair and you think—
Now what did I do in my life to get to the place
where I'm taking a lie detector test?
This is also the first time I was
ever fingerprinted
when I went to the FBI Building
uh
ya know

I just
I just
ya know you just feel like a common criminal
(she laughs)
is what you feel like
is like a common criminal.
But the uh
the test itself was horrible
and I thought once I had taken it
Well there
people will have to see
they'll have to see that
I'm telling the truth
and then of course by the time I had taken the second one and
    passed it
I said, Well you know this is you know a hands-down situation.
I actually do think it was at the lie—
the two detector tests
where you know nothing changed according to the
questioning and the treatment
in fact it got harsher.
What they care about is making a kind of a political point
and then they really didn't care about me
I was just in the way.
I mean I switched it from being so intent
on trying to remember things
and get ready
for these things
to just reading the Bible
because it was clear that they didn't care about anything that I had
    to say.
[I ask: "Did you think I was coming to Washington to fight?]
Oh no.
Oh no.
I wasn't going to Washington to fight.
I was going to Washington
and I was going to work for the first lady

because
I had just, I mean
my experience in having worked with her before
was—
you know, we had worked on I thought the most important issues
there were—
We worked on children and family issues.
And,
if she was going to keep doing that—
which I was sure that she was—
to me it seemed like
you know the most important thing I could do.
And she gave me such great hope
quite frankly.
And that's what I thought I would be doing.
And,
uhm,
I didn't think that I would
be having to
defend my
integrity
and—
Also the idea
that you have people chipping away—
at you know
this person that—
you and
your mother and your father
and all these other people have worked so hard to help
create.
And in an instant
they can
uhm—
I didn't think
that I would be wasting so much
time.

EVERYBODY'S TALKING

MONICA LEWINSKY

1998–1999
WASHINGTON, NEW YORK, SAN FRANCISCO,
LOS ANGELES, BOSTON

AT ANY RATE, EVERYBODY WAS TALKING. THE TONES OF STUDIED nonchalance were lifting. I heard trochees, I heard original breathing, I heard original language, and the moving rhythms and spontaneous pitches were even allowing me to hear music in the voices. As usual, when people start talking, finally, I ask myself which of the three questions I learned in the late seventies are being answered. Metaphorically, that is.

"Do you know the circumstances of your birth?" That wasn't the metaphor. "Have you ever been accused of something that you did not do?" That wasn't the metaphor. It was for the president but not for those who were watching him. "Have you ever come close to death?" That may have been the metaphor.

I took my tape recorder here and there, and plugged it into my phone. It took Monica Lewinsky to bring interesting language out of Washington. Why is that? I was reminded of a woman I interviewed who was dying of AIDS. She had been a prostitute, a drug addict, and an alcoholic. She has decided now, at age forty-nine, and in the midst of a full-blown disease, that she wanted to live. "Why did I have to come to this, to come this far to know this?" she said, as she burst into tears.

Why does it so often take extreme circumstances to get us to that which is original about us? There must be other ways of coming forward, of coming out of complacent language, of looking for more, of taking risks, of questioning the status quo.

BEN BRADLEE

FORMER EDITOR, *THE WASHINGTON POST*

"Lying"

Well, all right, sure.
Kennedy did it.
That is apparently true.
He apparently did it,
but the best
eh I can learn
there were no lawsuits.
There were no charges
of uh
rape.
There were no charges of uh
sexual misbehavior of any kind.
The rules were different
no question about it.
I mean people uh—
If there was discretion
and nobody got
hurt.
I'm in a jam because I didn't know about it
but uhm
I heard the stories certainly.
Well the times are different
and there have been several suits,
several accusations
in the current
uhm
incident.
Not to talk about lying.

Which I think is the most interesting part of this.
This is not the first lie.
This is not the first big lie.
Look
Vietnam certainly produced a, a uhm atmosphere where lying
was routine
routine by the government.
The counterculture examined—
they'd had it with churches,
schools,
institutions of all kinds,
businesses uh
colleges,
establishments.
It was very antiestablishment.
That's one of the things they were yelling about
McNamara!
Numero uno.

A MEDLEY

DAVID KENDALL

COUNSEL TO THE PRESIDENT

"Dream"

Boy.
[Exhales sharply]
I di——, I had a lotta dreams,
and I don't write them down.
I dream a lot.
I had dr——, yeah, I had dreams of peril.
And, uh, I can't say more.
I mean, a couple times I was awakened.
They weren't nightmares, but they were, uh, they were avala——
uh, one was an avalanche dream.
Because, I'd wanted to go skiing,
you know, I, I like to ski.
And, um, and I was skiing and there was an avalanche.
And there was one that I wanna say was,
wanted to go to the, uh, aaahhhh, the exhibit of, ah,

Edo art in the East Wing, which started in, like, November.
And, uh, friends had gone and my wife had gone and other
    people.
And there is a Hokusai print,
a very famous print,
showing the waves,
showing Mt. Fuji in the background,
but waves breaking over a boat.
And there was a dream I had about a tidal wave,
which combined the final scene in *Deep Impact*
with this Hokusai print, I think.
Those are the only two I remember.
And I can't remember, I c——, can't remember when——
they were always kind of near when I was gonna be up . . .

CHRIS VLASTO

INVESTIGATIVE REPORTER
ABC NEWS

"Chasing Me"

Even the first day,
even when we put [the Monica Lewinsky story] out on the radio,
and I flew.
I actually was in New York
so I hadda fly,
I was in New York—
and I flew down on the first shuttle.
And I remember the sun was comin up
and I knew that day that there were about—
Oh no actually I called my mother
and I said
"Oh, Mom, there's a big story, I broke a big story."

And she said
"Oh no."
She got very nervous,
and she got very nervous
and [whispering, urgent, sitting forward]
"Don't tell me these things."
And then I, when I saw
the sun
in Washington
I knew that everyone was going to wake up
that morning and start chasing
me.

PETER BAKER

THE WASHINGTON POST

"Netanyahu"

And if you remember, and I'm sure you do,
that was the day
uhm, uh Netanyahu was in town.
And he
was meeting with Clinton and their meeting during the day had
    been unproductive
but they decided to meet again, you know spontaneously, in the
    evening
So there was the President of the United States
meeting late into the night
with Bibi Netanyahu
trying desperately to put the Middle East peace process back on
    track.
And so the White House was already lit up with the late candles
    with people working late

and then suddenly from their perspective this kind of comes and hits
    them.
It was a scary story to put into the paper because it was so
    unpredictable and unimaginable
and uh, uh you know the very next day of course George
    Stephanopoulos goes on the air, the very first thing he says, he
    was talking about impeachment.

CHERYL MILLS

COUNSEL TO PRESIDENT CLINTON

Well, see
I don't think the law is necessarily about rightness and wrongness.
I mean, I think that's a large part of what the law tries to capture.
But it also tries to capture obligations and responsibilities,
or weed out obligations and responsibilities.
So, you know, it's that terrible paradigm of,
you see a baby facedown in the water, you don't turn it over, did
    you commit
murder?
No, our—our—our law says, we're going to preserve that level of
    space for
you and say, you have no, uh, affirmative duty in this particular
    instance.
Um, even though it would have taken you nothing—
and some states don't buy that, and have passed good samaritan
    laws, and
others haven't,
and they struggle with how to deal with that.
I think the law tries to do right and wrong,
but it also tries to preserve and protect certain freedoms,
and even the freedom not to do as much as we might think in a
    moral sense.

Because we all can't agree on the morality of that
and to the extent that a large number of us can, we might have
    made a choice
not to impose it on someone else.

MAXINE WATERS

CONGRESSWOMAN, CALIFORNIA

"How They Keep Everybody In Line"

When the Congressional Black Caucus
had a Democratic caucus
where we tried to convince our members not to vote with the
    Republicans
to release [the Ken Starr] material
when it hadn't been examined.
And they were all at that time basically
knew that they were going to vote to dump it out.
They were disgusted with the president.
They saw him as going down and they weren't going with him
and we made that argument within the Democratic caucus.
And it was silence you could hear a pin drop
and we changed a few minds.
And even with Dick Gephardt, he didn't get it.
The argument was
out there in Missouri
where people were
sick and tired of the discussion—
it was a sleazy affair between the president and a young lady
that kind of thing.
Rumor had it [Gephardt] was prepared to go to
the White House and ask him to resign with press in tow.
But the Congressional Black Caucus

representing
the most impoverished,
the most needy the most maligned the most everything
ended up on the point
to save a president based on principle.
I mean you see yourself
in terms of what your forefathers were doing with slavery.
You know what I'm saying?
The slaves who had made it to the house
had to still fight for the slaves
in the field.
I guess that's kind of our—
ya know?
Yeah,
ya know.
And I've thought about this thing
I tell you I was consumed
with thought about all aspects
and my own feelings
and I was on the Judiciary Committee and we were reviewing the
     appropriations for the next budget
and we had to look at the civil rights portion of the budget
and the same members of the Judiciary Committee
who led the fight, those thirteen managers were the ones who were
     all opposed to any
increases in the civil rights budget,
ya know the Canadys and the Barrs and the—
I just said
I mean I went way beyond where members are expected to go
I said, "No
I want a discussion on civil rights now!"
I said [she laughs]
"We've got police abuse cases
you've got gays who are being lynched and burned.
Don't you all have anything to say?"
And they sat there. And Barney Frank
[she laughs]

Barney said you know he wished it had been recorded because it
     told the story
of who these guys really are
Mr. Hyde said
"this is not the time or the place"
And it really pissed me off.
Because now we have two gays on that committee
we have one and a woman who's come on
I said "With all of the gays and the women and the blacks on this
     committee this is not the time?
To talk about civil rights?"
I said "When *is* the time, Mr. Chairman?"
But the relationships around here transcend the issues.
That's how they keep everybody in line.

MIKE ISIKOFF

NEWSWEEK

"Persistence"

You have to be persistent.
I mean
people hang up on you
people slam doors in your face.
One thing you do have to have that's important
particularly on this stuff—
I don't know
you have to have a really thick skin.
Now you're putting me on the couch and I don't wanna go there.
I don't know, I was less concerned about—
I don't know—
not so much in the slamming doors in your face
although it's not especially pleasant.
You knock on a door you know "I'd like to—"

I remember the trooper's wife in Arkansas
I went to Danny Ferguson's home
and, and ya know I was waiting for him to go home.
Then I figured out he was home.
I knocked on the door.
I was in a car outside
oh I don't know maybe an hour.
His wife came to the door
and I tried to you
know, and she said "No way, no how
get out of here
and leave us alone"
And I go away
I'm not a stalker.

CHRIS VLASTO

"Dirt"

There's tons of [dirt]
there's a lot of stuff that wouldn't air.
I mean, I mean the same that's what Mike, Mike Isikoff and I
I mean they killed the story on Saturday.
I had it
we had it nailed.
I called down to Cuba that night
and [they] killed it.
On, on January 20 the whole date would have changed
They didn't want to run it!
And then we put it out on the radio at 12:30.
I talked to the senior vice president,
whoever was down there at the time
I told him "Look I've got the story!"
[He's banging his hand on the table]

"We, we've got it we've got it nailed we've got to put it on
because I hear *The Washington Post* is gonna do it. We've got to
     do it now we've got to do it now!"
And then he goes "Okay we'll get back to you."
And then David Weston, who's the president, called back and said
     "We need a third source"
or a fourth source, or whatever source we had and um
we went and got it.
And I called back
about a half hour later an hour later and said "We have it this it, it,
     this is, I mean you've got to do this story." And they had some
     conference
which I would love to have been in on
down in Cuba
where I think Ted and Tom
killed it
said "Well we're down here . . ."

MIKE ISIKOFF

But for this story go back to the war room.
It was the shame card that they use.
"Serious journalists don't ask questions about stuff
like this you're telling me you're a tabloid reporter
you're asking me sleazy questions."
Look at the way Mike McCurry describes me to Howie Kurtz in
     Spin Cycle
That sleazy in the Kathleen Willey thing
this other new sleazy charge being promoted by another bimbo
     beat reporter Mike Isikoff
who goes around chasin sex stories
how cheap and tawdry
scum
they'll think you're scum

they'll make fun of you
you're a bimbo beat tabloid reporter
that's the way they use this to keep people off of
this stuff.
There's a tawdry element to this stuff
I just thought it was gonna be
it was a story
I thought that Clinton's private conduct was reckless
and for the most part most of these women were telling
the truth
and in that sense
they were lying
the Clinton people were lying and the women were telling the truth.

CHRIS VLASTO

"Running"

But when we found the dress—
well, well, well
I ran!
I literally was running in the streets of Washington.
And I run into
Jackie's office
I said
"Jackie
sit down . . .
it exists."
And she died.
She almost fell out of the chair when I told her.
And that's a great
that's a great story.

MIKE ISIKOFF

"You Use Me I Use You"

It doesn't mean that people weren't promoting this stuff
the kind of people you wouldn't want to invite to your
    home for dinner
but
there's a lot in my book that will provide ammunition to
    all sides of this.
There's probably nobody to like in this story.
It is the nature of reporting you know
that when you're talking to people and trying to get them
    to tell you shit
you like, you know, sound and act sympathetic.
I mean that's what we do.
I mean that's the way you do your job.
I mean you know
I tried to use them
they tried to use me.
This is the way the world works.
This is the way we operate.
This is the way journalism operates.
This is the way Washington works for that matter.
There was a lot of it that was hilarious.
I hope that
if you read the book
you'll find a lot entertaining.
There's a lot of funny stories.

JACKIE JUDD

ABC NEWS

The day that Monica turned the dress over was a,
    was a huge day for us
not only because of the significance that the dress
    played in the story
but the dress had become emblematic of all of our reporting
and because the dress had never been turned over
it never existed
for
those who were critical of our work
and it colored how all of our reporting was seen
and—
So once the dress was turned over
it suddenly lent credibility not only to our initial report that she had
    claimed that such a dress existed.
But to all of our reporting—it all became more credible because of
    that single act of her turning the dress over.
That's all I wanted to say.

CHRIS VLASTO

"Semen"

The—blue—dress.
Oh I knew about it the first day and nobody wanted to touch it
before
before we broke it.
I had known that she—
I had heard that she had sent up a dress

that had semen on it
and
with all the gifts
to her mother in New York
and I thought it should have been mentioned the very first day
but
Oh
we can't bring that up.
Oh come on Chris shut up.
You cannot talk—
We don't want to talk about semen
oh no.
And they're goin on and on
You can't talk about semen
go away.

BARNEY FRANK

CONGRESSMAN, MASSACHUSETTS

"Oral Sex"

What did the president touch and when did he touch it?
I mean,
that was the big account of perjury
was that Bill Clinton acknowledged that she had performed oral
    sex on him but he denied that he touched her breasts or
    vagina.
To impeach the president of the United States because he admitted
    that the woman sucked him, but he denied that he touched her.
At one point I said to Maxine,
[Congresswoman Maxine Waters] was standing with her full back
    to the committee room chatting with me,
and I said "I don't know, Max.
What's all this nonsense about?"

I said "I don't, I guess I don't understand why everybody gets so
    excited about whether
he touched her breasts.
I mean touching a woman's breast is no big deal as far as I can
    see."
She grabbed my hand and said "Well you want me to show you?"
I said "No, no."
And the last thing I think was, I think, and I with this, I think—
was on censure.
I think it would have been better for the House to have done
    censure and not gone to the Senate.
And one of their arguments was censure doesn't mean anything.
It's just a slap on the wrist.
Two it's a bad precedent because it'll cripple the president if he can
    be censured on a regular basis.
Well it can't be both—it can't be too little and then too much.
I reminded people that I myself had been reprimanded [because of
    involvement with a male prostitute].
And what I said was "Look,
you all, some of you are saying this doesn't mean anything.
I know it means something.
I was reprimanded, I know what it meant to me.
And I don't see how anybody who ever served here can say a
    reprimand from this place doesn't mean anything.
It memorializes the fact that you behaved very badly."
Formally in the House, a censure, you have to stand in the well of
    the House while it's read.
It's a vote, it's a resolution voted by the House.
"The House hereby reprimands you for bad conduct."
You know it's forever in the records.
"We hereby resolve that you are a, an embarrassment and you
    behaved very badly."
I mean, I, you don't, if you're totally indifferent to the expressed
    formal
opinion of the United States House of Representatives,
it's hard for me to think you'd run for Congress.
(Pause)

[I asked: "Did you have any dreams you'd be willing tell me?"]
Yes and no.
Yes I had dreams, no I won't tell you about them.
I mean I was uncomfortable really,
and there was this period but on August 17,
I went to Provincetown for vacation on Sunday the sixteenth,
I was going to stay for three or four days.
And then this hit the fan and
I found myself on Monday night doing CNN, Fox, ABC, CBS, and
NBC.
I did them all by remote in response to the Clinton piece.
Now why was I getting all five networks? Nobody else wanted to
do it.
I was the only one willing to defend Clinton.
I may have had a dream or two about being up there, relatively
isolated, defending Clinton. Um, and you know, there were
some other Democrats who were sort of distancing.
So somebody said "Gee I, that's kind of brave, you're out there all
alone defending Clinton."
And I said "Frankly, being in Provincetown and defending oral sex
is not a hard position."

A REMINISCENCE
BILL BARBEAU

FIREMAN, VIETNAM VET

"You Get All Your Dogs Together"

I was gonna stay wid my dog
I was gonna stay wid him
I mean I wanted to stay wid him.
It was him and I.
But you had local
animals

and the enemy
used to use
a local dog
from the village
that either ran out of
or come passin through
they'd feed the dog and the dog ed follow 'em
and the dog ed go out
and of course the dog wants to walk first on a trail
and if he stepped on a mine, so what.
But I took care of [Satan].
Thirteen months we ate
we ate out of the same plate.
We drank the same water
the same canteen cup.
We were like
tied together.
The end of that five-foot leash was the dog
that was him and I
and I'm not alone
it was all dog handlers were like that
all us scout dog handlers were like that
those of us that lived through it were close to your dog.
That's how your dog—
Sometimes the circumstances happen
that
you're gonna get killed
or the dog's gonna get shot.
Ya can't avoid that
but
you take care of that dog
the dog'll take care of you.
He kept me a-alive.
I kept that dog perfect
clean
fed.
We used to have um

circle jerks
for the dogs
for the male dogs.
You get four or five guys together and we bring our dogs in and
    you have circle jerks
and what it did was it kept your dog from
chasing
bitches in heat.
You get four or five dogs together and you jerk your dogs off.
I'm alive.
It's got its practical side.

ED BRADLEY

60 MINUTES HOST

"Captives"

Both are captives.
Um
I think the press is
individually and collectively a captive
of the White House.
[He puts a spoonful of yogurt in his mouth, and scrapes the cup]
In that
you go there every day.
And you stay there
Ehmm,
You, you don't leave because you have to look at these
photo ops.
As they're called.
That the president does during the course of the day.
And
[He scrapes the yogurt cup]
where there's an opportunity to throw a

question at him to which he doesn't always respond.
For example
a cabinet meeting.
A meeting with
some foreign leader
a meeting with congressional leaders
uhm
in which the press is ushered in—
for
a specific period of time—
a minute two minutes—
so they can get a picture—
they stand there with notes and pads—
eh—
"Mr. President, what about Bosnia?"
scream at him.
If he wants.
if he has something he wants to *say* then he'll use that opportunity
he'll take advantage of it.
If he doesn't
most of the time he'll ignore you.
Sometimes the president will say something when he has no
        intention of saying
something—
when it's not thought out,
and you get a free—
something.
But it's really a very limited exchange.
He's a captive
because
he's there.
Uhm
it's a very
controlled existence.
Uh
there's no freedom.
You can't just pick up and go,

uh
you can
rarely.
Uhm
without an announcement
that
the president is moving.
And the president moving
is not like you moving.
[He clears his throat]
You can't—
you can walk out here today and decide
"Well let me run over to Barney's I need to pick this thing up."
The president to do that has gotta take an entourage—
Somebody's gotta go there with dogs
and uh, eh—
ya know it just becomes uh, you, you
you are a captive of the White House!
True you have a lot of power and there's a lot you can do with it.
But you are a captive.
And the press
is very much a captive.
Because
[Hits his hand on the desk along with the next line in rhythm]
If he moves, we move.
If he sits, we sit.
[Hits the desk again]
And people don't like to say it
but everybody
particularly in those situations
and given the climate and the world we live in today
everybody's on the deathwatch.

PLAYING CLINTON

Perhaps Clinton's downfall was that he was too expressive in a time when studied nonchalance is the status quo. I don't know if that's Clinton's downfall, or the downfall of where we are as a society. People say that he should have had the moral courage to tell the truth when first confronted about Monica Lewinsky. I won't pretend to know what would have happened had he done that. I won't pretend to know if any of the people who have said what he should do would have done that had they been in his shoes.

The creation of language is the creation of a fiction. The minute we speak we are in that fiction. It's a fiction designed, we hope, to reveal a truth. There is no "pure" language. The only "pure language" is the initial sounds of a baby. All of us lose that purity, and as we get more "of" the world, we even lose sometimes the capacity to keep that breath moving in our language.

Our ability to create reality, by creating fictions with language, should not be abused. The abuse is called lying. Perhaps we understand the precariousness of our situation. We as linguistic animals. At the very least language is currency as we create "reality." To abuse language, to lie, is to fray reality, to tatter it. Those in public life who create our values are especially asked not to "lie." Yet most of us *say*, at least, that we believe we are often being lied to.

I am not satisfied to accept words at their face value. I don't really know what they mean, and I watch breakdowns of communication the way the morning helicopter looks for traffic delays. I assume them as a reality.

I take the words I can get and try to occupy them. Using the idea that my grandfather gave me—"If you say a word often enough it becomes you"—I borrow people for a moment, by borrowing their words. I borrow them for a moment to understand something about them, and to understand something about us. By "us," I mean humans.

In the course of occupying Clinton's words, I have learned only a few things so far. His idea was clear: The system is contentious. The press is aligned with power, and the pairing of the press with those who want power is bad for America—

"I told you what that Republican senator told me
and you can use this.
He said,
'Before you got elected
we were stupid enough to think the press was liberal
and then we realized
that they are liberal in the sense that most of 'em vote Democrat.'
He said 'They vote with you but they think like us.'
And I asked him what he meant and he said
"You're a Democrat
you come here thinkin you can do good.
You wanna use the power of the gubment to make good things happen,
improve people's lives."
He said "Republicans are suspicious
of the ability to make anybody's life better."
He said "We like this because we want power
and the press
they want power
so let 'em vote with you, they think like us.
When you're in they get power and we get power the same way.
We hurt you
so never mind what the truth is.
Hit the target!"

But Clinton is much more than that idea, and much more than his argument that "We really have to ask ourselves, Do we want to put our public officials in a position of having to bankrupt themselves just to survive in office?"

He is more than his confession "Now. I'm just like one those ol' Baby Huey dolls you had when you were a kid. You punch 'em and they come back up. So I'm fine."

And more than his warning

"But it's bad for the country.
It's bad
when the burden of proof is on the accused
and you're supposed to disprove all conceivable ac——
accusations
present
or future
and if you don't!
There's somethin wrong with ya.
That's bad."

I performed Clinton before the Monica Lewinsky scandal and after. It was harder to play it after. I was working against the disbelief of the audience. By my last performance of *House Arrest* in New York, I had learned something, in part because of the lighting designer. Lighting can do a lot to create a president, as Michael Deavere discovered when he brought lighting and the photo op into the White House.

My lighting designer had created an environment that made me look very far away from the audience. He wanted to show the power of the president. I decided that I should work with the image of power on the one hand but the feeling of powerlessness on the other. It was from that feeling of powerlessness, on an empty stage, in front of an audience that was predisposed *not* to believe me, that my work began.

In acting school we are told to play the play as if it were the first time. When I played Clinton, and ultimately when I played the entire play *House Arrest*, I began to play it as if it were the *last* time I would ever speak in public again. It was from that place that I began to get a feeling of what is at stake in the very powerful position of president of the United States.

It was my only way in. As an African American woman, I am actually not predisposed to know much about power. I am predisposed to identify with, and know a lot about, powerlessness. I was, from the outset, more comfortable playing an incarcerated child murderer, one who would be considered the lowest of the low, than I was playing the president of the United States.

So there I was, at the Public Theater in New York, every night. When it came time to be Clinton, I was looking out in the dark. And from out of the dark, I found a determination to find somebody out there in the darkness to talk to. I was going to find someone who would listen, someone who would hear my case. I was going to make my case. Whether I made my case or not was not the point, it was the activity of finding an ear upon which to rest my case. And my case was not really about the Republicans, and not really about the press, and not really about what they had done to Hillary and what they had done to me. My case was "I'm just like one those ol' Baby Huey dolls you had when you were a kid. You punch 'em and they come back up."

Inevitably someone, and sometimes many people, would laugh. Sometimes they would applaud. He had made his case. And he would continue with "So I'm fine." And again "I'm fine."

STUDS TERKEL

AMERICANIST

"Clowns"

Ya know when it gets back to as far as guys
presidents with dames.
My God!
Ya know
Kennedy my God
it wasn't so much Addison's disease
he suffered from satyriasis probably
In fact he said it.

So what?
And my favorite president
the one,
the one president of the century,
major league
FDR of course.
Well FDR is said to have had a fling with a socialite
and he had polio.
I said My God the man has polio
this might be very good therapy!
Long before McCarthy there was New Salem
I think Hillary has a point
about it being a right-wing—
[but]
that's too simple.
Well of course they're out to get him.
That's not what the issue is to me
the issue is
What the hell have we learned?
Where are we?
I was born in 1912
the year the *Titanic*
sank.
The greatest ship ever built!
It hits the tip of an iceberg and bam! It went down.
It went down
and I came up.
Wow some century!
But it's not this.
This almost becomes not the crowning touch
but the clowning touch!
It's the clowning touch!
It ends with a fright wig
putty nose
with baggy pants
and this is it!
It's not just Clinton and Monica

we all are wearing the fright wig and putty nose and baggy pants
we're all demeaned
by that I mean
all of us are clowns and that's what it's all about.
Instead of a new century
with all the discoveries made
in medicine
perhaps more to come.
And yet with fewer and fewer people controlling
more and more and more.
And the more and more and more feeling more and more and
        more
helpless.
And who runs the means of communication that condition these
        people to vote as they vote and think as they think?
We got Lewinsky-ism and Monica-ism
instead of what the hell we been doing to all these countries and to
        the have-nots in this country?
So we're wearing baggy pants putty nose
fright wigs.
We've been conditioned to wear them
by this time.
[Pause]
We've got to question official truth.
The thing that was so great about Mark Twain—
We honor Mark Twain ya know
and we don't read 'im.
We may read *Huck Finn,*
even Huck of course was tremendous.
Remember what Huck did?
That great scene on the raft you know
when Huck—
See
you have to
question official truth—
So truth—is the law was:
a black man is property, is a thing

and he's [Huck's] on with a property named Jim
a slave, see
on the raft.
And he heard that Jim says he's going to do a terrible thing.
And Huck is thirteen, twelve
and Jim said he's going to look for his wife and kids.
And he's gonna steal them
from the woman
or person who owns them.
And Huck says "That woman never did me any harm"
[Whispering]
I'm—
he's gonna steal!
In, in Huck's own mind—
Huck Finn is what it's all about.
The goodness of Huck you see.
He's an illiterate kid right
he's had no schoolin
but there's something in . . .
[Whispering, expressive, urgent]
and he says "Oh it's a terrible thing wow what an awful thing he's
    gonna steal."
And just then two slavers caught up—
the guys chasing the slaves,
looking for Jim
ya know.
And they come up "Anybody on that raft with ya?"
[Pause]
And Huck yeah (dibdebi) . . .
They know there's somebody there.
[Pause]
"Is he white or black?"
And Huck says
(Pause)
"White."
and they go off—
"Oh my God my conscience"

I lied!
Ya know
I lied
and he's gonna—
but if—
"I did a terrible thing"
(Pause)
"Why do I feel so good?"
There ya got it
in Huck
ya captured the human species.
That stuff that Huck is there
that part's been buried!
We're all demeaned.
We're all under the bed.
Who's under the bed?
The clowns are under the bed.
Clowns.
We're burlesque comics
the ringmasters
who is a ringmaster?
The guys who run the conglomerates whoever they are.
These ringmasters themselves are clowns too
except they happen to have power.
But they're also faceless.
The irony is most of these guys are faceless.
The ringmasters
in the old days
you knew in the old days,
this clown this brute
this—
But they're all there,
but they're faceless.
So there you have it!
So okay kid!
I've got to scram! I've got to go see my cardiologist!

ALSO BY ANNA DEAVERE SMITH

FIRES IN THE MIRROR
Crown Heights, Brooklyn, and Other Identities

In August 1991, simmering hostilities in the racially polarized neighborhood of Crown Heights in Brooklyn, New York, exploded forcefully after an African American boy was killed by a car in a rabbi's motorcade and a Jewish student was slain in retaliation. Derived from interviews with a wide range of people who experienced or observed the Crown Heights riots, *Fires in the Mirror* is Anna Deavere Smith's extraordinary portrayal of the events and emotions leading up to and following the incident.

"Electrifying. . . . A riveting work that captures the tensions of racial, class, and cultural conflict." —*Newsweek*

Current Affairs/Performing Arts/0-385-47014-2

TWILIGHT: LOS ANGELES, 1992
On the Road: A Search for American Character

Twilight: Los Angeles, 1992 is Anna Deavere Smith's stunning work of "documentary theater" in which she uses the exact words of people who experienced the Los Angeles riots to expose and explore the devastating human impact of that event. With brilliant emotional accuracy, *Twilight: Los Angeles, 1992* is as distinguished a commentary on racial conflict as it is a dramatic masterpiece.

"Dazzling and depressing, rich in details that subtly illuminate the problem of race." —*Time*

Current Affairs/Performing Arts/0-385-47376-1